Camping Wyoming and the Black Hills

Help Us Keep This Guide Up to Date

Every effort has been made by the author and editors to make this guide as accurate and useful as possible; however, many things can change after a guide is published—regulations change, facilities come under new management, and so forth.

We would love to hear from you concerning your experiences with this guide and how you feel it could be improved and kept up to date. While we may not be able to respond to all comments and suggestions, we'll take them to heart, and we'll also make certain to share them with the author. Please send your comments and suggestions to falconeditorial@rowman.com.

Thanks for your input!

Camping Wyoming and the Black Hills

A Comprehensive Guide to the State's Best Campgrounds

Second Edition

Kenneth L. Graham

FALCONGUIDES

ESSEX, CONNECTICUT

FALCONGUIDES®

An imprint of Globe Pequot, the trade division of
The Rowman & Littlefield Publishing Group, Inc.
4501 Forbes Blvd., Ste. 200
Lanham, MD 20706
www.rowman.com

Distributed by NATIONAL BOOK NETWORK

British Library Cataloguing in Publication Information available

Library of Congress Cataloging-in-Publication Data

Names: Graham, Kenneth Lee, author.
Title: Camping Wyoming and the Black Hills : a comprehensive guide to the state's best campgrounds / Kenneth L. Graham.
Description: Second Edition. | Essex, Connecticut : Falcon Guides, [2023] | Series: A FalconGuide | First edition: 2001. | Includes bibliographical references and index. | Summary: "This guide provides detailed information on more than 250 public campgrounds in Wyoming and South Dakota's Black Hills, accessible by car. For tenters and RVers alike, this guide will lead you to the perfect campground"—Provided by publisher.
Identifiers: LCCN 2022058833 (print) | LCCN 2022058834 (ebook) | ISBN 9781493069613 (Paperback : acid-free paper) | ISBN 9781493069620 (epub)
Subjects: LCSH: Camping—Wyoming—Guidebooks. | Black Hills (S.D. and Wyo.)—Guidebooks.
Classification: LCC GV191.42.W8 G73 2023 (print) | LCC GV191.42.W8 (ebook) | DDC 796.5409787—dc23/eng/20230112
LC record available at https://lccn.loc.gov/2022058833
LC ebook record available at https://lccn.loc.gov/2022058834

The authors and The Rowman & Littlefield Publishing Group, Inc., assume no liability for accidents happening to, or injuries sustained by, readers who engage in the activities described in this book.

Contents

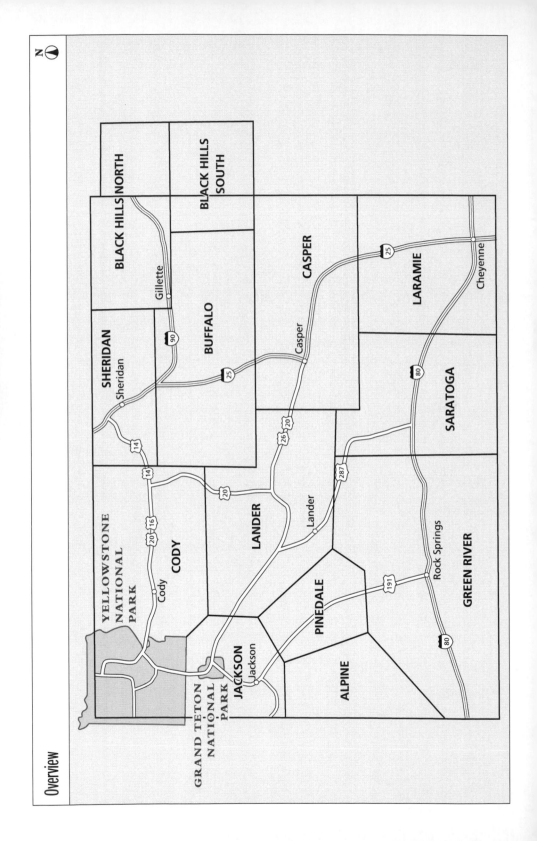

Acknowledgments

This has been a challenging and rewarding book to complete, with a lot of road miles. I wish to thank my wife, Sandy, for her unselfish contribution and patience. Without Sandy's support and help, this would still be a work in progress.

Meet Your Guide

I was born in Newcastle, Wyoming, in the shadow of the western edge of the Black Hills. The unique history and legends of the Old West came to life for me at a very young age. There were many trips into the forest and canyons role-playing what I thought the mountain men and Native Americans would have lived like. I wanted to walk in the footsteps of John Colter as he explored the wonders of Yellowstone and join the ranks of wagon train scouts as pioneers moved westward.

As I grew up, so did the country, with faster horses and homes on wheels. What once took years to travel through could now be done in weeks. I also discovered that in order to take those trips, money was required. Fur trapping and wagon scouting were no longer viable options. Instead, I found working as an underground miner not only gave me tramping funds but also allowed me to explore the artifacts and evidence left behind by my heroes in places the pioneers missed.

Getting older has made me more appreciative of the benefits of "tin teepees" with refrigerators, showers, and a dry place to cook, among other comforts. My days of staring into the stars from a sleeping bag in a mountain meadow as the campfire dwindled to a dull red glow changed to looking at the full moon through a skylight.

Now as a retired explorer, I wish to continue exploring and leave behind a "guidebook" that cuts through all the misinformation and left-out details to help direct those who wish to experience as many of the wonders of the West as they possibly can with limited time to get it done. As such I offer this menu of sorts as an explorer turned scout.

Introduction

About This Book

In the early days of Wyoming territory, scouts such as Jim Bridger and Jedediah Smith provided a valuable service for travelers, whether they were fortune seekers, homesteaders, or cavalry. These scouts blazed trails and directed travelers toward their goals along routes with food and water for man and beast within this unknown territory. Travel time was slow because the animals pulling the wagons required frequent stops for grazing, and travelers were able to explore areas near the paths their animals followed.

In many places little has changed, and for the most part travel today targets the unique features discovered by these previous visitors. But the sense of exploration does not end with days gone by. Today travelers use automobiles, synthetic tents, and "tin tepees." Campsites are no longer required to provide water and grass for livestock. Campfires are mostly used to roast marshmallows and to take off the evening chill at sundown, not for cooking dinner. And the nearby wildlife is an added attraction—not the evening meal.

Some of today's modern "wagons" are absolutely not equipped to make the trip into some spots. A 30-foot pull trailer behind a full-sized pickup does not easily fit on a mountain road hairpin turn. Neither do small tunnels and large RVs mix. Though the hazards are well marked and signed, it is usually very inconvenient to run across them in places involving a lot of backtracking. I have attempted to provide information on access requirements along with what you will find upon arrival. Out of almost 300 campgrounds, there are plenty that all vehicles can reach. This book allows you to plan your routes with your specific type of "wagon" in mind. This should eliminate hours of driving only to find that the last few miles are only accessible by short-wheelbase, all-terrain vehicles. There are too many wonderful things in Wyoming to spend precious time backtracking out of unannounced difficult country.

The appeal of camping for me is the relaxation offered in the fresh mountain air with an occasional wisp of campfire smoke and the smells of cowboy coffee and marshmallows roasted to a golden brown. For anglers there are plenty of trout in both lakes and streams offering both challenge and exploration. In Wyoming there are undesignated wilderness areas that have fewer visitors than designated ones. These hideaways are not openly advertised—adding to the thrill of discovery. This also implies an obligation to let others find these wild areas on their own, while we share the secret with only those that have been there before us.

Please keep in mind that Wyoming remains primitive by definition of modern camping practices. Hookups, with extremely few exceptions, do not exist. Drinking water is mostly produced through hard labor from ancient hand pumps and can have an unmistakable iron flavoring. Self-contained units offer alternatives; however, finding sources for filling holding tanks will take some research. There are a lot of miles between towns with no services available. In many places the only residents will be the wildlife common to the area. So, plan your route in advance, check out the features of available resources in this book, and get ready for an adventure.

Weather

Wyoming's high elevations result in a relatively cool climate. A hot sunny day will often require a coat by day's end. This is especially true of the high mountain country where most campgrounds in this book are found. Wyoming's lowest elevation is located near the northeastern corner and is 3,125 feet. The highest elevation tops off at over 13,000 feet with plenty of heights in between.

Wind in Wyoming leaves permanent impressions on any visitor. A story once circulated through a mining camp in central Wyoming about a local wind indicator. Supposedly, a half-inch log chain was left dangling just off the ground on a pole near a public gathering place. If the chain held steady at 45 degrees from the vertical, it was an ordinary day. A truly windy day was when this chain stretched out at 90 degrees like a bicycle streamer on a downhill ride. There are days when it is easy to believe this story, and the wind can create very dangerous driving conditions in bad weather.

Storms can be fast and furious in any part of Wyoming, though they seem to be much more severe in the wide-open desert. There is plenty of desert between campgrounds. If your travels take you into some backcountry, it might pay to sit out the storm.

Flora and Fauna

Bears and campgrounds just seem to match like frosting on brownies. Not all camping areas identified in this book have bears, but most do. The Yellowstone area offers a healthy number of grizzly bears. A variety of measures minimize human-bear encounters, including campground closure. Sleeping Giant Campground, west of Cody, has been closed for just that reason. Other areas no longer allow tents, and bear boxes provide safe storage in camping areas where tents are still allowed. Information on bear sightings and human-bear encounters gets posted on signs at key places in individual campgrounds. Usually this will be at the fee sign near the entrance.

Large game animals such as moose, deer, elk, pronghorn (antelope), and bison (buffalo) live in Wyoming. All are potentially dangerous, and interaction with humans can lead to fatal results. Buffalo are commonly seen in Yellowstone National Park and Custer State Park in and around campgrounds. Moose run a close second on the hazard list. These huge animals blatantly blunder past tents and trailers alike when they please, seeming to dare people to "knock the chip off." Do not get in their way.

As a rule, rattlesnakes are more talked about than seen. However, they are present and no less dangerous than larger wildlife. Late August or early September finds numerous snakes warming on the warm asphalt late in the evening. These dead-looking snakes are very much alive and can become contentious about their turf. At this time of year, a rattlesnake is preserving all the energy it can and will not necessarily warn you of its intentions by rattling its tail, so be wary of the not-so-dead snake on the road.

Even though larger animals and snakes represent potential dangers and/or death, the most annoying creature to me is the pesky mosquito. There are also ticks and horse and deer flies, although they don't buzz in my ear all night causing sleeplessness like mosquitos do. Adequate bug repellent is of great value. There are a lot of miles between stores in Wyoming, so stock up before you leave home.

Recreation

Technology has added a whole new perspective to outdoor recreation. Hunters, anglers, rock hounds, hikers, backpackers, horseback riders, and all those with a desire to explore and partake in a growing number of activities now have access to "real-time" information with respect to public versus private property. COVID-19 restrictions opened up a whole new perspective on outdoor entertainment as well. Camping offers the opportunity for plenty of "social distancing" and lots of room to move around in, whether in a campground or settling into a "dispersed" site. Motorized off-road activities have increased dramatically as well, with increasing designated trails of various difficulty providing access to some backcountry that would otherwise take many hours if not days to reach hiking on foot. Keep in mind that the internet is not always available so saving maps and information through one of the many apps on today's modern "smartphones" is required before venturing out using the GPS interaction provided by satellites.

Camping in Wyoming

Camping Restrictions/Regulations

Primitive camping used to mean laying out on the ground in a sleeping bag as sunlight turned to various versions of starlight or moonlight dependent on what time of the month it was. In today's world primitive camping includes RVs and/or trailers with no electric or water hookups. The high mountain country has an added issue: When the sun goes down, it can get downright cold. For those of you who have RVs or trailers with electrically controlled furnaces, almost all (98 percent) Wyoming campgrounds do not allow the running of generators during the quiet time hours, typically from 10 p.m. to 6 a.m. This can be a real uncomfortable situation. We have found a small propane catalytic heater can take the bite out of an unexpected chill, but it does come with some ventilation requirements. Be sure to study these and apply them. More than a few have died lighting a propane cooking oven for a heat source without proper ventilation.

Almost all of the public campgrounds in Wyoming do not allow dumping of refuse or waste, including gray water, from any source except in designated receptacles at specific locations that can be no small distance away. Holding tanks can fill up or, in the case of fresh water, empty long before the maximum stay limit is reached. Pets are also on the list of increasing restrictions and in some places require a nightly fee per animal. The length requirement for their leash varies depending on the management department, and pets cannot be left unattended. With RVs and camper trailers getting longer, wider (with slide-outs), and taller, the number of campgrounds that have camping spots that will accommodate them is greatly reduced. The reservation system does help identify specific campgrounds that will accommodate them, but it takes research along with an accurate knowledge of what your camping unit requires. It would also be wise to do a little investigating on the access roads leading to your designated spot. More than a few air conditioner parts have been found alongside the road where low-lying tree branches did not show any mercy.

Be Prepared

There are typically a lot of miles—some very slow-going, rough ones—to the backcountry camping spots that travelers find appealing. Be sure to have everything you need before venturing out. It can be a real bummer if the scenery is fabulous, wildlife plentiful, and fish are biting to discover your hours of grueling trekking across unforgiveable boulders and dodging canyon-deep potholes with a maximum stay designated in your selected campground finds the bug repellent insufficient on the first evening around the first campfire. It is always good to double-check all of your supplies, especially the fresh, gray, and black water tanks.

I learned the hard way that getting ready for a long weekend camping adventure in a remote high mountain area took enough time to force us to arrive well past dark. Typically, after every camping trip when we arrived home, I would open the drain valve on the freshwater tank with plans to shut it before venturing to the next campground. On this particular venture I did not check that valve and proceeded to fill the tank. It took an unusually long time to fill the tank. The incoming water quantity was greater than the outflow of the draining water from the valve I did not shut. It was not until we arrived at our little space of paradise with the camper leveled and supper under way that we discovered there was no water for the coffee or anything else. The tank had slowly drained out on the way. To make matters even worse, there was no available drinking water at the camping area.

Safety

Be sure to take a first-aid kit. As with other supplies, medical attention can be a long time in coming. Not to mention that even in today's cell phone world, there are a lot of miles with no cell phone service at all. Also pay attention to the road conditions, including low-hanging branches over the road. Low hanging can mean 12 or more feet above the road surface. Pay special attention to maps that show hairpin switchbacks on the access road. They are always associated with steep mountain conditions that, once embarked upon, offer no turning back. A call to the managing entity listed in the campground site descriptions could be time well spent to make sure your particular unit can make the trip.

Camping Etiquette

Use common sense when parking your unit. Before committing to a final positioning, take a look at the access with respect to campers that will be arriving after you. Longer units require a wider turning ratio. For those with slide-outs, a word of caution about parking apron widths: Just because the apron is 60 feet long does not mean it is wide enough for the slide-out. Unforgiving trees have a way of occupying the only spot your slide needs to go after getting the unit level. The added complication of having no room to park your towing unit has a chain-reaction effect when a larger camper arrives and can't get by you, with no way to back out. Try to think of things that annoy you when you're settled into a perfect place and the late-arriving "neighbors" tie their dog up to a tree and seem to be deaf to the continuous barking. Are there things that could prove irritating to your fellow campers?

How to Use This Guide

This book is intended for use as a planning guide to help find the best camping area to suit your specific individual needs and desires. First check out the site area descriptions. After finding an area that best matches your definition of paradise, check out the overview maps for an idea of what kind of travel and what route to take based upon where you will begin. Then study the quick-glance charts to verify the amenities and activities present. For example, should you be equipped with a 60-foot-long motor home and the quick-glance chart lists the campground selected as "tents only," there's no need to go there.

Detailed information found in the individual campground site specifications includes the location of a significant city easily found on a Wyoming map. The GPS coordinates are taken at the primary access to the campground and can in most cases be entered into a navigation system for maneuvering through difficult areas, such as unforeseen road closures or construction. However, keep in mind that not all navigation systems are equal. There are plenty of cases where the destination is not reached. Keep an eye on the map and any landmarks available. The "Facilities and amenities" section lists what is present at each site. If it is not listed, there is none available.

Elevation affects temperature. The higher the elevation, the colder the nights are. Road conditions control travel time. A gravel road in Wyoming is no interstate highway—a long gravel road will take more time. If it's getting dark and there are a large number of miles on a gravel road, a closer campground would likely be in order. Hookups, sites, and the maximum RV length each carry about the same level of importance. The majority of campgrounds in Wyoming do not have hookups, the smaller number of sites indicates an older campground, and the maximum RV length can vary for each individual campsite. There may be only one site that accommodates the listed maximum-sized RV. The season and fees can both provide deciding information, but keep in mind that the weather in Wyoming can vary quite a bit. Some years it can seem like winter never quits. The fees can also change. The following designations are used in the hopes of including any future increases: Below $9 = $; $10 to $19 = $$; $20 to $29 = $$$; $30 to $39 = $$$$; $40 to $49 = $$$$$; $50 and over = $$$$$$.

The maximum stay for campsites does change from area to area. The more popular areas are subject to shorter maximum stays during the peak seasons. Management and reservation specifications both provide important contact information and should be evaluated together for any differences, and then contact the appropriate department to make sure everything is acceptable before committing to embark on the journey. The pets, quiet hours, and ADA campsite specifications are pretty general but can be a deciding factor. For example, it may be unacceptable to you to pay a per pet, per night fee. "Finding the campground" is a detailed definition of travel dependent upon road and directional signs that may not be present for whatever reason. So, if the mileage gains from the listed number, there is a good chance your destination has been passed by. "About the campground" lists more detail about actual conditions—good or bad—as well as possible attractions to consider checking out during your stay.

Map Legend

≡(90)≡	Interstate Highway	●	Campground
≡(26)≡	US Highway	○	City/Town
≡(120)≡	State Highway	⬭	Body of Water
——	Local Road	∿	River/Creek
-------	State Border	▭	National Park/Recreation Area

Alpine Area

This area lives up to its name, with seemingly countless mountain meadows from creek bank to mountain peak. Pine forests stand watch in a timeless fashion, ambassadors of the native inhabitants. A generous helping of aspen trees weaves a golden lace throughout in the late summer and fall months as the very popular rafting activity starts to lose appeal, making August an excellent time to visit (unless you are a rafter). As the water levels increase Snake River intensity, rafting increases as well with all the services and personnel to support it. If rafting, high-traffic noise, and full campgrounds by noon are not desired, some of the less-visited "out-of-the-way" campgrounds should be considered. However, there is a price for this choice as well, given the gravel access roads are typically not well maintained and involve a great deal of distance between campgrounds. A large number of these primitive campgrounds have dropped out of service to become day-use-only areas to being nonexistent. Be sure to check the third-party reviews of specific campgrounds online if possible. In several cases we found "official" websites stating the campground to be open with full amenities only to arrive in front of a locked gate. Upon walking into the camping area, it appeared to have been unoccupied for several years.

Part of the access road to Cottonwood Lake.

#		Group sites	Tents	RV sites	Double sites	Total # of sites	Picnic area	Toilets	Showers	Drinking water	Dump station	Phone	Handicap	Recreation	Single unit fee	Double unit fee	Group unit fee	Season	Can reserve	Stay limit
1	Alpine	3		10	6	19	X	V		X				FBP	$$	$$$	$$$$$	5/1-9/30	X	14
2	Wolf Creek			20		20		V		X				FW	$$			5/1-9/30		16
3	Station Creek			16		16		V		X				FR	$$			7/1-8/31	X	14
4	East Table Creek			20		20	X	V		X				FRP	$$			6/1-8/31		14
5	Hoback			14		14		V		X				FP	$$			6/1-8/31		14
6	Kozy			8		8		V		X				FHW	$$	$$		5/1-9/30		16
7	Granite Creek			51		51		V		X				FHMP	$$			6/1-9/30		16
8	Murphy Creek			10		10		V		X				FHW	$			5/1-9/30		16
9	Moose Flat			10		10		V		X				FHW	$			5/1-9/30		16
10	Forest Park			13		13		V		X				FHW	$			5/1-9/30		16
11	Cottonwood Lake		10	8		18	X	V		X				FHHr	$			5/1-9/1		14
12	Allred Flat			32		32		V		X				HW	$			5/1-9/1		10

B = boating, F = fishing, H = hiking, Hr = horseback riding, M = mountain biking, P = picnicking, R = rafting, V = vault toilet, W = wildlife viewing

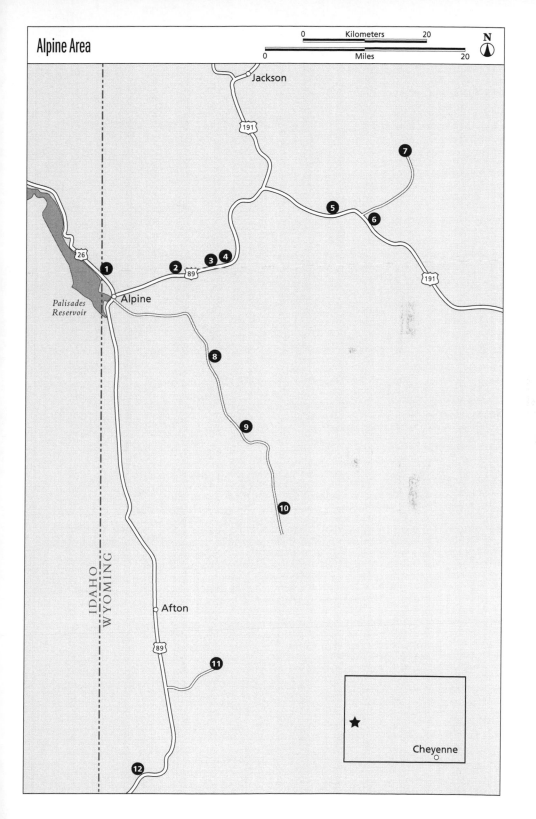

Alpine Area

Kilometers

Miles

N

Jackson

191

7

5

6

191

26

1

2

89

3

4

Alpine

Palisades
Reservoir

8

9

10

IDAHO
WYOMING

Afton

89

11

12

Cheyenne

★

1 Alpine

Location: 2 miles north of Alpine
GPS: N43 49.58' / W111 2.47'
Facilities and amenities: Vault toilets, fire rings, picnic tables, trash receptacles, drinking water, picnic area
Elevation: 5,694 feet
Road conditions: Gravel
Hookups: None
Sites: 10 basic sites, 6 double sites, 3 group sites
Maximum RV length: 40 feet long
Season: May–Sept, weather permitting
Fees: $$ per night for single units, $$$ per night for double units, $$$$$$ per night for group area, $ per night per extra vehicle
Maximum stay: 14 days
Management: Palisades Ranger District, 3659 E. Ririe Hwy., Idaho Falls, ID 83423; (208) 523-1412. AuDi Campground Services Inc., HC 82 Box 1158, Duck Creek Village, UT 84762; (541) 351-1182; audi1@scinternet.net (concessionaire).
Reservations: National Recreation Reservation Service toll-free at (877) 444-6777 or online at recreation.gov
Pets: Pets must be kept on a leash and under control at all times.
Quiet hours: 10 p.m. to 6 a.m.
ADA compliance: No
Activities: Fishing, boating, picnicking
Finding the campground: Take US 26 north out of Alpine. The campground is on the left side of the road near the Idaho border.
About the campground: Mature lodgepole pine dominate the campground, with a smattering of spruce and tall aspen trees mixed in. Rosebushes and tall grass fill the gaps between parking units. Boating and fishing are available in the nearby Palisades Reservoir and can be seen from select spots. However, access to the water and boat launching will require some travel. This area is very close to the Idaho border; only 20 percent of the lake lies in Wyoming so be aware of permit requirements.

2 Wolf Creek

Location: 8 miles northeast of Alpine
GPS: N43 11.91' / W110 54.20'
Facilities and amenities: Host on-site, vault toilets, fire rings, food-storage locker, picnic tables, trash receptacles, drinking water
Elevation: 5,795 feet
Road conditions: Gravel
Hookups: None
Sites: 20 basic sites, including 6 pull-through sites

Maximum RV length: 45 feet long
Season: May–Sept, weather permitting
Fees: $$ per night, $ per night per extra vehicle
Maximum stay: 16 days
Management: Jackson Ranger District, 25 Rosencrans Lane, PO Box 1689, Jackson, WY 83001; (307) 739-5400. AuDi Campground Services Inc., HC 82 Box 1158, Duck Creek Village, UT 84762; (541) 351-1182; audi1@scinternet.net (concessionaire).
Reservations: First-come, first-served
Pets: Pets must be on a leash and under control at all times.
Quiet hours: 10 p.m. to 6 a.m.
ADA compliance: No
Activities: Wildlife viewing, fishing
Finding the campground: Take US 26/89 northeast out of Alpine for 8 miles. The campground is on the left side of the road.
About the campground: Lodgepole pine line up along the Snake River and drink from the cold mountain water. Memorable views are found on the way to and from the campground, with some on-site as well. There is a "people's tube" for access to the river without crossing the very active highway. Fishing will take some thought, and be on the lookout for rafters passing by. Leveling can be a challenge in certain units, so be sure to evaluate the conditions carefully.

3 Station Creek

Location: 11 miles northeast of Alpine
GPS: N43 12.30' / W110 50.07'
Facilities and amenities: Vault toilets, fire rings, picnic tables, trash receptacles, drinking water
Elevation: 5,800 feet
Road conditions: Gravel
Hookups: None
Sites: 16 basic sites
Maximum RV length: 40 feet long
Season: July–Aug
Fees: $$ per night, $ per night per extra vehicle
Maximum stay: 14 days
Management: Jackson Ranger District, 25 Rosencrans Lane, PO Box 1689, Jackson, WY 83001; (307) 739-5400. AuDi Campground Services Inc., HC 82 Box 1158, Duck Creek Village, UT 84762; (541) 351-1182; audi1@scinternet.net (concessionaire).
Reservations: National Recreation Reservation Service toll-free at (877) 444-6777 or online at recreation.gov
Pets: Pets must be on a leash and under control at all times.
Quiet hours: 10 p.m. to 6 a.m.
ADA compliance: No
Activities: Fishing, rafting
Finding the campground: Take US 26/89 northeast out of Alpine for 11 miles. The campground is on the right (south) side of the road.

About the campground: A few spruce trees mingle with the lodgepole pine in this busy little place. Being early is a key factor in getting a spot here, so if it's getting dark, it would be best to pass this spot by. Traffic could get noisy at times even with the raging waters of the Snake River echoing through the canyon.

4 East Table Creek

Location: 12 miles northeast of Alpine
GPS: N43 12.77' / W110 48.46'
Facilities and amenities: Vault toilets, fire rings, picnic tables, drinking water, trash receptacles, picnic area (The picnic area is separate and typically has multiple tables for large groups.)
Elevation: 5,788 feet
Road conditions: Gravel
Hookups: None
Sites: 20 basic sites
Maximum RV length: 30 feet long
Season: June–Aug
Fees: $$ per night, $ per night per extra vehicle
Maximum stay: 14 days
Management: Jackson Ranger District, 25 Rosencrans Lane, PO Box 1689, Jackson, WY 83001; (307) 739-5400. AuDi Campground Services Inc., HC 82 Box 1158, Duck Creek Village, UT 84762; (541) 351-1182; audi1@scinternet.net (concessionaire).
Reservations: First-come, first-served
Pets: Pets must be on a leash and under control at all times.
Quiet hours: 10 p.m. to 6 a.m.
ADA compliance: No
Activities: Fishing, rafting, picnicking
Finding the campground: Take US 26/89 northeast out of Alpine for 12 miles. The campground is on the right side of the road.
About the campground: There are five pull-throughs that accommodate longer RVs, with the remaining units all back-in. Shade can be found under the mature lodgepole pine like the other nearby campgrounds.

5 Hoback

Location: 60 miles west of Pinedale
GPS: N43 12.89' / W110 48.62'
Facilities and amenities: Vault toilets, fire rings, picnic tables, drinking water, trash receptacles, picnic area
Elevation: 6,188 feet
Road conditions: Gravel
Hookups: None

Sites: 14 basic sites

Maximum RV length: 28 feet long

Season: June–Aug

Fees: $$ per night, $ per additional vehicle

Maximum stay: 14 days

Management: Jackson Ranger District, 25 Rosencrans Lane, PO Box 1689, Jackson, WY 83001; (307) 739-5400. AuDi Campground Services Inc., HC 82 Box 1158, Duck Creek Village, UT 84762; (541) 351-1182; audi1@scinternet.net (concessionaire).

Reservations: First-come, first-served

Pets: Pets must be on a leash and under control at all times.

Quiet hours: 10 p.m. to 6 a.m.

ADA compliance: No

Activities: Fishing, picnicking

Finding the campground: Take US 191 west out of Pinedale for 60 miles. The campground is on the left (south) side of the road.

About the campground: The paved, level parking area fills quickly here. The Hoback River meanders by, inviting anglers to test their skills. Spruce trees grow tall and offer some privacy with their bushy lower branches. Rosebushes fill some of the leftover space. This campground settles tightly into the canyon bottom with the Hoback River swiftly passing under the forest shade.

6 Kozy

Location: 55 miles west of Pinedale

GPS: N43 16.22' / W110 35.02'

Facilities and amenities: Vault toilet, fire rings, picnic tables, trash receptacles, drinking water

Elevation: 6,500 feet

Road conditions: Gravel

Hookups: None

Sites: 8 basic sites

Maximum RV length: 30 feet long

Season: May–Sept, weather permitting

Fees: $$ per night, $ per night per extra vehicle

Maximum stay: 16 days

Management: Jackson Ranger District, 25 Rosencrans Lane, PO Box 1689, Jackson, WY 83001; (307) 739-5400. AuDi Campground Services Inc., HC 82 Box 1158, Duck Creek Village, UT 84762; (541) 351-1182; audi1@scinternet.net (concessionaire).

Reservations: First-come, first-served

Pets: Pets must be on a leash and under control at all times.

Quiet hours: 10 p.m. to 6 a.m.

ADA compliance: No

Activities: Fishing, hiking, wildlife viewing

Finding the campground: Take US 191 west out of Pinedale for 55 miles. The campground is on the right (north) side of the road.

About the campground: When this campground was constructed, long, wide RVs with slide-outs were nonexistent. The one site listed for a 30-foot-long RV reportedly can accommodate a longer one, though leveling and getting an ideal position for all the added features will come with challenges that take time. The highway passes close by this compact area, creating some unwanted noise, though for the most part, as the sun sets so too does the noise. A host is available at a nearby campground. The other campgrounds in this area fill quickly, so if you are passing along on your way toward Jackson with a more classic "vintage" type of camper in the evening, you might consider setting up in an available unit.

7 Granite Creek

Location: 65 miles west of Pinedale
GPS: N43 21.57' / W110 26.80'
Facilities and amenities: Vault toilets, fire rings, picnic tables, trash receptacles, drinking water
Elevation: 7,100 feet
Road conditions: Gravel
Hookups: None
Sites: 51 basic sites
Maximum RV length: 28 feet long
Season: June–Sept, weather permitting
Fees: $$ per night, $ per night per extra vehicle
Maximum stay: 16 days
Management: Jackson Ranger District, 25 Rosencrans Lane, PO Box 1689, Jackson, WY 83001; (307) 739-5400. AuDi Campground Services Inc., HC 82 Box 1158, Duck Creek Village, UT 84762; (541) 351-1182; audi1@scinternet.net (concessionaire).
Reservations: National Recreation Reservation Service toll-free at (877) 444-6777 or online at recreation.gov
Pets: Pets must be on a leash and under control at all times.
Quiet hours: 10 p.m. to 6 a.m.
ADA compliance: No
Activities: Hiking, fishing, mountain biking, picnicking
Finding the campground: Take US 191 west out of Pinedale for 56 miles. Turn right just after crossing the bridge at the Granite Creek Recreation Area sign onto the gravel road and travel 9 miles.
About the campground: The campground loops circle around lengthwise above Granite Creek. Lodgepole pine fills the camping area, with a few units just outside the timber. Sagebrush, rocks, and a little grass take over from there. High, rocky mountains plunge into the canyon floor providing scenic views for those who seek them. Granite Falls drops off one of the outcrops almost within sight of the camping area. Farther upstream former visitors from the Civilian Conservation Corps constructed a concrete containment for the hot spring oozing out of the mountainside. This living piece of history shows its age but still holds the water.

8 Murphy Creek

Location: 13 miles southeast of Alpine
GPS: N43 04.42' / W110 50.16'
Facilities and amenities: Vault toilets, fire rings, picnic tables, drinking water
Elevation: 6,300 feet
Road conditions: Gravel
Hookups: None
Sites: 10 basic sites
Maximum RV length: 30 feet long, not including towing unit
Season: May–Sept, weather permitting
Fees: $ per night
Maximum stay: 16 days
Management: Greys River Ranger District, 671 N. Washington St., Afton, WY 83110; (307) 886-5300
Reservations: First-come, first-served
Pets: Pets must be on a leash and under control at all times.
Quiet hours: 10 p.m. to 6 a.m.
ADA compliance: No
Activities: Fishing, hiking, wildlife viewing
Finding the campground: In Alpine turn at the sign onto Greys River Road and travel 13 miles. Greys River Road turns to gravel and becomes FR 10138 at the forest boundary. The campground is on the right side of the road.
About the campground: Both the river and toilets are near the entrance to this campground. The back parking areas lack use and close access to the toilet. Lodgepole pines shelter the picnic tables and fire rings alike.

9 Moose Flat

Location: 22 miles southeast of Alpine
GPS: N42 58.30' / W110 46.12'
Facilities and amenities: Vault toilets, fire rings, picnic tables, drinking water
Elevation: 6,400 feet
Road conditions: Gravel
Hookups: None
Sites: 10 basic sites
Maximum RV length: 30 feet long, not including towing unit
Season: May–Sept, weather permitting
Fees: $ per night
Maximum stay: 16 days
Management: Greys River Ranger District, 671 N. Washington St., Afton, WY 83110; (307) 886-5300

Reservations: First-come, first-served
Pets: Pets must be on a leash and under control at all times.
Quiet hours: 10 p.m. to 6 a.m.
ADA compliance: No
Activities: Fishing, hiking, wildlife viewing
Finding the campground: In Alpine turn at the sign onto Greys River Road and travel 22 miles. Greys River Road turns to gravel and becomes FR 10138 at the forest boundary. The campground is on the right side of the road.
About the campground: Aspen and rosebushes share the forest with pine trees in this campground. A host site was filled, though as of our visit was not present. There was one occupied unit, though this was not a weekend so that's probably normal. The road has become quite full of washboard and annoying dust, but the camping units closer to the river are also farthest from the dust and traffic noise, with plenty of shade. ORVs, pack animals, and horses are not allowed in the campground, though there is designated parking for ORVs outside the camping area.

10 Forest Park

Location: 35 miles southeast of Alpine
GPS: N42 49.87' / W110 41.50'
Facilities and amenities: Vault toilets, fire rings, picnic tables, drinking water
Elevation: 6,930 feet
Road conditions: Gravel
Hookups: None
Sites: 13 basic sites
Maximum RV length: 30 feet long, not including towing unit
Season: May–Sept, weather permitting
Fees: $ per night
Maximum stay: 16 days
Management: Greys River Ranger District, 671 N. Washington St., Afton, WY 83110; (307) 886-5300
Reservations: First-come, first-served
Pets: Pets must be on a leash and under control at all times.
Quiet hours: 10 p.m. to 6 a.m.
ADA compliance: No
Activities: Fishing, hiking, wildlife viewing
Finding the campground: In Alpine turn at the sign onto Greys River Road and travel 35 miles. Greys River Road turns to gravel and becomes FR 10138 at the forest boundary. The campground is on the left side of the road.
About the campground: The forest hides this campground a short distance off of the road, almost within sight of an elk feeding ground. A host with an abundance of gallon water jugs occupied one of the units near the entrance. Lodgepole pines line the continuous meadow following the creek on the opposite side of the road. This campground showed the most activity of this group in spite of being the farthest away from the pavement. Perhaps the ability to park longer RVs brings more campers. Plentiful firewood came into sight at occupied campsites, but it was difficult to tell where

it came from. The forest stretches out behind and beyond, presenting the possibility of deadfall. The main road was not oiled as it was in other places in this area, but the camping is far enough off that the dust presented no major problem.

11 Cottonwood Lake

Location: 12 miles southeast of Afton
GPS: N42 38.32' / W110 49.09'
Facilities and amenities: Vault toilets, fire rings, picnic tables, drinking water, picnic area, trailhead
Elevation: 7,254 feet
Road conditions: Very rough gravel to rocky road
Hookups: None
Sites: 10 for tents, 8 basic sites
Maximum RV length: 38 feet long
Season: Memorial Day through Labor Day, weather permitting
Fees: $ per night
Maximum stay: 14 days
Management: Greys River Ranger District, 671 N. Washington St., Afton, WY 83110; (307) 886-5300
Reservations: First-come, first-served
Pets: Pets must be on a leash and under control at all times.
Quiet hours: 10 p.m. to 6 a.m.
ADA compliance: No
Activities: Fishing, hiking, horseback riding
Finding the campground: Take US 89 south out of Afton for about 8 miles. Turn left (east) at the sign onto the semi-paved CR 153/Cottonwood Creek Road and travel 6 miles to the campground entrance. About 1.5 miles from the highway, the road turns to gravel. The road goes from bad to worse for the remainder of the journey.
About the campground: Three separate areas divide the campground. Seven units allow horses with tent camping, eight units accommodate tents or RVs in a fairly flat location with large spruce standing guard, and three walk-in sites require footwork to access. Steep, forested mountains wall both Cottonwood Lake and the campground secretly into this almost enchanted area. The willow brush gets high close to the water. The picnic area takes up a portion of the lakeshore, while the camping area is a short hike away. Obviously, horses are a popular part of the recreation.

12 Allred Flat

Location: 20 miles south of Afton
GPS: N42 29.11' / W110 57.69'
Facilities and amenities: Vault toilets, fire rings, picnic tables, drinking water
Elevation: 6,726 feet

Road conditions: Gravel

Hookups: None

Sites: 32 basic sites

Maximum RV length: 30 feet long

Season: Memorial Day weekend through Labor Day weekend, weather permitting

Fees: $ per night

Maximum stay: 10 days

Management: Greys River Ranger District, 671 N. Washington St., Afton, WY 83110; (307) 886-5300

Reservations: First-come, first-served

Pets: Pets must be on a leash and under control at all times.

Quiet hours: 10 p.m. to 6 a.m.

ADA compliance: No

Activities: Hiking, wildlife viewing

Finding the campground: Take US 89 south out of Afton for 20 miles. The campground is on the right side of the highway.

About the campground: Both pull-through and back-in sites are stretched out in this mixed forest. Lodgepole pines and aspens of various ages share the sun with rosebushes and other grasses. Salt Creek meanders past on the opposite side of the highway, enticing anglers.

Black Hills North

The Black Hills attract millions every summer to visit Mount Rushmore alone. When touring this national monument and any of the other multiple attractions in the area, it would be wise to avoid traveling during the last two weeks of July through the first two weeks of August. The annual Sturgis Motorcycle Rally dominates every camping spot, public and private, along with what seems like every square foot of highway. Early spring is not too crowded, but bugs get very aggressive with an insatiable hunger for human blood—don't forget the bug spray. We have found over the course of time that late fall, when leaves change color and the daylight hours are warm but not hot, is the most desirable time to visit this popular destination.

History hides in seemingly every draw and canyon in these hills. Many tales and log cabins of the Old West are shared among the ponderosa pine trees blanketing the hillsides. Such colorful characters as "Wild Bill" Hickok and "Calamity Jane," among others, have become permanent residents at Mount Moriah Cemetery in Deadwood, should you decide to visit.

Wary trout can often be viewed in the crystal-clear waters, many of which are within very short distances of camping areas. When fishing is frustrating, it is most refreshing to pull off your boots and roll up your pants for an old-fashioned wading spree. The ice-cold water, combined with pine-scented fresh air, puts a different perspective on life instantly.

Legends live on the Black Hills of the Wyoming side. Native Americans once gathered in the shadow of a most impressive mountain and danced. The dance has in fact left its mark on both the mountain and the name of the town now occupying the area. Sundance also boasts of outlaw tales, such as the escape of the "Sundance Kid" from the local jail. Not too far away from Sundance, Devils Tower snuggles up against the western edge of the Black Hills in Wyoming.

This ancient geological wonder is reported by Native American legend to have been created when a monolithic bear attacked seven girls. To protect these girls, the ground rose under them while the bear clawed at the sides attempting to reach them; the credibility of this tale increases with your visit. However, my inquisitive mind still has questions as to how the girls got safely down.

		Group sites	Tent sites	RV sites	Total # of sites	Picnic area	Toilets	Showers	Drinking water	Dump station	Phone	Handicap	Electric hookups	Water hookups	Recreation	Fee	Season	Can reserve	Stay limit
1	Beaver Creek			8	8		V		X			Y			FHi	$$	5/15-9/15		14
2	Black Fox			9	9		V								FHi	$$	5/15-9/15		14
3	Castle Peak			9	9		V								FHiW	$$	5/15-9/15		14
4	Robaix Lake		16	37	53	X	FlV		X			Y			FBoSBi	$$$	5/15-9/15	X	14
5	Boxelder Forks			14	14		V		X						FH	$$	5/15-9/15		14
6	Dalton Lake			10	10	X	V		X						FHS	$$	5/15-9/15		14
7	Hanna		6	7	13		V		X						FH	$$$	5/22-8/28		14
8	Rod and Gun			7	7		V		X						FH	$$	5/1-9/30		14
9	Timon			7	7		V		X						FH	$$	5/1-9/30		14
10	Reuter			24	24		V		X						HiMhrC	$-$$	Year-round	X	14
11	Cook Lake Recreation Area			32	32	X	V		X						FBoWPhHiMPiD	$-$$$	Year-round	X	14
12	Bearlodge			8	8		V								Camping	$$	Year-round		10
13	Belle Fourche River	3		43	46		Fl		X			Y			HiWPh	$$-$$$$	5/15-10/15		14
	Keyhole State Park																		
14	Arch Rock			14	14		V		X			Y			FWsHi	$-$$	4/14-11/1	X	14
15	Tatanka		11	32	43	X	V		X			Y	X	X	FBoWsHiPi	$-$$	4/14-11/1	X	14
16	Pat's Point		8	28	36	X	V		X			Y			FBoWsHiPi	$-$$	4/14-11/1	X	14
17	Pronghorn			35	35		V		X						FBoSHi	$-$$	4/14-11/1	X	14
18	Beach Area			8	8		V		X			Y			FSHi	$-$$	4/14-11/1	X	14
19	Homestead		11	34	45		V		X			Y			FSHuHrHi	$-$$	4/14-11/1	X	14
20	Cottonwood Area	2	10	37	49	X	V		X			Y			FSHiPiPl	$-$$	4/14-11/1	X	14
21	Rocky Point		6		6		V								FSHi	$-$$	4/14-11/1	X	14
22	Coulter Bay		7	27	34	X	V		X						FBoSPiBr	$-$$	4/14-11/1	X	14
23	Wind Creek			14	14		V								FBoS	$-$$	4/14-11/1	X	14

Black Hills North

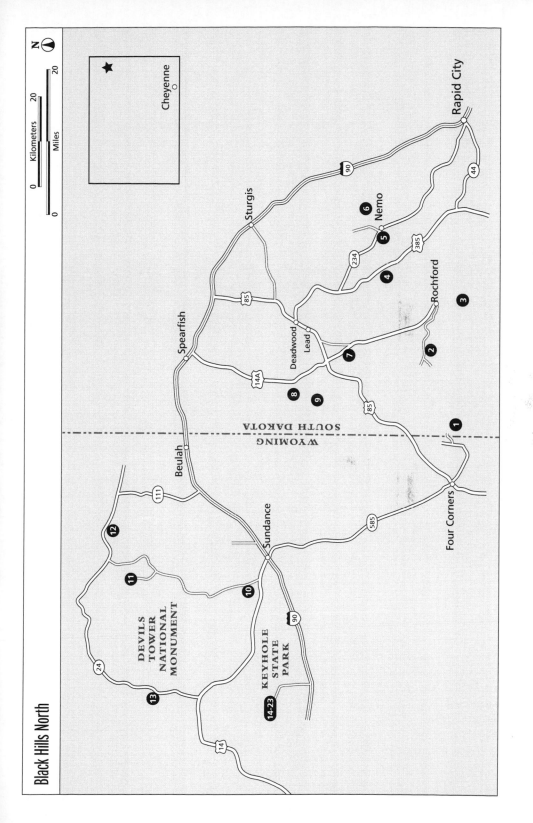

1 Beaver Creek

Location: 6 miles east of Four Corners
GPS: N44 4.48' / W104 2.99'
Facilities and amenities: Vault toilet, fire rings, picnic tables, drinking water
Elevation: 6,155 feet
Road conditions: Gravel
Hookups: None
Sites: 8 basic sites
Maximum RV length: 25 feet long
Season: Mid-May through mid-Sept
Fees: $$ per night
Maximum stay: 14 days
Management: Black Hills National Forest, Custer Ranger District, (605) 673-4853 (concessionaire). Forest Recreation Management Inc., PO Box 1168, Hill City, SD 57745; (605) 574-4402.
Reservations: First-come, first-served
Pets: Pets must be leashed and under control at all times. A per-night pet fee is required upon check-in.
Quiet hours: 10 p.m. to 6 a.m. (Generators cannot be run during this time.)
ADA compliance: No
Activities: Fishing, hiking
Finding the campground: Four Corners is about 20 miles north of Newcastle, Wyoming, or about 34 miles southwest of Lead, South Dakota. Follow the signs to Mallo Camp for 4.5 miles; it's just across from the Four Corners Store. Turn right to enter the Mallo Camp, and follow the road past the motel and later the lodge to the Wyoming–South Dakota border for 1.5 miles. Continue on this otherwise unmarked gravel road for 0.5 mile to the campground.
About the campground: Spruce trees and high banks offer plenty of shade for the trout in Beaver Creek. The picnic tables and fire rings are located close to the creek, with parking a bit of a walk. Aspen appears at different places, with granite outcrops defining the water flow. Directions to this campground are not well posted, which probably helps promote a sense of remoteness. The road is narrow and steep in places, so take your time.

2 Black Fox

Location: 49 miles south of Spearfish
GPS: N44 8.76' / W103 50.72'
Facilities and amenities: Vault toilets, fire rings, picnic tables
Elevation: 5,900 feet
Road conditions: Gravel
Hookups: None
Sites: 9 basic sites
Maximum RV length: 45 feet long

Season: Mid-May through mid-Sept, weather permitting

Fees: $$ per night

Maximum stay: 14 days

Management: Black Hills National Forest, Forest Recreation Management, PO Box 1168, Hill City, SD 57745; frm.fb@aol.com; (605) 574-4402 (concessionaire)

Reservations: First-come, first-served

Pets: $ per night, payable upon check-in

Quiet hours: 10 p.m. to 6 a.m. (Generators are not allowed to run during quiet hours.)

ADA compliance: No

Activities: Fishing, hiking

Finding the campground: Take US 14 Alternate south out of Spearfish for 20 miles. Turn left onto US 85 and travel 5 miles. Turn right onto the paved FR 17 and travel 15 miles to Rochford. Stay to the right in Rochford and follow FR 231 for 9 miles. Turn left onto FR 233 and travel 0.5 mile. The campground is along the road on the left side.

About the campground: There is likely little traffic along the road where the majority of the parking units are. The ancient hand pump is no longer used to provide water, so be sure to bring plenty. Rapid Creek meanders past spruce trees and willow brush with semi-deep pools inviting anglers and hot feet alike. The trout spook easily, making for a greater challenge and offering evidence of continued use of this seemingly forgotten refuge.

3 Castle Peak

Location: 6.3 miles southwest of Rochford

GPS: N44 4.79' / W103 43.70'

Facilities and amenities: Vault toilet, fire rings, picnic tables

Elevation: 5,496 feet

Road conditions: Very rough rocky road

Hookups: None

Sites: 9 basic sites

Maximum RV length: 20 feet long

Season: Mid-May through mid-Sept

Fees: $$ per night

Maximum stay: 14 days

Management: Forest Recreation Management Inc., PO Box 1168, Hill City, SD 57745; (605) 574-4402

Reservations: First-come, first-served

Pets: Pets must be leashed and under control at all times. A pet fee of $2 per pet per night is required upon check-in.

Quiet hours: 10 p.m. to 6 a.m. (Generators are not allowed to run during quiet hours.)

ADA compliance: No

Activities: Fishing, hiking, wildlife viewing

Finding the campground: Take US 14 Alternate south out of Spearfish for 20 miles. Turn left onto US 85 and travel 5 miles. Turn right onto the paved FR 17 and travel 15 miles to Rochford. Go west of Rochford for 0.7 mile and turn left onto the gravel South Rochford Road. Travel for 2.8 miles to the Castle Peak Road and turn left. Travel down this single-lane sharp, rocky, rough road for another 2.8 miles.

About the campground: The gold might be gone, but the pot at the end of the rainbow is still here. Moss droops off of the spruce trees, making them look like old men of the mountains. Rust-stained Castle Creek pleasantly clashes with the vertical granite cliffs further sheltering the sun. If the weather looks threatening, you would be well advised to have extra supplies. Mosquitoes can be very plentiful, so come prepared. Trailers do make the journey; however, it is going to be a test of equipment and nerves, especially if the roof extends above the pickup cab.

4 Robaix Lake

Location: 45 miles northwest of Rapid City
GPS: N44 12.47' / W103 39.20'
Facilities and amenities: Vault and flush toilets, fire rings, picnic tables, drinking water, picnic area (The picnic area is separate with multiple tables for large groups.)
Elevation: 5,471 feet
Road conditions: Paved
Hookups: None
Sites: 16 for tents and 37 basic sites
Maximum RV length: 45 feet long
Season: Mid-May through mid-Sept; 13 units are open year-round
Fees: $$$ per night
Maximum stay: 14 days
Management: Black Hills National Forest, Forest Recreation Management, PO Box 1168, Hill City, SD 57745; frm.fb@aol.com; (605) 574-4402 (concessionaire)
Reservations: National Recreation Reservation Service toll-free at (877) 444-6777 or online at recreation.gov
Pets: $ per night, payable upon check-in
Quiet hours: 10 p.m. to 6 a.m. (Generators are not allowed to run during quiet hours.)
ADA compliance: Yes
Activities: Fishing, boating, swimming, biking
Finding the campground: Take US 44 south out of Rapid City for 24 miles. Turn right onto US 385 and travel 23 miles. Turn left onto FR 255 and travel 0.5 mile. The campground is on the left.
About the campground: The refreshing waters of this small lake lure picnickers, anglers, and swimmers from near and far. All three of the camping loops are a short hike from the lake. The units are scattered among tall ponderosa pine. The sandy beaches along these 5 acres of mountain water have a specially designated swimming area with no lifeguard. A campground host is present. Firewood should be purchased or obtained elsewhere.

5 Boxelder Forks

Location: 25 miles northwest of Rapid City
GPS: N44 11.84' / W103 32.13'
Facilities and amenities: Vault toilets, fire pits, picnic tables, drinking water
Elevation: 4,750 feet
Road conditions: Gravel
Hookups: None
Sites: 14 basic sites
Maximum RV length: 45 feet long
Season: Mid-May through mid-Sept, weather permitting
Fees: $$ per night, $ per night per extra vehicle
Maximum stay: 14 days
Management: Black Hills National Forest, Forest Recreation Management, PO Box 1168, Hill City, SD 57745; frm.fb@aol.com; (605) 574-4402 (concessionaire)
Reservations: First-come, first-served
Pets: $ per night, payable upon check-in
Quiet hours: 10 p.m. to 6 a.m. (Generators are not allowed to run during quiet hours.)
ADA compliance: No
Activities: Fishing, hiking
Finding the campground: Take US 44 west out of Rapid City. Turn right onto US 385. Turn right onto Nemo Road/CR 234. At Nemo turn right onto FR 140 (going past the Nemo Store) and travel for 2 miles. *Note:* The more-traveled Ford Road just past the Nemo Store bears dead ahead, but it is not the road you want. Look for the bridge crossing the creek.
About the campground: The campground is nestled quietly within the pines, with Boxelder Creek bubbling through the shadows. Spruce and large ponderosa pine block out the burning sun's rays for most of the units. Where the shade is not too thick, the tall grass is. The fairly swift creek cuts the campground in two, with a footbridge shortcut to the toilets. A host stays at the campground. Firewood could take some energy and climbing, unless you purchase it from the host.

6 Dalton Lake

Location: 25 miles northwest of Rapid City
GPS: N44 13.81' / W103 28.44'
Facilities and amenities: Vault toilet, fire rings, picnic tables, picnic area, drinking water
Elevation: 4,400 feet
Road conditions: Groomed gravel
Hookups: None
Sites: 10 basic sites
Maximum RV length: 45 feet long
Season: Mid-May through mid-Sept, weather permitting
Fees: $$ per night, $ per night per extra vehicle
Maximum stay: 14 days

Management: Black Hills National Forest, Forest Recreation Management, PO Box 1168, Hill City, SD 57745; frm.fb@aol.com; (605) 574-4402 (concessionaire)

Reservations: First-come, first-served

Pets: $ per night, payable upon check-in

Quiet hours: 10 p.m. to 6 a.m. (Generators are not allowed to run during quiet hours.)

ADA compliance: No

Activities: Fishing, hiking, swimming

Finding the campground: Take US 44 west out of Rapid City. Turn right onto US 385 and travel 29 miles. Turn right onto Nemo Road/CR 234 and travel 11 miles. Turn left onto FR 26 and travel 4 miles. Turn right at the campground sign onto the otherwise unmarked gravel road and travel 4 miles.

About the campground: A rustic pole fence designates parking and units alike. Large spruce trees share the ground with younger aspen, resulting in plenty of shade. An old log structure shelters a huge fireplace to keep rain off any picnickers. Plenty of trout live in little Dalton Lake, but the water is a little cloudy. Between the moss and muddy-looking water, swimming might not be to your liking.

7 Hanna

Location: 20 miles south of Spearfish

GPS: N44 16.46' / W103 51.03'

Facilities and amenities: Vault toilets, fire rings, picnic tables, drinking water

Elevation: 5,550 feet

Road conditions: Gravel

Hookups: None

Sites: 7 basic sites, 6 tent sites

Maximum RV length: 55 feet long

Season: 1 week before Memorial Day through 1 week before Labor Day. Walk-in tent sites open year-round.

Fees: $$$ per night, $ per night per extra vehicle

Maximum stay: 14 days

Management: Black Hills National Forest; Forest Recreation Management, PO Box 1168, Hill City, SD 57745; (605) 574-4402; frm.fb@aol.com (concessionaire)

Reservations: First-come, first-served

Pets: $ per night, payable upon check-in

Quiet hours: 10 p.m. to 6 a.m. (Generators are not allowed to run during quiet hours.)

ADA compliance: No

Activities: Fishing, hiking

Finding the campground: Take US 14 Alternate south out of Spearfish for 18 miles. Turn right onto US 85 and travel a short distance (the turn is almost in sight). At the Hanna Campground sign, turn left and travel 2 miles.

About the campground: The crystal-clear waters of Spearfish Creek make their way past grassy meadows and tall spruce trees. Ponderosa pines blanket the mountains overlooking this peaceful place. The six tent sites require crossing the creek via a footbridge, creating a little more isolation.

The longer units are in the sun. This out-of-the-way place seems to get less traffic than other nearby campgrounds do.

8 Rod and Gun

Location: 15 miles south of Spearfish
GPS: N44 20.29' / W103 57.58'
Facilities and amenities: Vault toilets, fire rings, picnic tables, drinking water
Elevation: 5,600 feet
Road conditions: Gravel
Hookups: None
Sites: 7 standard sites
Maximum RV length: 50 feet long
Season: May–Sept, weather permitting
Fees: $$ per night, $ per night per extra vehicle
Maximum stay: 14 days
Management: Black Hills National Forest, Forest Recreation Management, PO Box 1168, Hill City, SD 57745; frm.fb@aol.com; (605) 574-4402 (concessionaire)
Reservations: First-come, first-served
Pets: $ per night, payable upon check-in
Quiet hours: 10 p.m. to 6 a.m. (Generators are not allowed to run during quiet hours.)
ADA compliance: No
Activities: Fishing, hiking
Finding the campground: Take US 14 Alternate south out of Spearfish for 12 miles. At Savoy turn right onto FR 222 and travel 3 miles.
About the campground: The grass gets high here and the temperature can, too. The spruce and aspen trees hug the banks of the crystal-clear Little Spearfish Creek rushing past. Roughlock Falls is an attraction you will pass by on your way, and is well worth taking some time to explore. The falls are quite well hidden and require wading in the ice-cold, almost knee-deep water for a full view. A developed trail leads to the water's edge, where you must continue on ancient stones positioned with seekers and photographers in mind. Homestake Mining Company maintains the Roughlock Falls Picnic Area. Before embarking on this little adventure, it would be a good idea to secure your site. The campgrounds just past the falls fill quickly any time of the week.

9 Timon

Location: 16 miles south of Spearfish
GPS: N44 19.72' / W103 59.29'
Facilities and amenities: Vault toilets, fire rings, picnic tables, drinking water
Elevation: 5,558 feet
Road conditions: Gravel
Hookups: None

Sites: 7 standard sites
Maximum RV length: 60 feet long
Season: May–Sept, weather permitting
Fees: $$ per night, $ per night per extra vehicle
Maximum stay: 14 days
Management: Black Hills National Forest; Forest Recreation Management, PO Box 1168 Hill City, SD 57745; frm.fb@aol.com; (605) 574-4402 (concessionaire)
Reservations: First-come, first-served
Pets: $ per night, payable upon check-in
Quiet hours: 10 p.m. to 6 a.m. (Generators are not allowed to run during quiet hours.)
ADA compliance: No
Activities: Fishing, hiking
Finding the campground: Take US 14 Alternate south out of Spearfish for 12 miles. At Savoy turn right onto FR 222 and travel 4 miles.
About the campground: Shade is plentiful but room is not. Huge spruce trees and tall grass crowd the units even more. Don't get in a hurry. Deadfall is nearby, making the gathering of firewood less work than at other areas. This campground tends to fill first, possibly due to the better shade on hot days. If you prefer to have isolation and inactivity, this is not the best choice. Spectacular Spearfish Canyon and Roughlock Falls draw plenty of visitors, almost creating an overworked appearance. No doubt there will be quiet moments, but there is plenty of activity between.

10 Reuter

Location: 4 miles west of Sundance
GPS: N44 25.65' / W104 25.44'
Facilities and amenities: Vault toilets, fire rings, picnic tables, drinking water
Elevation: 5,540 feet
Road conditions: Gravel
Hookups: None
Sites: 24 basic sites
Maximum RV length: 30 feet long
Season: Year-round with limitations
Fees: Mid-May to mid-Sept $$ per night (concessionaire); mid-Sept to mid-May $ per night (no water)
Maximum stay: 14 days
Management: Black Hills National Forest, Forest Recreation Management, PO Box 1168, Hill City, SD 57745; frm.fb@aol.com; (605) 574-4402 (concessionaire)
Reservations: National Recreation Reservation Service toll-free at (877) 444-6777 or online at recreation.gov
Pets: $ per night, payable upon check-in
Quiet hours: 10 p.m. to 6 a.m. (Generators are not allowed to run during quiet hours.)
ADA compliance: No
Activities: Hiking, mountain biking, horseback riding, cross-country skiing

Finding the campground: Take US 14 at exit 185 on I-90 for 1 mile west of Sundance. Turn right onto the paved FR 838 and travel about 3 miles.

About the campground: Huge ponderosa pine trees are spaced just right so that too much sun can't get in. Chipmunks, scolding pine squirrels, and multiple birds share their home with an occasional whitetail deer. Please keep in mind that this is truly their home and we are the visitors. This campground rarely fills up because of nearby Cook Lake. The long and somewhat tricky road back to the lake suggests you stay here at Reuter and take advantage of the excellent picnic area on the lakeshore via access in a more compact vehicle, assuming you have that option.

11 Cook Lake Recreation Area

Location: 21 miles north of Sundance
GPS: N44 35.35' / W104 24.22'
Facilities and amenities: Vault toilets, fire rings, picnic tables, drinking water, picnic areas, carry-down nonmotorized boat access
Elevation: 4,861 feet
Road conditions: Gravel
Hookups: None
Sites: 32 basic sites and 33 picnic sites
Maximum RV length: 45 feet long
Season: Year-round with limitations
Fees: Mid-May to mid-Sept $$$ per night, $ per day for day-use activities; $ per night mid-Sept to mid-May
Maximum stay: 14 days
Management: Black Hills National Forest, Forest Recreation Management, PO Box 1168, Hill City, SD 57745; frm.fb@aol.com; (605) 574-4402 (concessionaire)
Reservations: National Recreation Reservation Service toll-free at (877) 444-6777 or online at recreation.gov
Pets: $ per night, payable upon check-in
Quiet hours: 10 p.m. to 6 a.m. (Generators are not allowed to run during quiet hours.)
ADA compliance: No
Activities: Fishing, boating, wildlife viewing, photography, hiking, mountain biking, picnicking, day-use area
Finding the campground: Take US 14 at exit 185 on I-90 west of Sundance for 1 mile. At the Cook Lake Recreation Area sign, turn right onto FR 838 and travel 13 miles. FR 838 turns to gravel in about 7 miles. Turn right onto FR 843 and travel about 2.5 miles. Bear left to continue on FR 843 and travel 3.5 miles. Turn left onto FR 842 and travel 1 mile to Cook Lake.
About the campground: Tall ponderosa pines are far apart between cut grass. The Cliff Swallow Trail takes off from this area and offers 3.5 miles of backcountry exploration. Beaver lodges and big pine trees share the shoreline with the picnic area. Aspen sneak between pine and grass at different places along the 30 acres of the Cook Lake Recreation Area. This area fills fast on weekends, so reservations are recommended.

12 Bearlodge

Location: 24 miles north of Sundance
GPS: N44 39.38' / W104 19.68'
Facilities and amenities: Vault toilets, fire rings, picnic tables
Elevation: 4,682 feet
Road conditions: Gravel
Hookups: None
Sites: 8 basic sites
Maximum RV length: 25 feet long
Season: Year-round
Fees: $$ per night
Maximum stay: 10 days
Management: Black Hills National Forest, Forest Recreation Management, PO Box 1168, Hill City, SD 57745; frm.fb@aol.com; (605) 574-4402 (concessionaire)
Reservations: First-come, first-served
Pets: $ per night, payable upon check-in
Quiet hours: 10 p.m. to 6 a.m. (Generators are not allowed to run during quiet hours.)
ADA compliance: No
Activities: Camping
Finding the campground: Take I-90 east out of Sundance for 8 miles to the Alladin exit/exit 199. Turn left onto WY 111 and travel 9 miles. Turn left onto WY 24 and travel 7 miles. The campground is on the left side of the road.
About the campground: Even without water, this forgotten campground is a real prize for those who want to avoid the "herd." The grass and brush grow unhindered by many feet. Deadfall is plentiful, though be careful to clear away weeds and dry grass from the unused fire rings. The back road to Devils Tower offers wildlife viewing and a side of the monument few will see. If you have a taste for the unique or unusual with respect to discovering the life beyond billboards and fast-food places, this is a good option.

13 Belle Fourche River

Location: 26 miles northwest of Sundance
GPS: N44 35.03' / W104 42.86'
Facilities and amenities: Flush toilets, fire rings, picnic tables, drinking water
Elevation: 3,859 feet
Road conditions: Paved with gravel aprons
Hookups: None
Sites: 43 pull-through, 3 tents-only group sites
Maximum RV length: 35 feet long. *Note:* Loop B is recommended for long vehicles with trailers.
Season: Mid-May through mid-Oct
Fees: $$ per night, $$$ per night for group sites

Devils Tower.

Maximum stay: 14 days
Management: Devils Tower National Monument, 149 WY 110, Devils Tower, WY 82714; (307) 467-5283
Reservations: First-come, first-served
Pets: Pets must be leashed at all times and may not be left unattended.
Quiet hours: 10 p.m. to 6 a.m. *Note:* Generators permitted only from 8 a.m. to 8 p.m.
ADA compliance: Yes
Activities: Hiking, wildlife viewing, photography
Finding the campground: Take US 14 at exit 185 on I-90 west of Sundance for 20 miles. Turn right onto WY 24 and travel 6 miles. The monument is on the left side of the road.
About the campground: Legend states that seven Native American girls took refuge from a bear on a rock at this site long ago. As the aggressive bear clawed at the rock, it shot upward, keeping the girls from its grasp. The claw marks are still very visible today. Huge cottonwood trees shade the paved road of the campground. Visitors pulling trailers must unhook them in special parking areas before proceeding to the end of the park road. Campers should find a spot and set up first. The second week of August is very crowded.

Keyhole State Park

14 Arch Rock

Location: 6.8 miles north of I-90 exit 165
GPS: N44 21.66' / W104 45.83'
Facilities and amenities: Vault toilets, fire rings, picnic tables, trash receptacles, drinking water
Elevation: 4,128 feet
Road conditions: Paved to the campground entrance, gravel after
Hookups: None
Sites: 14 basic sites
Maximum RV length: 40 feet long
Season: Apr 15 through Nov 1, weather permitting
Fees: Wyoming residents: $ per day + $ per night per vehicle. Nonresidents: $$ per day + $$ per night per vehicle. *Note:* Extra charges apply for additional vehicles and electric and water hookups.
Maximum stay: 14 days
Management: Keyhole State Park, 22 Marina Rd., Moorcroft, WY 82721; (307) 756-3596
Reservations: All campsites must be reserved. Call (877) 996-7275 or go online at wyoparks.wyo .gov.
Pets: All pets must be on a leash.
Quiet hours: 10 p.m. to 6 a.m.
ADA compliance: Yes
Activities: Fishing, water sports, hiking
Finding the campground: Go north off of I-90 at the Pine Ridge Road exit/exit 165 for about 6 miles. Turn left onto Marina Road (there may not be a sign there) and travel a short distance to the fee booth. Drive past the fee booth for 0.8 mile on the access road. The campground access is on the right.
About the campground: For those who don't want or need the electric and water hookups, this campground has the same attraction as Tatanka. The pine trees offer shade and the hint of wind whispering through them when it slows down enough.

15 Tatanka

Location: 7.3 miles north of I-90 exit 165
GPS: N44 21.85' / W104 46.07'
Facilities and amenities: Vault toilets, drinking water, fire rings, picnic tables, trash receptacles, picnic area, group picnic shelter, boat ramp, water and electric hookups
Elevation: 4,088 feet

Road conditions: Paved to campground entrance, gravel after

Hookups: Water and electric

Sites: 32 RV sites with water and electric hookups, 11 tents-only sites, 4 cabins

Maximum RV length: 40 feet long

Season: Apr 15 through Nov 1, weather permitting

Fees: Wyoming residents: $ per day + $ per night per vehicle. Nonresidents: $$ per day + $$ per night per vehicle. *Note:* Extra charges apply for additional vehicles and electric and water hookups.

Maximum stay: 14 days

Management: Keyhole State Park, 22 Marina Rd., Moorcroft, WY 82721; (307) 756-3596

Reservations: All campsites must be reserved. Call (877) 996-7275 or go online at wyoparks.wyo.gov.

Pets: All pets must be on a leash.

Quiet hours: 10 p.m. to 6 a.m.

ADA compliance: Yes

Activities: Fishing, boating, water sports, hiking, picnicking

Finding the campground: Go north off of I-90 at the Pine Ridge Road exit/exit 165 for about 6 miles. Turn left onto Marina Road (there may not be a sign there) and travel a short distance to the fee booth. Drive past the fee booth for 1.3 miles on the access road. The campground access is on the right.

About the campground: This is a very popular camping spot with pine tree shade available to minimize the electricity needed to run the air conditioner. There is also good access to the cold water of the reservoir to partake of the many water sports that are the main attraction for this area. Keep in mind that these spots must be reserved, and weekends and holidays are filled well in advance.

16 Pat's Point

Location: 7.4 miles north of I-90 exit 165

GPS: N44 21.94' / W104 46.15'

Facilities and amenities: Vault toilets, fire rings, picnic tables, trash receptacles, picnic area, group picnic shelter, boat ramp, drinking water

Elevation: 4,128 feet

Road conditions: Paved to campground entrance, gravel after

Hookups: None

Sites: 28 basic sites, 8 tents-only sites

Maximum RV length: 40 feet long

Season: Apr 15 through Nov 1, weather permitting

Fees: Wyoming residents: $ per day + $ per night per vehicle. Nonresidents: $$ per day + $$ per night per vehicle. *Note:* Extra charges apply for additional vehicles and electric and water hookups.

Maximum stay: 14 days

Management: Keyhole State Park, 22 Marina Rd., Moorcroft, WY 82721; (307) 756-3596

Reservations: All campsites must be reserved. Call (877) 996-7275 or go online at wyoparks.wyo.gov.

Pets: All pets must be on a leash.

Quiet hours: 10 p.m. to 6 a.m.

ADA compliance: Yes

Activities: Fishing, boating, water sports, hiking

Finding the campground: Go north off of I-90 at the Pine Ridge Road exit/exit 165 for about 6 miles. Turn left onto Marina Road (there may not be a sign there) and travel a short distance to the fee booth. Drive past the fee booth for 1.4 miles on the access road. The campground access is on the left.

About the campground: Shade from the few pine trees is available but not abundant. The major attraction of this camping area is the relatively easy access to the water.

17 Pronghorn

Location: 7.4 miles north of I-90 exit 165

GPS: N44 21.96' / W104 46.16'

Facilities and amenities: Vault toilets, fire rings, picnic tables, trash receptacles, drinking water

Elevation: 4,140 feet

Road conditions: Paved to campground entrance, gravel after

Hookups: None

Sites: 35 basic sites

Maximum RV length: 40 feet long

Season: Apr 15 through Nov 1, weather permitting

Fees: Wyoming residents: $ per day + $ per night per vehicle. Nonresidents: $$ per day + $$ per night per vehicle. *Note:* Extra charges apply for additional vehicles and electric and water hookups.

Maximum stay: 14 days

Management: Keyhole State Park, 22 Marina Rd., Moorcroft, WY 82721; (307) 756-3596

Reservations: All campsites must be reserved. Call (877) 996-7275 or go online at wyoparks.wyo.gov.

Pets: All pets must be on a leash.

Quiet hours: 10 p.m. to 6 a.m.

ADA compliance: No

Activities: Fishing, boating, swimming, hiking

Finding the campground: Go north off of I-90 at the Pine Ridge Road exit/exit 165 for about 6 miles. Turn left onto Marina Road (there may not be a sign there) and travel a short distance to the fee booth. Drive past the fee booth for 1.4 miles on the access road. The campground access is on the right.

About the campground: Mature pine trees provide shade—it's better in some spots than others, but it can be found pretty much everywhere. Boat ramps are available but not at this camping area.

18 Beach Area

Location: 7.8 miles north of I-90 exit 165
GPS: N44 21.22' / W104 46.45'
Facilities and amenities: Vault toilets, fire rings, picnic tables, trash receptacles, beach, drinking water
Elevation: 4,150 feet
Road conditions: Paved to campground entrance, gravel after
Hookups: None
Sites: 8 basic sites
Maximum RV length: 40 feet long
Season: Apr 15 through Nov 1, weather permitting
Fees: Wyoming residents: $ per day + $ per night per vehicle. Nonresidents: $$ per day + $$ per night per vehicle. *Note:* Extra charges apply for additional vehicles and electric and water hookups.
Maximum stay: 14 days
Management: Keyhole State Park, 22 Marina Rd., Moorcroft, WY 82721; (307) 756-3596
Reservations: All campsites must be reserved. Call (877) 996-7275 or go online at wyoparks.wyo .gov.
Pets: All pets must be on a leash.
Quiet hours: 10 p.m. to 6 a.m.
ADA compliance: Yes
Activities: Fishing, swimming, hiking
Finding the campground: Go north off of I-90 at the Pine Ridge Road exit/exit 165 for about 6 miles. Turn left onto Marina Road (there may not be a sign there) and travel a short distance to the fee booth. Drive past the fee booth for 1.8 miles on the access road. The campground access is on the left.
About the campground: The primary attraction here is the beach. The marina is not that far away as well, adding to the popularity of this spot, especially on sunny weekends and holidays.

19 Homestead

Location: 6.6 miles north of I-90 exit 165
GPS: N44 21.83' / W104 45.16'
Facilities and amenities: Vault toilets, fire rings, picnic tables, drinking water
Elevation: 4,124 feet
Road conditions: Gravel
Hookups: None
Sites: 32 basic sites, 11 tents-only sites, 2 first-come, first-served basic sites
Maximum RV length: 50 feet long
Season: Apr 15 through Nov 1, weather permitting
Fees: Wyoming residents: $ per day + $ per night per vehicle. Nonresidents: $$ per day + $$ per night per vehicle. *Note:* Extra charges apply for additional vehicles and electric and water hookups.

Maximum stay: 14 days

Management: Keyhole State Park, 22 Marina Rd., Moorcroft, WY 82721; (307) 756-3596

Reservations: All campsites must be reserved. Call (877) 996-7275 or go online at wyoparks.wyo .gov.

Pets: All pets must be on a leash.

Quiet hours: 10 p.m. to 6 a.m.

ADA compliance: Yes

Activities: Fishing, swimming, hunting, hiking, horse facility

Finding the campground: Go north off of I-90 at the Pine Ridge Road exit/exit 165 for about 6.6 miles. The campground access is on the left.

About the campground: Water sports are available, but the primary attraction here is horse related including activities associated with them. Shade is available but not at every site.

20 Cottonwood Area

Location: 7.4 miles north of I-90 exit 165

GPS: N44 22.51' / W104 45.68'

Facilities and amenities: Vault toilets, fire rings, picnic tables, trash receptacles, group picnic shelter, playground, drinking water

Elevation: 4,189 feet

Road conditions: Gravel

Hookups: None

Sites: 37 basic sites, 10 tents-only sites, 2 group sites

Maximum RV length: 40 feet long

Season: Apr 15 through Nov 1, weather permitting

Fees: Wyoming residents: $ per day + $ per night per vehicle. Nonresidents: $$ per day + $$ per night per vehicle. *Note:* Extra charges apply for additional vehicles and electric and water hookups.

Maximum stay: 14 days

Management: Keyhole State Park, 22 Marina Rd., Moorcroft, WY 82721; (307) 756-3596

Reservations: All campsites must be reserved. Call (877) 996-7275 or go online at wyoparks.wyo .gov.

Pets: All pets must be on a leash.

Quiet hours: 10 p.m. to 6 a.m.

ADA compliance: Yes

Activities: Fishing, swimming, hiking, picnicking, playground

Finding the campground: Go north off of I-90 at the Pine Ridge Road exit/exit 165 for about 7.4 miles. Turn left onto the Cottonwood/Rocky Point access road and travel 0.4 mile. The campground access is on the left.

About the campground: There are pine trees here, but not many are situated for any shade benefit. Weeds are tall enough in places to indicate a lack of use and maintenance in places. It could be a rather quiet place to settle in if you're the type who likes isolation. There was no water on-site, but we did not venture any distance from the camping units so it may not be that far away.

21 Rocky Point

Location: 7.8 miles north of I-90 exit 165
GPS: N44 22.74' / W104 46.12'
Facilities and amenities: Vault toilet, fire rings, picnic tables
Elevation: 4,131 feet
Road conditions: Gravel to dirt
Hookups: None
Sites: 6 tents-only
Maximum RV length: No RVs allowed
Season: Apr 15 through Nov 1, weather permitting
Fees: Wyoming residents: $ per day + $ per night per vehicle. Nonresidents: $$ per day + $$ per night per vehicle. *Note:* Extra charges apply for additional vehicles and electric and water hookups.
Maximum stay: 14 days
Management: Keyhole State Park, 22 Marina Rd., Moorcroft, WY 82721; (307) 756-3596
Reservations: All campsites must be reserved. Call (877) 996-7275 or go online at wyoparks.wyo .gov.
Pets: All pets must be on a leash.
Quiet hours: 10 p.m. to 6 a.m.
ADA compliance: No
Activities: Fishing, swimming, hiking
Finding the campground: Go north off of I-90 at the Pine Ridge Road exit/exit 165 for about 7.4 miles. Turn left onto the Cottonwood/Rocky Point access road and travel 0.4 mile. The campground access is on the right.
About the campground: Mature pine trees are well represented in this rocky hillside, but shade will be determined by the time of day with respect to where your tent is placed. The sign at the entrance indicated drinking water was available but we did not find the source.

22 Coulter Bay

Location: Fee booth located 12 miles northeast of Moorcroft
GPS: N44 21.55' / W104 48.05'
Facilities and amenities: Vault toilets, fire rings, picnic tables, trash receptacles, boat ramp, group picnic shelter, drinking water
Elevation: 4,128 feet
Road conditions: Paved to campground entrance, gravel after
Hookups: None
Sites: 27 basic sites, 7 tents-only sites
Maximum RV length: 40 feet long
Season: Apr 15 through Nov 1, weather permitting

Fees: Wyoming residents: $ per day + $ per night per vehicle. Nonresidents: $$ per day + $$ per night per vehicle. *Note:* Extra charges apply for additional vehicles and electric and water hookups.

Maximum stay: 14 days

Management: Keyhole State Park, 22 Marina Rd., Moorcroft, WY 82721; (307) 756-3596

Reservations: All campsites must be reserved. Call (877) 996-7275 or go online at wyoparks.wyo .gov.

Pets: All pets must be on a leash.

Quiet hours: 10 p.m. to 6 a.m.

ADA compliance: No

Activities: Fishing, boating, swimming, picnicking

Finding the campground: Take either exit 153 or exit 154 to enter Moorcroft from I-90. Be on the lookout for US 14 and turn to go north and travel under I-90, with no on- or off-ramps for 5 miles. Turn right onto the paved Pine Haven Road/WY 113 and travel 5 miles east. Turn left onto the paved Pine Haven Road and travel 2 miles. Once in Pine Haven, be on the lookout for Hays Boulevard—it is easy to miss. Turn right and travel to the fee booth.

About the campground: There are pine trees close to the shoreline with most of the camping units in the open flat country some distance away. Wind could be a real issue to deal with here. The water, trash, and toilets are some distance away as well. This might be a spot to consider if all the other camping units are full. The ADA site was not paved, and there was evidence of muddy conditions for a previous camper. It could be a bit tricky to navigate. The official map does not show the accessible site, but there is a sign posted defining it as such.

23 Wind Creek

Location: 13.7 miles northeast of Moorcroft

GPS: N44 21.86' / W104 50.09'

Facilities and amenities: Vault toilets, fire rings, picnic tables, trash receptacles

Elevation: 4,128 feet

Road conditions: Gravel

Hookups: None

Sites: 14 basic sites

Maximum RV length: 40 feet long

Season: Apr 15 through Nov 1, weather permitting

Fees: Wyoming residents: $ per day + $ per night per vehicle. Nonresidents: $$ per day + $$ per night per vehicle. *Note:* Extra charges apply for additional vehicles and electric and water hookups.

Maximum stay: 14 days

Management: Keyhole State Park, 22 Marina Rd., Moorcroft, WY 82721; (307) 756-3596

Reservations: First-come, first-served

Pets: All pets must be on a leash.

Quiet hours: 10 p.m. to 6 a.m.

ADA compliance: No

Activities: Fishing, boating, swimming

Finding the campground: Take either exit 153 or exit 154 to enter Moorcroft from I-90. Be on the lookout for US 14 and turn to go north and travel under I-90, with no on- or off-ramps for 5 miles. Turn right onto the paved Pine Haven Road/WY 113 and travel 5 miles east. Turn left onto the paved Pine Haven Road and travel 2 miles. Once in Pine Haven, be on the lookout for a directional sign to the Wind Creek Campground pointing to the left. The map says it is Lakeview Drive, but we failed to see any sign. Turn to the left here and travel 1.7 miles.

About the campground: The first five camping units are scattered somewhat haphazardly in a group of pine trees with a vault toilet next to the road. It is a pretty fair distance to the lakeshore, but it's doable. The boat ramp comes next, with the remaining nine units pretty well spaced in the pine trees a lot closer to the water. Wind might get noticeable at times, but it seems a much better choice over the flat open areas of Coulter Bay. Be sure to bring plenty of drinking water as there is none provided here.

Black Hills South

Please note the information in the Black Hills North section, above, with regard to the Sturgis Motorcycle Rally. Camping may be a more realistic option in the southern hills if reservations are made far enough in advance. However, the unending traffic and seemingly endless "heavy-metal thunder" will still be present.

Lakes and reservoirs are available in this section, which also holds popular, more recently built attractions. The Mount Rushmore National Monument and the Crazy Horse Monument are obvious destinations, but for the more inquisitive, there are numerous other treasures to discover. Before his defeat at the Battle of the Little Bighorn in 1876, Lieutenant Colonel George Armstrong Custer camped in various places throughout this area, and members of his party discovered gold here, opening the area up to exploration, mining, and settlement.

Water sports abound in the many reservoirs with scenic pine-forested hills for a background. In the evening, crackling fires and cool breezes make an excellent setting for roasting marshmallows. The gentle lapping of waves along the shoreline can be a soothing addition to a brilliantly starlit night as well.

Custer State Park presents camping and abundant wildlife in the midst of spectacular geologic formations. Narrow tunnels push through adequately named needle spires of hard granite with countless cubbyholes to explore. An old fire-lookout tower invites visitors to hike up Black Elk Peak (formerly known as Harney Peak), the highest point in the Black Hills, for the chance to see five states from one spot. Naturally the weather conditions must smile favorably on the endeavor. All the same, a moderately difficult hike rewards the conquerors.

Sylvan Lake.

#	Name	Group sites	Tents	RV sites	Total # of sites	Picnic area	Toilets	Showers	Drinking water	Dump station	Phone	Handicap	Recreation	Fee	Season	Can reserve	Stay limit
1	Dutchman			40	40		V		X			Y	FBoHiMW	$$–$$$$	5/15–9/15	X	14
2	Whitetail			17	17		V		X			Y	FBoHiMWBr	$$$	5/15–9/15	X	14
3	Custer Trails		9	16	25		V		X				FBoHiMBr	$$	5/15–9/15	X	14
4	Ditch Creek			13	13		V		X				FHi	$$	5/15–9/15	X	14
5	Red Bank Springs			4	4		Po						Hi	$$–$	5/15–9/15	X	14
6	Horsethief Lake		8	28	36		V		X			Y	FHiM	$$$	5/15–9/15	X	14
7	Oreville			26	26		V		X			Y	HiMW	$$$	5/15–9/15	X	14
8	Bismarck Lake			21	21		V		X			Y	FBoHiBIWDFp	$$$	5/15–9/15	X	14
9	Comanche Park			34	34		V		X				HiBIW	$$	5/15–9/15	X	14
10	Sheridan Lake South Shore		2	125	127		V		X			Y	FBoSBiWD	$$$	5/15–9/15	X	14
11	Pactola			83	83		V		X			Y	FBoSBiW	$$$	5/15–9/15	X	14
Custer State Park																	
12	Blue Bell			31	31		FIV	X	X		X	Y	FHrHi	$$–$$$	5/1–10/14	X	14
13	Center Lake	1	14	57	72		V	X	X		X		FBoS	$–$$$	5/1–9/30	X	14
14	Game Lodge			57	57		Fl	X	X	X	X	Y	FSHi	$$–$$$	4/1–11/15	X	14
15	Grace Coolidge		10	17	27		Fl	X	X			Y	FSHi	$$–$$$	4/17–10/31	X	14
16	Legion Lake			21	21		Fl	X	X				FSHiPl	$$$	4/1–10/13	X	14
17	Stockade Lake North			42	42		FIV	X	X				FBSHi	$$$	4/1–10/7	X	14
18	Stockade Lake South			25	25		FIV	X	X				FBSHiPl	$$–$$$	4/17–10/7	X	14
19	Sylvan Lake		12	27	39		FIV	X	X				FSHi	$$–$$$	4/17–9/30	X	14
20	Elk Mountain	2	62	48	112		FIV		X			Y	HiW	$–$$	Year-round	X	14
21	Cold Brook Reservoir		12	12	12		V		X				FBoBrSHiWPiPlABe	$$	4/15–9/14	X	14
22	Cottonwood Springs Recreation Area			17	17		FIV		X				FBoHiWDPiPl	$$	4/15–9/14	X	14

A = archery range
Be = beach
Bi = biking
Bo = boating
Br = boat ramp
C = comfort station
D = day use area
F = fishing
Fl = flush toilet
Fp = fishing pier
Hi = hiking
Hr = horseback riding
M = mountain biking
Pi = picnicking
Pl = playground
Po = portable toilet
R = rock climbing
S = swimming
V = vault toilet
W = wildlife viewing

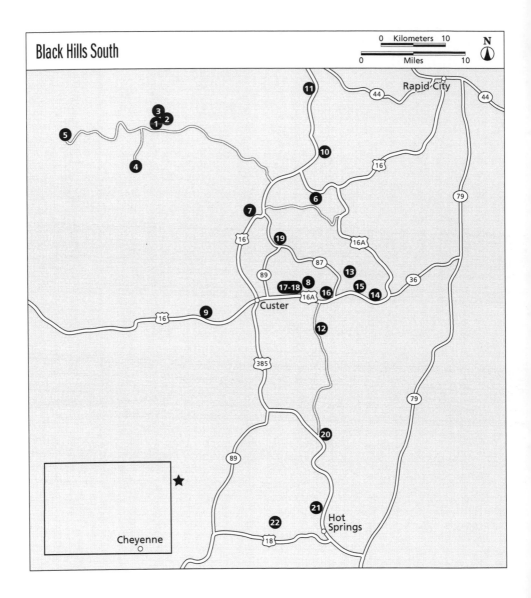

Black Hills South

0   Kilometers   10

0   Miles   10

N

Rapid City

11

44   44

10

16

79

6

7

16A

16

19

87

16

89   13

17-18 8   15

16   14

16A   36

Custer

9   12

16

385

20

89

★

21

Cheyenne   22   Hot
                         Springs

18

79

1 Dutchman

Location: 16 miles west of Hill City
GPS: N44 1.15' / W103 46.81'
Facilities and amenities: Vault toilets, fire rings, picnic tables, drinking water
Elevation: 6,055 feet
Road conditions: Gravel
Hookups: None
Sites: 40 basic sites
Maximum RV length: 50 feet long
Season: Mid-May through mid-Sept
Fees: $$ per night per unit, $$$$ per night per double unit
Maximum stay: 14 days
Management: Forest Recreation Management Inc., PO Box 1168, Hill City, SD 57745; (605) 574-4402
Reservations: National Recreation Reservation Service toll-free at (877) 444-6777 or online at recreation.gov
Pets: Pets must be leashed and under control at all times. A pet fee of $2 per pet per night is required upon check-in.
Quiet hours: 10 p.m. to 6 a.m. (Generators are not allowed to run during quiet hours.)
ADA compliance: Yes
Activities: Fishing, boating, hiking, mountain biking, wildlife viewing
Finding the campground: From Hill City go west on Highway 17/Deerfield Road approximately 14 miles to FSR 607, turn right (north) onto FSR 607, and travel 2 miles to the campground.
About the campground: The pine trees are tall and far enough apart to allow some grass to grow in between. The camping units are also separated well enough to create a sort of isolation without being too far away should you want to visit a neighbor to share a fire and roast some hot dogs. There is an available boat ramp not that far away. However, the Deerfield shoreline is a pretty good hike away.

2 Whitetail

Location: 16 miles west of Hill City
GPS: N44 0.75' / W103 48.17'
Facilities and amenities: Vault toilets, fire rings, picnic tables, drinking water, boat ramp
Elevation: 5,988 feet
Road conditions: Gravel
Hookups: None
Sites: 17 basic sites
Maximum RV length: 50 feet long
Season: Mid-May through mid-Sept
Fees: $$$ per night
Maximum stay: 14 days

Management: Forest Recreation Management Inc., PO Box 1168, Hill City, SD 57745; (605) 574-4402

Reservations: National Recreation Reservation Service toll-free at (877) 444-6777 or online at recreation.gov

Pets: Pets must be leashed and under control at all times. A pet fee of $ per pet per night is required upon check-in.

Quiet hours: 10 p.m. to 6 a.m. (Generators are not allowed to run during quiet hours.)

ADA compliance: Yes

Activities: Fishing, boating, hiking, mountain biking, wildlife viewing

Finding the campground: From Hill City take Deerfield Road (CR 308/FR 17) west for 15.1 miles to the Whitetail Campground sign (FR 421). Turn right onto FR 421 and travel 0.9 mile to the campground.

About the campground: The Whitetail Loop Road divides this campground with the north loop closer to the shoreline, although it is downhill. Pine trees dominate the camping area, and the units closest to the lake tend to fill up first. There is a boat ramp available, but it is a bit of a drive away.

3 Custer Trails

Location: 16 miles west of Hill City

GPS: N44 1.64' / W103 47.99'

Facilities and amenities: Vault toilets, fire rings, picnic tables, drinking water, boat ramp

Elevation: 5,988 feet

Road conditions: Gravel

Hookups: None

Sites: 16 basic sites, 9 tents-only sites

Maximum RV length: 50 feet long

Season: Mid-May through mid-Sept

Fees: $$ per night

Maximum stay: 14 days

Management: Forest Recreation Management Inc., PO Box 1168, Hill City, SD 57745; (605) 574-4402

Reservations: First-come, first-served

Pets: Pets must be leashed and under control at all times. A pet fee of $2 per pet per night is required upon check-in.

Quiet hours: 10 p.m. to 6 a.m. (Generators are not allowed to run during quiet hours.)

ADA compliance: No

Activities: Fishing, boating, hiking, mountain biking

Finding the campground: From Hill City take Deerfield Road west for about 23 miles to FR 417 on the northwest side of the lake. Turn right onto FR 417 and travel 1.5 miles. The campground is at the end of the road.

About the campground: The only shade available here is in the tents-only section just to the right as you enter the campground. The major attraction here is the boat ramp, with the RV camping units within walking distance of it. So if you are a boater, this is the place to stay.

4 Ditch Creek

Location: 21 miles northwest of Hill City (5 miles south of Deerfield Reservoir)
GPS: N43 57.60' / W103 50.48'
Facilities and amenities: Vault toilet, fire rings, picnic tables, drinking water (water not available during non-peak season)
Elevation: 6,248 feet
Road conditions: Gravel to improved dirt
Hookups: None
Sites: 13 basic sites
Maximum RV length: 50 feet long
Season: Mid-May through mid-Sept
Fees: $$ per night
Maximum stay: 14 days
Management: Forest Recreation Management Inc., PO Box 1168, Hill City, SD 57745; (605) 574-4402
Reservations: First-come, first-served
Pets: Pets must be leashed and under control at all times. A pet fee of $2 per pet per night is required upon check-in.
Quiet hours: 10 p.m. to 6 a.m. (Generators are not allowed to run during quiet hours.)
ADA compliance: No
Activities: Fishing, hiking
Finding the campground: From Hill City travel west on Deerfield Road 16.8 miles. Turn left onto the gravel Ditch Creek Road and travel 4 miles. The campground is on the right.
About the campground: Spruce trees and willow brush compete for space on the banks of Ditch Creek. Lush grass flourishes where the sun can find its way through. A large shade-free meadow takes up one side of the campground, which also contains the best units for larger RVs. Tents and pickup campers are better suited for the opposite side. The ice-cold waters of Ditch Creek are equally close to all of the units. Pools ranging from knee- to waist-deep offer refreshment for waders and fish for anglers. For the adventurous the limestone cliffs above the campground provide a place to explore. This is an excellent hideaway to drink in a portion of the Black Hills that is not visited by the masses seeking to touch ground at every attraction available. When the sun sets in the evening, be sure to have a coat handy. It can get chilly.

5 Red Bank Springs

Location: 29 miles west of Hill City
GPS: N43 59.45' / W103 58.85'
Facilities and amenities: Portable toilets (seasonal), fire rings, picnic tables
Elevation: 6,600 feet
Road conditions: Gravel
Hookups: None
Sites: 4 basic sites

Maximum RV length: 40 feet long

Season: Mid-May through mid-Sept

Fees: $$ per night during the regular season, $ per night during the off-season (Sept 12 through Oct 31) (The off-season is only in Sept and Oct—the campground closes Oct 31.)

Maximum stay: 14 days

Management: Forest Recreation Management Inc., PO Box 1168, Hill City, SD 57745; (605) 574-4402

Reservations: First-come, first-served

Pets: Pets must be leashed and under control at all times.

Quiet hours: 10 p.m. to 6 a.m. (Generators cannot be run during this time.)

ADA compliance: No

Activities: Hiking

Finding the campground: From Hill City take the paved Deerfield Road west for 16.8 miles. Turn left onto the gravel Ditch Creek Road and travel about 0.1 mile. Turn to the right onto the gravel South Castle Creek Road and travel 11.6 miles to the campground access road. Turn right and travel 0.7 mile.

About the campground: For those who like to camp as far away as possible from the noise and high-speed hassles of modern living, this would be a good place to spend some time. Pine and aspen trees are both well represented in this old campground with remnants of a time when it had more available camping spots. If it is late in the day, this would not be a good destination, as more than likely, it will be full. However, if the appeal of being more "primitive" than the majority of other campgrounds is worth the trip, an early morning arrival would be in order—but do have an alternate spot in mind.

6 Horsethief Lake

Location: 6.5 miles west of Keystone

GPS: N43 53.86' / W103 29.04'

Facilities and amenities: Vault toilets, fire rings, picnic tables, drinking water

Elevation: 4,957 feet

Road conditions: Paved

Hookups: None

Sites: 28 basic sites, 8 tents-only sites

Maximum RV length: 50 feet long. *Note:* RVs and trailer combinations over 25 feet total length are not allowed in the area of sites 23 through 28.

Season: Mid-May through mid-Sept

Fees: $$$ per night, $ per night per extra vehicle, $ per pet per night

Maximum stay: 14 days

Management: Forest Recreation Management Inc., PO Box 1168, Hill City, SD 57745; (605) 574-4402

Reservations: National Recreation Reservation Service toll-free at (877) 444-6777 or online at recreation.gov

Pets: Pets must be leashed and under control at all times. A pet fee of $ per pet per night is required upon check-in.

Quiet hours: 10 p.m. to 6 a.m. (Generators cannot be run during this time.)
ADA compliance: Yes
Activities: Fishing, hiking, mountain biking
Finding the campground: From Hill City take US 16/385 south 3 miles to SD 244. Turn left and travel 5.9 miles. The campground is on the right.
About the campground: The pine trees are thick here with an abundant amount of foliage in between. The paved access and parking units offer convenient walking alternatives. This is a very popular spot with Mount Rushmore close by. There are tent units closer to the Horsethief Lake shoreline, though they fill quickly.

7 Oreville

Location: 6 miles south of Hill City
GPS: N43 52.67' / W103 36.76'
Facilities and amenities: Vault toilets, fire rings, picnic tables, drinking water
Elevation: 5,313 feet
Road conditions: Paved
Hookups: None
Sites: 26 standard sites
Maximum RV length: 50 feet long
Season: Mid-May through mid-Sept
Fees: $$$ per night
Maximum stay: 14 days
Management: Forest Recreation Management Inc., PO Box 1168, Hill City, SD 57745; (605) 574-4402
Reservations: National Recreation Reservation Service toll-free at (877) 444-6777 or online at recreation.gov
Pets: Pets must be leashed and under control at all times. A pet fee of $ per pet per night is required upon check-in.
Quiet hours: 10 p.m. to 6 a.m. (Generators cannot be run during this time.)
ADA compliance: Yes
Activities: Hiking, mountain biking, wildlife viewing
Finding the campground: From Hill City take US 16 south for 5.2 miles. The campground is on the left.
About the campground: The units have plenty of space between pine trees, with aspen thickets sprinkled haphazardly about. Granite outcrops invite young and old explorers alike. The forest quietly hides special formations from passersby. Spring Creek sneaks past this area just out of sight across the highway, and as a result the trout here have far less pressure than other spots. Be very careful when crossing the highway; traffic is very active and has a reputation for going well over the speed limit. This campground is centrally located for most points of interest in the Black Hills. If you want to stay here, reservations must be made well in advance. Firewood can be purchased from the host present at the campground.

8 Bismarck Lake

Location: 5 miles east of Custer
GPS: N43 46.29' / W103 30.67'
Facilities and amenities: Vault toilets, fire rings, picnic tables, drinking water, fishing pier
Elevation: 5,207 feet
Road conditions: Paved with gravel parking aprons
Hookups: None
Sites: 21 basic sites
Maximum RV length: 55 feet long
Season: Mid-May through mid-Sept
Fees: $$$ per night, $ per night per extra vehicle
Maximum stay: 14 days
Management: Forest Recreation Management Inc., PO Box 1168, Hill City, SD 57745; (605) 574-4402
Reservations: National Recreation Reservation Service toll-free at (877) 444-6777 or online at recreation.gov
Pets: Pets must be leashed and under control at all times. A pet fee of $ per pet per night is required upon check-in.
Quiet hours: 10 p.m. to 6 a.m. (Generators are not allowed to run during quiet hours.)
ADA compliance: Yes
Activities: Fishing, boating, hiking, biking, wildlife viewing, day-use area
Finding the campground: In Custer, SD, at the intersection of SD 89/US 16A (Mount Rushmore Road) and US 16/ 385 (5th Street), take US 16A east for 4.8 miles (past Custer State Park entrance) to the Bismarck Lake Campground sign. Turn left at the sign into the campground.
About the campground: Old ponderosa pine trees and granite outcrops collide, with resulting rough terrain. An occasional aspen grove appears at random. There are three loops of parking to choose from. Units 18 through 23 are closest to the lake and boat ramp. Canoeing is the activity of choice, but electric motors are also allowed. A picnic area shares the boat ramp for a daily-use fee. A host occupies one of the available units. Firewood would best be bought or brought, depending on your capacity. This is a pleasant area to spend some time exploring. Bismarck Lake has a "no-wake" restriction that limits motorized boating, making canoeing a popular choice. There is a boat launch available. Ponderosa pine and aspen trees share the available soil among the granite rocks and grassy meadows.

9 Comanche Park

Location: 6 miles west of Custer
GPS: N43 44.17' / W103 42.74'
Facilities and amenities: Vault toilets, fire rings, picnic tables, drinking water
Elevation: 5,496 feet
Road conditions: Single lane, gravel
Hookups: None

Sites: 34 basic sites
Maximum RV length: 55 feet long
Season: Mid-May through mid-Sept
Fees: $$ per night, $ per night per extra vehicle
Maximum stay: 14 days
Management: Forest Recreation Management Inc., PO Box 1168, Hill City, SD 57745; (605) 574-4402
Reservations: National Recreation Reservation Service toll-free at (877) 444-6777 or online at recreation.gov
Pets: Pets must be leashed and under control at all times. A pet fee of $ per pet per night is required upon check-in.
Quiet hours: 10 p.m. to 6 a.m. (Generators are not allowed to run during quiet hours.)
ADA compliance: No
Activities: Hiking, biking, wildlife viewing
Finding the campground: From Custer, SD, go west on US 16 for approximately 6 miles. The campground is on the left (south) side of the highway.
About the campground: Tall pine trees populate this campground, with grassy spaces between. This campground is named for a horse named Comanche, the only survivor of Lieutenant Colonel George Armstrong Custer's 7th Cavalry, defeated at the Battle of the Little Bighorn. Captain Keogh captured this horse from the Comanches previously, and it camped near here with Custer's expedition during the winter of 1874. The tent sites are separated from the RVs by a fair distance; however, they are located close to the highway. If you have tents to break away from reminders of modern conveniences, a different campground could be more appealing. A host is available.

10 Sheridan Lake South Shore

Location: 7 miles northeast of Hill City
GPS: N43 57.99' / W103 28.70'
Facilities and amenities: Vault toilets, fire rings, picnic tables, drinking water
Elevation: 4,685 feet
Road conditions: Paved and gravel
Hookups: None
Sites: 2 for tents, 125 basic sites
Maximum RV length: 75 feet long
Season: Mid-May through mid-Sept
Fees: Peak season: $$$ per night
Maximum stay: 14 days
Management: Forest Recreation Management Inc., PO Box 1168, Hill City, SD 57745; (605) 574-4402
Reservations: National Recreation Reservation Service toll-free at (877) 444-6777 or online at recreation.gov
Pets: Pets must be leashed and under control at all times. A pet fee of $ per pet per night is required upon check-in.
Quiet hours: 10 p.m. to 6 a.m. (Generators are not allowed to run during quiet hours.)

ADA compliance: Yes
Activities: Fishing, boating, swimming, biking, wildlife viewing, day-use area
Finding the campground: Take US 16 south out of Rapid City for 18 miles to Three Forks; turn right (north) onto US 385 and travel 2 miles. Turn right onto Calumet Road and travel 1 mile to the campground.
About the campground: Ponderosa pines offer shade with plenty of space in between camping units to offer a sort of isolation. The rather gentle sloping of the geography also offers pleasant views, though the upper loops can be quite a distance from the lake shoreline.

11 Pactola

Location: 19 miles west of Rapid City
GPS: N44 3.55' / W103 29.88'
Facilities and amenities: Vault toilets, fire rings, picnic tables, drinking water
Elevation: 4,625 feet
Road conditions: Gravel
Hookups: None
Sites: 83 basic sites
Maximum RV length: 30 feet long
Season: Mid-May through mid-Sept
Fees: $$$ per night
Maximum stay: 14 days
Management: Forest Recreation Management Inc., PO Box 1168, Hill City, SD 57745; (605) 574-4402
Reservations: National Recreation Reservation Service toll-free at (877) 444-6777 or online at recreation.gov
Pets: Pets must be leashed and under control at all times. A pet fee of $ per pet per night is required upon check-in.
Quiet hours: 10 p.m. to 6 a.m. (Generators are not allowed to run during quiet hours.)
ADA compliance: Yes
Activities: Fishing, boating, swimming, biking, wildlife viewing
Finding the campground: Travel west on SD 44 for 15 miles. Turn left (south) onto US 385 and travel 2 miles. Turn right (west) onto Custer Gulch Road and travel 2 miles.
About the campground: The 30-foot-long maximum length is more of an average. Longer units can fit here, if the site is not already occupied. Mature ponderosa pine populate this campground, with shorter new growth seedlings sprouting up in the grass between them. The camping units can be a little close to each other in some spots but not all. The lake can be a bit of a hike, but it's well worth the effort.

Custer State Park

12 Blue Bell

Location: 12 miles southwest of Custer
GPS: N43 43.01' / W103 28.94'
Facilities and amenities: Host on-site, flush and vault toilets, showers, drinking water, full-service restaurant, hayride and chuckwagon cookouts, fishing licenses, horseback riding, Laundromat, resort cabins, convenience store and gift shop, fuel
Elevation: 4,877 feet
Road conditions: Paved
Hookups: Electric
Sites: 31 basic sites
Maximum RV length: 50 feet
Season: May 1 through Oct 14
Fees: $$ per night non-electric site, $$$ per night per electric site
Maximum stay: 14 days
Management: Custer State Park, (605) 255-4515; CusterStatePark@state.sd.us
Reservations: (800) 710-2267 or online at campsd.com. *Note:* Be sure to check out the "top 10 things to remember" on the website.
Pets: Pets need to be on a leash no longer than 10 feet and are not allowed in any park buildings or on designated swimming beaches. Service animals are welcome.
Quiet hours: 11 p.m. to 6 a.m. Disturbances caused by loud music, bright lights, or disorderly conduct can lead to expulsion from the park. Generators can be operated limitedly from 8 a.m. to 8 p.m. but for no more than 2 hours at a time.
ADA compliance: Yes
Activities: Fishing, horseback riding, hiking
Finding the campground: Take SD 79 south out of Rapid City for 18 miles. Turn right onto SD 36 and travel 9 miles. Turn left onto Alternate US 16 and travel 12 miles. Turn left onto SD 87 and drive 6 miles.
About the campground: There are numerous activities available in this camping area. Towering ponderosa pines provide shade with plenty of room for grass to grow and sunshine to warm up if you so choose. It all depends on where you want to place your seating arrangement. Fishing is available within 2 miles and as such will take some planning. This is mountain country with rocky hilly features that can be an adventure in motorized vehicles, but the hiking, biking, and horseback riding put things in a different light.

13 Center Lake

Location: 12.3 miles northeast of Custer
GPS: N43 48.32' / W103 25.19'
Facilities and amenities: Vault toilets, showers, fire rings, picnic tables, playground, drinking water
Elevation: 4,718 feet
Road conditions: Paved and gravel pads
Hookups: None
Sites: 57 basic sites, 14 tents-only sites, 1 youth group site
Maximum RV length: 35 feet long
Season: May 1 through Sept 30
Fees: $ tents-only, no electricity; $$ per night no electricity: $$$ per night with electricity
Maximum stay: 14 days
Management: Custer State Park, (605) 255-4515; CusterStatePark@state.sd.us
Reservations: This campground has same-day reservations with stipulations. Call (800) 710-2267.
Pets: Pets need to be on a leash no longer than 10 feet and are not allowed in any park buildings or on designated swimming beaches. Service animals are welcome.
Quiet hours: 11 p.m. to 6 a.m. Disturbances caused by loud music, bright lights, or disorderly conduct can lead to expulsion from the park. Generators can be operated limitedly from 8 a.m. to 8 p.m. but for no more than 2 hours at a time.
ADA compliance: No
Activities: Fishing, boating, swimming
Finding the campground: Take SD 79 south out of Rapid City for 18 miles. Turn right onto SD 36 and travel 9 miles. Turn left onto Alternate US 16 and travel 9 miles. Turn right onto the Needles Highway and travel 3 miles. Turn right at the Center Lake sign and travel 1 mile.
About the campground: Upper and Lower Center Lake Campgrounds are separated from the tent area. Shade is plentiful under the thick ponderosa pine. The hike from the upper campground can seem fairly long, but the shock of cold water on hot feet will drown the memory. The extremely scenic drive along the Needles Highway is a must, but be advised of very narrow, short tunnels.

14 Game Lodge

Location: 14 miles east of Custer
GPS: N43 45.64' / W103 22.26'
Facilities and amenities: Flush and vault toilets, showers, RV dump station, fire rings, picnic tables, playground, Laundromat, concessions, fuel
Elevation: 4,155 feet
Road conditions: Paved
Hookups: Electric (50 amp)
Sites: 57 basic sites
Maximum RV length: 50 feet long

Season: Apr 1 through Nov 15 with full facilities (dependent upon weather); Nov 16 through Mar 31 with comfort station closed, vault toilets, and water hydrant available
Fees: $$ per night tents-only, no electricity; $26 per night no electricity; $$$ per night with electricity
Maximum stay: 14 days
Management: Custer State Park, 13329 US Highway 16A, Custer, SD 57730; (605) 255-4515; CusterStatePark@state.sd.us
Reservations: (800) 710-2267 or online at campsd.com. $ fee for all phone reservations, $ fee for nonresidents.
Pets: Pets need to be on a leash no longer than 10 feet and are not allowed in any park buildings or on designated swimming beaches. Service animals are welcome.
Quiet hours: 11 p.m. to 6 a.m. Disturbances caused by loud music, bright lights, or disorderly conduct can lead to expulsion from the park. Generators can be operated limitedly from 8 a.m. to 8 p.m. but for no more than 2 hours at a time.
ADA compliance: Yes
Activities: Fishing, swimming, hiking
Finding the campground: Take US 16 A east out of Custer for 14 miles. The campground access road is on the right just past the visitor center.
About the campground: Ash trees are liberally planted among the paved parking units. Short grass testifies to the use of mowers for upkeep. Cold water is available for a refreshing dip in the small pool near the entrance. The pine forest borders one side of the campground, offering some shade, though most units are in the sun.

15 Grace Coolidge

Location: 11.8 miles east of Custer
GPS: N43 46.65' / W103 24.31'
Facilities and amenities: Flush toilets, showers, Laundromat, concessions, fuel, fire rings, picnic tables, drinking water
Elevation: 4,364 feet
Road conditions: Paved
Hookups: None
Sites: 17 basic sites, 10 tents-only
Maximum RV length: 40 feet long
Season: May 17 through Oct 13
Fees: $$ per night tents-only, no electricity; $$$ per night with electricity
Maximum stay: 14 days
Management: Custer State Park, 13329 US Highway 16A, Custer, SD 57730; (605) 255-4515; CusterStatePark@state.sd.us
Reservations: (800) 710-2267 or online at campsd.com. $ fee for all phone reservations, $ fee for nonresidents.
Pets: Pets need to be on a leash no longer than 10 feet and are not allowed in any park buildings or on designated swimming beaches. Service animals are welcome.

Quiet hours: 11 p.m. to 6 a.m. Disturbances caused by loud music, bright lights, or disorderly conduct can lead to expulsion from the park. Generators can be operated limitedly from 8 a.m. to 8 p.m. but for no more than 2 hours at a time.

ADA compliance: Yes

Activities: Fishing, swimming, hiking

Finding the campground: Take SD 79 south out of Rapid City for 18 miles. Turn right onto SD 36 and travel 9 miles. Turn left onto Alternate US 16 and travel 4 miles.

About the campground: Four tent sites are located across the highway in a secluded area. The shower offers a very refreshing place to visit after hiking all day. Oak trees dominate the area.

16 Legion Lake

Location: 7.4 miles east of Custer

GPS: N43 45.07' / W103 27.91'

Facilities and amenities: Flush toilets, showers, fishing dock, playground, concessions, fire rings, picnic tables, drinking water

Elevation: 5,039 feet

Road conditions: Paved

Hookups: Electric

Sites: 21 basic sites

Maximum RV length: 60 feet long

Season: May 1 through Oct 13

Fees: $$$ per night with electricity

Maximum stay: 14 days

Management: Custer State Park, 13329 US Highway 16A, Custer, SD 57730; (605) 255-4515; CusterStatePark@state.sd.us

Reservations: (800) 710-2267 or online at campsd.com. $ fee for all phone reservations, $ fee for nonresidents.

Pets: Pets need to be on a leash no longer than 10 feet and are not allowed in any park buildings or on designated swimming beaches. Service animals are welcome.

Quiet hours: 11 p.m. to 6 a.m. Disturbances caused by loud music, bright lights, or disorderly conduct can lead to expulsion from the park. Generators can be operated limitedly from 8 a.m. to 8 p.m. but for no more than 2 hours at a time.

ADA compliance: No

Activities: Fishing, swimming, hiking

Finding the campground: Take SD 79 south out of Rapid City for 18 miles. Turn right onto SD 36 and travel 9 miles. Turn left onto Alternate US 16 and travel 15 miles.

About the campground: These units are well spaced, with huge ponderosa pines scattered between the two sections. Legion Lake is just across the highway along with a store. The picnic area is closer to the lake, offering a pleasant place for a sandwich. This is a good place to set up a central base camp for large trailers and RVs. A host is present but does not offer firewood.

17 Stockade Lake North

Location: 4 miles east of Custer
GPS: N43 46.41' / W103 31.25'
Facilities and amenities: Flush and vault toilets, showers, concessions
Elevation: 5,254 feet
Road conditions: Gravel
Hookups: Electric
Sites: 42 basic sites
Maximum RV length: 60 feet long
Season: May 1 through Oct 7
Fees: $$$ per night no electricity, $$$ per night with electricity
Maximum stay: 14 days
Management: Custer State Park, 13329 US Highway 16A, Custer, SD 57730; (605) 255-4515; CusterStatePark@state.sd.us
Reservations: (800) 710-2267 or online at campsd.com. $ fee for all phone reservations, $ fee for nonresidents.
Pets: Pets need to be on a leash no longer than 10 feet and are not allowed in any park buildings or on designated swimming beaches. Service animals are welcome.
Quiet hours: 11 p.m. to 6 a.m. Disturbances caused by loud music, bright lights, or disorderly conduct can lead to expulsion from the park. Generators can be operated limitedly from 8 a.m. to 8 p.m. but for no more than 2 hours at a time.
ADA compliance: No
Activities: Fishing, boating, swimming, hiking
Finding the campground: Take SD 79 south out of Rapid City for 18 miles. Turn right onto SD 36 and travel 9 miles. Turn left onto Alternate US 16 and travel 20 miles. Follow the signs to Stockade Lake North.
About the campground: Sites must be reserved if you want to stay here, though if there is a cancellation, a stay of one night is allowed with no guarantee of another. A host is present at the campground. The pine forest housing this campground appears to have been thinned, but not enough to lose any shade. Juniper pops up here and there among the rock outcrops. Larger RVs may have some work involved in leveling up in this uneven terrain. Members of Custer's expedition reported finding gold on their way through here. As a result, John Gordon illegally led a group of gold seekers here in the fall of 1874. The group eluded army patrols assigned to keep "white men" out of the Black Hills. Seven cabins and the stockade walls were constructed in three weeks. A bitter winter and little gold found many of the original party leaving the following year. The Gordon party was eventually evicted and escorted to Fort Laramie in an attempt to honor the treaty allowing the Native Americans to possess the Black Hills. All too soon, however, gold fever infected more people than the army could dissuade. The stockade has been rebuilt and is standing at its original place a short distance from the lake named for it.

18 Stockade Lake South

Location: 4.2 miles east of Custer
GPS: N43 45.87' / W103 31.36'
Facilities and amenities: Flush and vault toilets, showers, fishing dock, playground, fire rings, picnic tables, drinking water
Elevation: 5,293 feet
Road conditions: Gravel
Hookups: Electric
Sites: 25 basic sites
Maximum RV length: 25 feet long
Season: May 17 through Oct 7
Fees: $$ per night tents-only, no electricity; $$$ per night with electricity
Maximum stay: 14 days
Management: Custer State Park, 13329 US Highway 16A, Custer, SD 57730; (605) 255-4515; CusterStatePark@state.sd.us
Reservations: (800) 710-2267 or online at campsd.com. $ fee for all phone reservations, $ fee for nonresidents.
Pets: Pets need to be on a leash no longer than 10 feet and are not allowed in any park buildings or on designated swimming beaches. Service animals are welcome.
Quiet hours: 11 p.m. to 6 a.m. Disturbances caused by loud music, bright lights, or disorderly conduct can lead to expulsion from the park. Generators can be operated limitedly from 8 a.m. to 8 p.m. but for no more than 2 hours at a time.
ADA compliance: No
Activities: Fishing, boating, swimming, hiking
Finding the campground: Take SD 79 south out of Rapid City for 18 miles. Turn right onto SD 36 and travel 9 miles. Turn left onto Alternate US 16 and travel 20 miles. Follow the signs to Stockade Lake South.
About the campground: Fireplaces built by the Civilian Conservation Corps of the 1930s both fit in this historic place and pleasantly add a striking contrast to the wild surroundings. At first glance, you might think these stone structures are left over from a cabin burning down. Yellow-bellied marmots willingly share their home with ever-changing visitors and scurry from one place to another, stopping now and then for a picture. The heated comfort station becomes a popular meeting place on a chilly day.

19 Sylvan Lake

Location: 7.3 miles northeast of Custer
GPS: N43 50.44' / W103 33.46'
Facilities and amenities: Flush and vault toilets, showers, fire rings, picnic tables, drinking water, Laundromat, concessions
Elevation: 6,282 feet
Road conditions: Paved

Hookups: Electric
Sites: 27 basic sites, 12 for tents
Maximum RV length: 27 feet long
Season: May 17 through Sept 30
Fees: $$ per night tents-only, no electricity; $$$ per night with electricity
Maximum stay: 14 days
Management: Custer State Park, 13329 US Highway 16A, Custer, SD 57730; (605) 255-4515; CusterStatePark@state.sd.us
Reservations: (800) 710-2267 or online at campsd.com. $ fee for all phone reservations, $ fee for nonresidents.
Pets: Pets need to be on a leash no longer than 10 feet and are not allowed in any park buildings or on designated swimming beaches. Service animals are welcome.
Quiet hours: 11 p.m. to 6 a.m. Disturbances caused by loud music, bright lights, or disorderly conduct can lead to expulsion from the park. Generators can be operated limitedly from 8 a.m. to 8 p.m. but for no more than 2 hours at a time.
ADA compliance: No
Activities: Fishing, swimming, hiking
Finding the campground: Take US 16A east out of Custer for 2 miles. Turn left onto SD 89 and travel 7 miles.
About the campground: Spruce trees separate the compact sites and also provide a green curtain for isolation. Parking units accommodate tents and cab-over campers best. Shower facilities add to the desire for a longer stay, but reservations are advised if you want to stay here at all. Generally, as one camper pulls out, another is waiting to pull in. Sylvan Lake is a short distance away. A very active picnic area clings to the shoreline, with backcountry trails beckoning those who want to temporarily escape the crowd. The spectacular Needles Highway is a must. Keep in mind that very narrow, low tunnels do not accommodate large vehicles. Take your time and camera when traveling this stretch.

20 Elk Mountain

Location: 19 miles south of Custer at Wind Cave National Park
GPS: N43 33.84' / W103 28.21' *Note:* Many GPS navigation systems locate the park visitor center incorrectly—pay attention to the road signs.
Facilities and amenities: Flush and vault toilets, fire rings, picnic tables, drinking water
Elevation: 4,203 feet
Road conditions: Gravel
Hookups: None. RV dump stations are in Hot Springs and Custer.
Sites: 62 tents-only sites, 48 RV-only, 2 group sites
Maximum RV length: 40 feet long
Season: Year-round (water is weather dependent)
Fees: $$ per night. Golden Age and Access Passport holders half price. When water is not available, the fee is half price for all campers.
Maximum stay: 14 days
Management: Wind Cave National Park, (605) 745-4600

Reservations: First-come, first-served

Pets: Pets must be leashed at all times.

Quiet hours: 10 p.m. to 6 a.m. (Turn off generators during quiet hours. Generators allowed from 8 a.m. to 8 p.m.)

ADA compliance: Yes

Activities: Hiking, wildlife viewing

Finding the campground: From Hot Springs drive north on US 385 for 12 miles. Turn left at the Wind Cave National Park sign and travel 0.5 mile. Turn right at the campground sign and travel 0.5 mile.

From Custer drive south on US 385 for 20 miles and follow the signs.

About the campground: Wind tends to miss this sheltered grassy draw. Perhaps you will find it in the cave that is directly under the campground. Ponderosa pines grow haphazardly throughout, with thicker stands on the higher places. The grass grows so fast that mowing is required. Firewood is sold on an honor system. Gathering wood for fires is not allowed here. Daily guided hikes are offered, and a talk is presented at the amphitheater in the evening. Five comfort stations, two of them accessible to persons with disabilities, are conveniently located in the campground. These stations offer tap water, flush toilets, electricity, and slop sinks. Keep in mind that Wind Cave is underneath, so don't just dump your gray water on the ground. Not many visitors camp here, though it is hard to understand why. Perhaps it is just not known.

21 Cold Brook Reservoir

Location: 1 mile north of Hot Springs

GPS: N43 27.84' / W103 29.49'

Facilities and amenities: Vault toilets, fire rings, grills, picnic tables, trash receptacles, drinking water, boat ramp, beach, picnic shelters, archery range, playground

Elevation: 3,603 feet

Road conditions: Gravel

Hookups: None

Sites: 12 basic sites

Maximum RV length: 50 feet long

Season: May 15 through Sept 14

Fees: $$ per night

Maximum stay: 14 days

Management: US Army Corps of Engineers, Hot Springs Office, PO Box 664, Hot Springs, SD; (605) 745-5476

Reservations: National Recreation Reservation Service toll-free at (877) 444-6777 or online at recreation.gov

Pets: Pets must be on a leash no longer than 6 feet while in the campground.

Quiet hours: 10 p.m. to 6 a.m. (turn off generators)

ADA compliance: No

Activities: Fishing, boating, swimming, hiking, wildlife viewing, picnicking

Finding the campground: From Rapid City, SD, take US 79 South, turn right onto US 18W/US 385N, and follow US 385N through Hot Springs. Shortly after the speed limit increases to 35

mph, turn left onto Badger Clark Road. At the T intersection turn right onto Evans Street and follow that road as it takes a sharp curve to the left. Then as the road splits, stay to the right and go up the hill. The road will turn to gravel—follow it to the campground and day-use area.

About the campground: At the entrance a large sign warns individuals of flash-flood hazard. Should you encounter such an event in this area, follow the instructions and find higher ground. The water level fluctuates a great deal, as the warning implies, and as a result, the elm trees are a considerable distance from the lakeshore. The reservoir sits in a scenic, red-colored, cliff-sided canyon. Motorized boats are not allowed on this lake.

22 Cottonwood Springs Recreation Area

Location: 5 miles west of Hot Springs
GPS: N43 26.64' / W103 34.34'
Facilities and amenities: Flush and vault toilets, fire rings, grills, trash receptacles, picnic tables, drinking water, lake access, picnic shelters, playground
Elevation: 3,902 feet
Road conditions: Paved
Hookups: None
Sites: 17 basic sites
Maximum RV length: 60 feet long
Season: May 15 through Sept 14
Fees: $$ per night
Maximum stay: 14 days
Management: US Army Corps of Engineers, Hot Springs Office, PO Box 664, Hot Springs, SD; (605) 745-5476
Reservations: National Recreation Reservation Service toll-free at (877) 444-6777 or online at recreation.gov
Pets: Pets must be on a leash no longer than 6 feet while in the campground.
Quiet hours: 10 p.m. to 6 a.m. (turn off generators)
ADA compliance: No
Activities: Fishing, boating, hiking, wildlife viewing, picnicking, day-use area
Finding the campground: From Rapid City, SD, take US 79 south for 57 miles to US 18W/US 385N. Turn right onto US 18 and travel 10 miles, passing through Hot Springs, to CR 17/Memorial Road. Turn right onto this gravel road and travel about 1 mile, staying to the left as the road Y's. The campground entrance is on the right.
About the campground: The comfort station includes flush toilets, electricity, and sinks. The centrally located station shares a mowed grassy slope with climbing bars and other playground equipment. Shade is short and for the most part, the sun is intense. Cedarlike trees stand on the rim along with ponderosa pines some distance from the lakeshore. This is a good place to gaze at distant stars while listening to the crackle of your campfire.

Buffalo Area

Both Native Americans and outlaws took refuge in this area, which has changed little since the days of the Wild West. The "Wild Bunch," which included Butch Cassidy and the Sundance Kid, used Outlaw Caves near Hole-in-the-Wall as a hideout. The difficult access still discourages more than a few travelers. The desertlike prairie dominating the Hole-in-the-Wall area rapidly develops into alpine meadows with thick evergreen forests of Douglas fir and lodgepole pine in the Bighorn Mountains. Outlaws were not the only contributors to the scattered artifacts of the vicinity. Chief Red Cloud of the Sioux effectively drove the US Cavalry out of the area in 1858, and you can see abandoned forts and headstones along the eastern slope. Further evidence of the Native Americans who camped in the area lives on along the western slope of the Bighorn Mountains—the town of Ten Sleep was so named for the ten sleeps it took to arrive in the area from across the mountains. The beauty and uniqueness of this area will undoubtedly create a desire to spend more time exploring the region.

Mountain lakes reflect snowy peaks contrasted against blue skies, and massive canyons hold the echoes of voices and whitewater rapids alike. Excellent fishing awaits anglers in this relatively unknown portion of Wyoming. Classic western trout streams boast unforgettable mountain scenery for a backdrop. This wonderful area is no longer a secret, so be sure to make reservations or be prepared to make changes in your ultimate destination.

Camping units can be close, but the easy access is welcome.

#		Tents	RV sites	Total # of sites	Picnic area	Toilets	Showers	Drinking water	Dump station	Handicap	Recreation	Fee	Season	Can reserve	Stay limit
1	Middle Fork		9	9		V		X			FHMW	$$	5/15–9/15	X	14
2	Circle Park		10	10		V		X			HMW	$$	6/1–8/31	X	14
3	Tie Hack		20	20		V		X		Y	FBHMW	$$	5/15–9/15	X	14
4	South Fork	5	9	14		V		X		Y	FHM	$$	6/1–9/15	X	14
5	Doyle		18	18		V		X			FHMW	$$	6/1–9/30	X	14
6	Lost Cabin		20	20		V		X			FH	$$	6/1–9/30	X	14
7	Lake View	8	12	20		V		X		Y	FBH	$$	6/1–9/30	X	14
8	Sitting Bull		43	43		V		X			FHMW	$$	6/1–9/30	X	14
9	Boulder Park		32	32		V		X			FHM	$$	6/1–9/30	X	14
10	Island Park	2	10	10		V		X			FHW	$$	6/1–9/30	X	14
11	Deer Park		7	7		V		X			FHW	$$	6/1–9/30		14
12	West Tensleep Lake	1	9	10		V		X			FBHW	$$	6/1–9/30	X	14
13	Leigh Creek	5	6	11		V		X			FHM	$$	6/1–9/30	X	14
14	Castle Gardens		4	4		V					HMPhPi	none	Year-round		14
15	Outlaw Caves		12	12		V					FHPh	none	4/15–12/31		14

B = boating, F = fishing, H = hiking, M = mountain biking, Ph = photography, Pi = picnicking, V = vault toilet, W = wildlife viewing

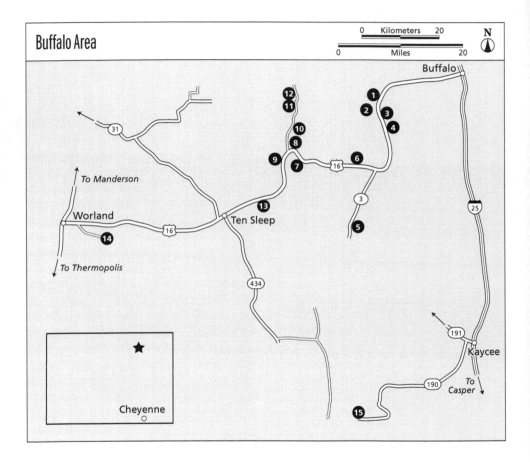

Buffalo Area

0 Kilometers 20

0 Miles 20

N

1 Middle Fork

Location: 13 miles west of Buffalo
GPS: N44 18.08' / W106 56.84'
Facilities and amenities: Host travels from South Fork Campground; vault toilets, fire rings, grills, trash receptacles, picnic tables, drinking water
Elevation: 7,414 feet
Road conditions: Gravel
Hookups: None
Sites: 8 basic sites, 1 double site
Maximum RV length: 20 feet long
Season: Mid-May through mid-Sept
Fees: $$ per night, Golden Age and Access Passport holders half price
Maximum stay: 14 days
Management: Bighorn National Forest, Powder River Ranger District, (307) 684-7806. Gallatin Canyon Campgrounds, (406) 587-9054; gccampgrounds13@gmail.com (concessionaire).
Reservations: National Recreation Reservation Service toll-free at (877) 444-6777 or online at recreation.gov
Pets: Pets must be on a leash.
Quiet hours: 10 p.m. to 6 a.m. (turn off generators)
ADA compliance: No
Activities: Fishing, hiking, mountain biking, wildlife viewing
Finding the campground: Take US 16 west out of Buffalo for 13 miles. The campground access is at the bottom of a steep and long stretch with just enough of a corner to make the access road easy to miss, so be on the lookout for the sign and slow down beforehand, carefully. The traffic coming up behind can be challenging, especially if the rigs behind are towing a heavy load. If the rear-view mirror is filled to capacity with the vehicle behind it, it would be wise to continue on the highway to the Hettinger Group Campground and turn around.
About the campground: Douglas fir, lodgepole pine, and aspen trees settle in on both sides of the Middle Fork Clear Creek. Some trees are almost in the water. The cold mountain water varies in width dependent on just how big the multitude of granite boulders are that have been placed in the way. The camping units are carefully arranged to take advantage of the best possible parking, resulting in creating an individual unit with its own identity. Trailers were present, but getting them in position must have taken more than a little maneuvering. For those with a desire to see panoramic mountain views, a hike up the steep hillside on the north will provide some "boulder piles" to climb for a great view. Toward evening, provided you are prepared with the proper lighting to get back to camp, the elk and deer can be watched coming out into the meadow for supper, with a majestic view of the Bighorn Mountains.

2 Circle Park

Location: 18 miles west of Buffalo
GPS: N44 16.89' / W106 59.20'

Facilities and amenities: Host on-site, vault toilet, fire rings, trash receptacles, picnic tables, drinking water
Elevation: 8,107 feet
Road conditions: Gravel to improved dirt
Hookups: None
Sites: 10 basic sites
Maximum RV length: 20 feet long
Season: June–Aug
Fees: $$ per night, Golden Age and Access Passport holders half price
Maximum stay: 14 days
Management: Bighorn National Forest, Powder River Ranger District, (307) 684-7806. Gallatin Canyon Campgrounds, (406) 587-9054; gccampgrounds13@gmail.com (concessionaire).
Reservations: National Recreation Reservation Service toll-free at (877) 444-6777 or online at recreation.gov
Pets: Pets must be on a leash.
Quiet hours: 10 p.m. to 6 a.m. (turn off generators)
ADA compliance: No
Activities: Hiking, mountain biking, wildlife viewing
Finding the campground: From the stop light on Main Street in Buffalo, turn right (west) onto US 16 and travel for about 14.5 miles. At FR 20 (Circle Park Road), turn right (west) onto the gravel-to-improved dirt road and travel 2.4 miles.
About the campground: Photography should be another activity listed for this area. Lodgepole pine and aspen shade the camping units to various degrees, with excellent views of the adjacent meadows. These units are spaced well enough to offer a sense of isolation. Granite pokes out in multiple places, calling to young and old alike to do some climbing. Moose, elk, and deer have all been spotted from the camping units at various times during the year. Trailer-leveling skills will be exercised to various degrees depending upon which unit is chosen.

The Circle Park Trailhead is a popular jumping-off point to enter the Cloud Peak Wilderness area near the campground. Dispersed camping is allowed in the area as well, which may be appealing when the campground is full. Stream fishing is also available and will take some effort, but the exploration can be even more rewarding. While the multitudes are working their way into the backcountry, campers can find special places few will ever see.

3 Tie Hack

Location: 15.5 miles west of Buffalo
GPS: N44 17.04' / W106 56.69'
Facilities and amenities: Host on-site, vault toilets, fire rings, grills, trash receptacles, picnic tables, drinking water
Elevation: 7,759 feet
Road conditions: Gravel
Hookups: None
Sites: 20 basic sites
Maximum RV length: 45 feet long

Season: Mid-May through mid-Sept
Fees: $$ per night, Golden Age and Access Passport holders half price
Maximum stay: 14 days
Management: Bighorn National Forest, Powder River Ranger District, (307) 684-7806. Gallatin Canyon Campgrounds, (406) 587-9054; gccampgrounds13@gmail.com (concessionaire).
Reservations: National Recreation Reservation Service toll-free at (877) 444-6777 or online at recreation.gov
Pets: Pets must be on a leash.
Quiet hours: 10 p.m. to 6 a.m. (turn off generators)
ADA compliance: Yes
Activities: Fishing, boating, hiking, mountain biking, wildlife viewing
Finding the campground: From the stop light on Main Street in Buffalo, turn right (west) onto US 16 and travel for about 15 miles to the campground sign. Turn left (east) onto FR 21 and travel on this gravel road for about 0.25 mile to the campground entrance and turn right. Continue on the gravel access road for 0.25 mile to the campground.
About the campground: The access road and parking aprons are relatively wide and well graveled, though trailers will need to be backed in. The lodgepole pines have been well thinned, leaving plenty of space in between without eliminating shade. It is much easier to see any wildlife (like the local deer). As of our visit, a returning campground host was on-site and the best source for firewood. The Tie Hack Reservoir is a short distance away and offers fishing and nonmotorized boating in combination with a scenic view. With today's smartphones, taking pictures can be easy, but be sure to take time to look around without the view screen, as there is a lot to see.

4 South Fork

Location: 16 miles west of Buffalo
GPS: N44 16.64' / W106 56.89'
Facilities and amenities: Host on-site, vault toilets, fire rings, grills, trash receptacles, picnic tables, drinking water
Elevation: 7,660 feet
Road conditions: Gravel
Hookups: None
Sites: 9 basic sites, 5 tents-only
Maximum RV length: 35 feet long
Season: June through mid-Sept
Fees: $$ per night, Golden Age and Access Passport holders half price, $ per additional vehicle
Maximum stay: 14 days
Management: Bighorn National Forest, Powder River Ranger District, (307) 684-7806. Gallatin Canyon Campgrounds, (406) 587-9054; gccampgrounds13@gmail.com (concessionaire).
Reservations: National Recreation Reservation Service toll-free at (877) 444-6777 or online at recreation.gov
Pets: Pets must be leashed and kept under physical control at all times.
Quiet hours: 10 p.m. to 6 a.m. (turn off generators)

ADA compliance: Yes
Activities: Fishing, hiking, mountain biking
Finding the campground: From the stop light on Main Street in Buffalo, turn right (west) onto US 16 and travel for about 15.5 miles. At the campground sign turn left (east) onto the gravel FR 337 and travel 0.25 mile to the campground.
About the campground: South Fork Clear Creek crashes through this campground with no shame, providing its own form of music for those who are listening. Granite cliffs confine fir and aspen trees and define the shoreline for this cold mountain water stream. Nights can get chilly here even in the summer, making it difficult to crawl out of a pleasantly warm sleeping bag. A coat of sorts will be required until a campfire is available for warming up. It takes a while for sunlight to make its way into this secluded gem. Water does take some manual labor from a hand pump, but that seems to make the cold drink even tastier.

5 Doyle

Location: 32 miles west and south of Buffalo
GPS: N44 4.39' / W106 59.33'
Facilities and amenities: Host travels from Lost Cabin Campground; vault toilets, fire rings, grills, trash receptacles, picnic tables, water
Elevation: 8,130 feet
Road conditions: Gravel to improved dirt
Hookups: None
Sites: 18 basic units
Maximum RV length: 30 feet long
Season: June–Sept
Fees: $$ per night, Golden Age and Access Passport holders half price
Maximum stay: 14 days
Management: Bighorn National Forest, Powder River Ranger District, (307) 684-7806. Gallatin Canyon Campgrounds, (406) 587-9054; gccampgrounds13@gmail.com (concessionaire).
Reservations: National Recreation Reservation Service toll-free at (877) 444-6777 or online at recreation.gov
Pets: Pets must be leashed and kept under physical control at all times.
Quiet hours: 10 p.m. to 6 a.m. (turn off generators)
ADA compliance: No
Activities: Fishing, hiking, mountain biking, wildlife viewing
Finding the campground: From the stop light on Main Street in Buffalo, turn right (west) onto US 16 and travel for about 26 miles. At the campground sign turn left (southwest) onto CR 3 and travel 6 miles. At the campground sign turn left and travel 0.3 mile.
About the campground: This campground is kind of a drive to get to. The hand-pump water can have an iron taste that is not all that uncommon in older campgrounds. But if you find that feature unpleasant, bringing your own would be worth the extra effort. The quiet and relative seclusion, barring any ATV special events that do occasionally occur, make for a very pleasant experience. There can be issues with longer trailers with slide-outs with respect to reservations. For the most

part, smaller trailers are much easier to position and level in this hard to very difficult leveling terrain. Ancient lodgepole pines stand guard and offer shade in the camping area with granite boulders shooting out at various places. Doyle Creek glides just past the entrance area to the campground, then makes a shift to the south into a sort of meadow away from the camping area. Two of the eighteen sites are pull-through, one short and one long. All of the other units are back-in.

6 Lost Cabin

Location: 25 miles west of Buffalo
GPS: N44 8.72' / W106 57.02'
Facilities and amenities: Host on-site, vault toilets, fire rings, trash receptacle, picnic tables, drinking water
Elevation: 8,215 feet
Road conditions: Gravel
Hookups: None
Sites: 8 basic sites, 10 pull-through sites, 1 double site
Maximum RV length: 50 feet long
Season: June–Sept, weather permitting
Fees: $$ per night, Golden Age and Access Passport holders half price; $$$$ per night, no discount, for double site; $ per night per additional vehicle
Maximum stay: 14 days
Management: Bighorn National Forest, Powder River Ranger District, (307) 684-7806. Gallatin Canyon Campgrounds, (406) 587-9054; gccampgrounds13@gmail.com (concessionaire).
Reservations: National Recreation Reservation Service toll-free at (877) 444-6777 or online at recreation.gov
Pets: Pets must be leashed and kept under physical control at all times.
Quiet hours: 10 p.m. to 6 a.m. (turn off generators)
ADA compliance: No
Activities: Fishing, hiking
Finding the campground: From the stop light on Main Street in Buffalo, turn right (west) onto US 16 and travel for about 25 miles. At the campground sign turn right (north) and travel 0.3 mile.
About the campground: Thick lodgepole pines tower above the relatively level units and dominate this quiet place. The grass and underbrush are green and thick, with plenty of water oozing from the ground within the central part on a wet year, so hiking can get wet in the campground proper. There is plenty of hiking territory to explore in the adjacent forest. Fishing in the stream, on the other hand, will require crossing the road. Be very careful as traffic can be extremely unpredictable and fast. Drinking water is provided by way of a hand pump, which can add to the exercise agenda or keep young ones occupied at least for a little time. A host is available. The stars and moon will not be easy to see in this thick timber, but when a gentle breeze strums the chords of the pine needles for a soothing serenade with an occasional whiff of campfire perfume, all is forgiven.

7 Lake View

Location: 20 miles east of Ten Sleep
GPS: N44 10.61' / W107 12.86'
Facilities and amenities: Host on-site, vault toilets, fire rings, trash receptacles, picnic tables, drinking water
Elevation: 8,750 feet
Road conditions: Gravel
Hookups: None
Sites: 11 basic sites, 8 tents-only, 1 double site
Maximum RV length: 60 feet long
Season: June–Sept, weather permitting
Fees: $$ per night, Golden Age and Access Passport holders half price; $$$ per night, no discount, for double site; $ per night per additional vehicle
Maximum stay: 14 days
Management: Bighorn National Forest, Powder River Ranger District, (307) 684-7806. Gallatin Canyon Campgrounds, (406) 587-9054; gccampgrounds13@gmail.com (concessionaire).
Reservations: National Recreation Reservation Service toll-free at (877) 444-6777 or online at recreation.gov
Pets: Pets must be leashed and kept under physical control at all times.
Quiet hours: 10 p.m. to 6 a.m. (turn off generators)
ADA compliance: Yes
Activities: Fishing, boating, hiking
Finding the campground: From Ten Sleep take US 16 east for about 20 miles and turn right at the campground sign.
About the campground: Meadowlark Lake is the primary attraction for this well-developed campground. The tent-camping area is a good distance away from the main campground. Highway noise may still linger in the background on a busy day. There are grassy areas with thick Douglas fir that offer a pleasant feature to the landscape for picture-postcard photos, especially if one of the local residents, such as a moose, wanders in for a snack. With respect to boating, it will take getting back on the highway and traveling back toward Ten Sleep. It is not that far, but traffic can make it difficult to make the left-hand turn; that does change on the return at the end of the day, however. Firewood can be an issue at times so bringing some from a local vendor might be a good idea, especially for the early morning chill and late summer temperature drops.

8 Sitting Bull

Location: 21 miles east of Ten Sleep
GPS: N44 11.42' / W107 12.66'
Facilities and amenities: Host on-site, vault toilets, fire rings, barbecue grills, trash receptacles, picnic tables, drinking water
Elevation: 8,686 feet

Road conditions: Gravel

Hookups: None

Sites: 41 basic sites, 1 double site

Maximum RV length: 50 feet long

Season: June–Sept, weather permitting

Fees: $$ per night, Golden Age and Access Passport holders half price; $$$$ per night, no discount, for double site; $ per night per additional vehicle

Maximum stay: 14 days

Management: Bighorn National Forest, Powder River Ranger District, (307) 684-7806. Gallatin Canyon Campgrounds, (406) 587-9054; gccampgrounds13@gmail.com (concessionaire).

Reservations: National Recreation Reservation Service toll-free at (877) 444-6777 or online at recreation.gov

Pets: Pets must be leashed and kept under physical control at all times.

Quiet hours: 10 p.m. to 6 a.m. (turn off generators)

ADA compliance: No

Activities: Fishing, hiking, mountain biking, wildlife viewing

Finding the campground: From Ten Sleep take US 16 east for about 19.9 miles to FR (FSR) 432. Turn left and travel about 1 mile to campground.

About the campground: Keep the camera handy with an eye on the rear-view mirror after turning off the main highway. Moose were seen multiple times on the access road. Keep in mind that not everyone traveling that road wants to stop and take pictures so be aware of the traffic. It can be a very busy road.

Willow brush and mountain meadows line the banks of Lake Creek as it passes by this campground. Tall lodgepole pines populate the camping area along with a pleasant mixture of Douglas fir. Inviting trails take off into the surrounding area. Four-wheel-drive roads are present, though many have been gated, limiting use to bikes, horses, and feet. Mountain biking is not allowed in wilderness areas, but this campground has some distance between it and the Cloud Peak Wilderness, if you want to bring your knobby tires. Firewood is for purchase at the host site.

9 Boulder Park

Location: 18 miles east of Ten Sleep

GPS: N44 10.14' / W107 15.09'

Facilities and amenities: Host on-site, vault toilets, fire rings, trash receptacles, picnic tables, drinking water

Elevation: 8,100 feet

Road conditions: Gravel

Hookups: None

Sites: 32 basic sites

Maximum RV length: 45 feet long

Season: June–Sept, weather permitting

Fees: $$ per night, $ per night per additional vehicle

Maximum stay: 14 days

Management: Bighorn National Forest, Powder River Ranger District, (307) 684-7806. Gallatin Canyon Campgrounds, (406) 587-9054; gccampgrounds13@gmail.com (concessionaire).

Reservations: National Recreation Reservation Service toll-free at (877) 444-6777 or online at recreation.gov

Pets: Pets must be leashed and kept under physical control at all times.

Quiet hours: 10 p.m. to 6 a.m. (turn off generators)

ADA compliance: No

Activities: Fishing, hiking, mountain biking

Finding the campground: From Ten Sleep take US 16 east for about 17 miles to FR 27. Turn left (north) onto the gravel FR 27, cross the bridge, go 0.2 mile, and turn left (west) at the sign.

About the campground: This campground is well named for the boulders that defiantly try to keep the raging Tensleep Creek from going any farther down the canyon. The irritated waters voice their disapproval loudly enough to echo off the nearby majestic limestone cliffs. The highway traffic does offer some competition with the complaining stream, but in the end the mountain music always prevails. Douglas fir shares the banks with lodgepole pine, with a narrow strip of grassy meadow centered in the camping area. Fishing might be a bit complicated with the large assortment of boulders, but not impossible. Hiking, biking, and relaxing in front of a campfire early in the evening as a cool breeze tickles the trees for a forest symphony, combined with the "hard rock" background river music, make it easy to forgive all the difficulties and delays involved on the journey.

10 Island Park

Location: 20.5 miles northeast of Ten Sleep

GPS: N44 12.32' / W107 14.27'

Facilities and amenities: Host on-site, vault toilet, fire rings, trash receptacles, picnic tables, drinking water

Elevation: 8,564 feet

Road conditions: Gravel

Hookups: None

Sites: 10 basic sites

Maximum RV length: 22 feet long (longer units can fit but will take some course-plotting)

Season: June–Sept, weather permitting

Fees: $$ per night, $ per night per additional vehicle

Maximum stay: 14 days

Management: Bighorn National Forest, Powder River Ranger District, (307) 684-7806. Gallatin Canyon Campgrounds, (406) 587-9054; gccampgrounds13@gmail.com (concessionaire).

Reservations: National Recreation Reservation Service toll-free at (877) 444-6777 or online at recreation.gov

Pets: Pets must be leashed and kept under physical control at all times.

Quiet hours: 10 p.m. to 6 a.m. (turn off generators)

ADA compliance: No

Activities: Fishing, hiking, wildlife viewing

Finding the campground: From Ten Sleep take WY 16 east for about 17 miles to FR 27. Turn left (north) onto the gravel FR 27, cross the bridge, go 0.2 mile. Turn left (west) at the sign and travel 3 miles.

About the campground: West Tensleep Creek is much more user-friendly for anglers here. Campers can settle in with the creek within view and watch the fish jump for lunch a short distance away. Lodgepole pine, spruce, and Douglas fir shade the tables and fire pits while willow brush bordered by aspen trees outlines the crystal-clear, trout-infested creek. Moose and other wildlife are often viewed having their own dinner in the lush meadows and brush as well. Highway traffic has no representation here, though there can be plenty of solitude seekers making their way to the backcountry; on a typical weekday as the sun sets so does the dust.

11 Deer Park

Location: 24 miles northeast of Ten Sleep
GPS: N44 14.66' / W107 13.36'
Facilities and amenities: Host travels from Island Park Campground; vault toilet, fire rings, trash receptacle, picnic tables, drinking water
Elevation: 8,898 feet
Road conditions: Gravel
Hookups: None
Sites: 7 basic units
Maximum RV length: 20 feet long
Season: June–Sept, weather permitting
Fees: $$ per night, Golden Age and Access Passport holders half price, $ per night per additional vehicle
Maximum stay: 14 days
Management: Bighorn National Forest, Powder River Ranger District, (307) 684-7806. Gallatin Canyon Campgrounds, (406) 587-9054; gccampgrounds13@gmail.com (concessionaire).
Reservations: First-come, first-served
Pets: Pets must be leashed and kept under physical control at all times.
Quiet hours: 10 p.m. to 6 a.m. (turn off generators)
ADA compliance: No
Activities: Fishing, hiking, wildlife viewing
Finding the campground: From Ten Sleep travel on US 16 east for about 17 miles to FR 27 and turn left (north). Cross the bridge and travel 7 miles. The campground is on the left side of the road.
About the campground: A classic western trout stream sleepily passes by this little place in a lush grassy meadow. Douglas fir inhabit the camping area proper, with firewood within walking distance. The gravel road leading to and past the campground can get busy, creating a dusty situation. Deer and moose are frequently seen in the area, and an assortment of wildflowers is present from late June through early July. A campground host is available at a nearby camping area. This is an excellent area to sit in the shade next to a campfire and scout the meadows for native inhabitants.

12 West Tensleep Lake

Location: 25 miles northeast of Ten Sleep
GPS: N44 15.42' / W107 12.92'
Facilities and amenities: Host travels from Island Park Campground; vault toilet, fire rings, trash receptacle, picnic tables, hand-pump drinking water
Elevation: 9,082 feet
Road conditions: Gravel
Hookups: None
Sites: 1 for tent, 9 basic sites
Maximum RV length: 45 feet long RV including towing unit
Season: June–Sept, weather permitting
Fees: $$ per night, Golden Age and Access Passport holders half price, $ per night per additional vehicle
Maximum stay: 14 days
Management: Bighorn National Forest, Powder River Ranger District, (307) 684-7806. Gallatin Canyon Campgrounds, (406) 587-9054; gccampgrounds13@gmail.com (concessionaire).
Reservations: National Recreation Reservation Service toll-free at (877) 444-6777 or online at recreation.gov
Pets: Pets must be leashed and kept under physical control at all times.
Quiet hours: 10 p.m. to 6 a.m. (turn off generators)
ADA compliance: No
Activities: Fishing, boating, hiking, wildlife viewing
Finding the campground: From Ten Sleep travel on US 16 east for about 17 miles to FR 27. Turn left (north) and cross the bridge, then go about 1 mile to a Y intersection. Bear right, continuing on FR 27, and go another 6 miles.
About the campground: This compact place is well situated on the shores of the postcard-quality West Tensleep Lake. Mature fir trees are well spaced, with some willow brush and grass in between. Snowcapped mountains often reflect off of the lake surface, and trout shatter the image in airborne attempts to eat lunch. Reservations are definitely the way to go, especially for larger RVs since this campground was developed long before RVs were even thought of. The nearby trailhead attracts a lot of visitors with a very noticeable amount of traffic. Purchase of firewood may involve a stop at the Island Park Campground as that is where the host is stationed. Most of the local deadfall has been picked up over the years. Keep in mind that firewood needs to be obtained at or near your destination, so keep an eye out for availability with an awareness of traffic conditions. Things can get complicated in a hurry.

Nonmotorized boating is allowed in the lake, which offers some very special photography opportunities. Be sure to bring warm clothing as the elevation in this high mountain country will have no mercy on those who don't. We can always take layers off if we have them.

13 Leigh Creek

Location: 8 miles east of Ten Sleep
GPS: N44 4.84' / W107 18.88'
Facilities and amenities: Host on-site, vault toilet, fire pits, trash receptacle, picnic tables, hand-pump drinking water
Elevation: 5,339 feet
Road conditions: Paved highway to the gravel campground access
Hookups: None
Sites: 6 basic sites, 5 tents-only
Maximum RV length: 35 feet long total length including towing unit
Season: June–Sept, weather permitting
Fees: $$ per night, Golden Age and Access Passport holders half price, $ per night per additional vehicle
Maximum stay: 14 days
Management: Bighorn National Forest, Powder River Ranger District, (307) 684-7806. Gallatin Canyon Campgrounds, (406) 587-9054; gccampgrounds13@gmail.com (concessionaire).
Reservations: National Recreation Reservation Service toll-free at (877) 444-6777 or online at recreation.gov
Pets: Pets must be leashed and kept under physical control at all times.
Quiet hours: 10 p.m. to 6 a.m. (turn off generators)
ADA compliance: No
Activities: Fishing, hiking, mountain biking
Finding the campground: From Ten Sleep travel east on US 16 for 7.5 miles. At the campground sign stay to the right and travel down the old US 16 road, now called FR 18, for 1 mile. The campground is on the right. *Note:* The old US 16 can be difficult to identify. Just before heading up grade into the canyon, a wide asphalt area will be present on the right (south) side of the highway.
About the campground: This is an older campground settled in among the willow brush, some aspen, and a few cedar trees that compete for the limited available parking space at the lower end of the canyon. Roaring Tensleep Creek drowns out any sounds from the nearby highway, providing a smashing orchestra for those who relish nature's unashamed revelation of power. Fishing and hiking are listed as activities here, though the raging creek will take some evaluation with respect to finding the fish, not to mention the thick brush and multitude of various-sized boulders that will require some forethought as well. A 35-foot trailer will fit in some parking areas but will require unhooking and some creative parking for the towing unit. In addition, slide-outs could have some extra planning involved.

The lower elevation here offers a warmer nighttime temperature, especially in the fall when the higher elevation campgrounds drop below freezing. When the leveling is all done, a campfire is crackling with hot dogs warming up in preparation for a waiting bun and marshmallows, chocolate, and graham crackers next in line, and all will be forgiven. The traffic passes by unseen and unheard thanks to the roaring waters, thick brush, and trees.

14 Castle Gardens

Location: 7 miles west and south of Ten Sleep
GPS: N43 57.42' / W107 31.03'
Facilities and amenities: Vault toilet, fire rings, barbecue grills, picnic tables, shade structures
Elevation: 5,600 feet
Road conditions: Gravel
Hookups: None
Sites: 4 basic sites
Maximum RV length: 40 feet long
Season: Year-round
Fees: None
Maximum stay: 14 days
Management: Bureau of Land Management, Worland Field Office, (307) 347-5100; worland_wymail@blm.gov
Reservations: First-come, first-served
Pets: Pets welcome; please keep them under control at all times and pick up the poop.
Quiet hours: Campers courtesy
ADA compliance: No
Activities: Hiking, mountain biking, photography, picnicking
Finding the campground: From Ten Sleep, take the first street (Old Ten Sleep Highway) west for 3 miles, then turn left on 2 Mile Hill Road and drive south approximately 4.5 miles. Veer right onto Castle Gardens Road and drive southwest 1 mile to the parking area.
About the campground: This camping area is a sort of seek-and-discover place for those who would prefer to spend some time exploring. The unique formations and panoramic snowcapped mountain backdrop have their own identity that will not be forgotten. Keep in mind that there are certain dangers, like cliffs, loose rocks, and other related features, that must be treated with the utmost caution. It is no place to be in a hurry.

Bring plenty of water as none is provided. This is a "pack it in, pack it out" place, and quite frankly, if a soda can be packed in full, it can be packed out empty even easier.

15 Outlaw Caves

Location: 81 miles south of Buffalo
GPS: N43 35.34' / W106 56.84'
Facilities and amenities: Vault toilet, fire rings, picnic tables
Elevation: 6,065 feet
Road conditions: Improved all-weather access. *Note:* High-profile 4-wheel-drive recommended for the last 3 miles.
Hookups: None
Sites: 12 primitive sites
Maximum RV length: NA, the limiting factor for trailers is clearance height.

Season: Apr 15 through Dec 31, weather permitting
Fees: None
Maximum stay: 14 days
Management: Bureau of Land Management, Buffalo Field Office, (307) 684-1100
Reservations: First-come, first-served
Pets: Pets must be kept under physical control at all times.
Quiet hours: Common courtesy
ADA compliance: No
Activities: Hiking, fishing, photography
Finding the campground: Kaycee is 45 miles south of Buffalo on I-25. Take exit 254 at Kaycee and turn right (west) on WY 191 and travel about 1 mile. Turn left (south) onto WY 190W and travel about 16 miles to Barnum. Turn left onto Bar C Road (sign for Middle Fork Powder River Management Area). This road travels directly through the headquarters of the Hole-in-the-Wall ranch. Please respect private property rights and all posted signs. Follow it for about 8 miles to the campground.

About the campground: The outlaws did not choose this location to "camp" in because of easy access. In today's world we have a more comfortable ride, but there are some that would argue that horseback would be quicker when the road gets rough. Even with high-profile vehicles and RVs, including ten-ply tires, things arrive in much better shape with the added benefit of taking in a lot more of the scenic views at a slower pace that would otherwise be missed. Don't forget your camera. There are picnic tables available, but it will take some searching to find an acceptable one for use. Bringing a suitable portable table will eliminate the search and open up additional camping spots, perhaps with a more desirable view. There are plenty of fantastic views to consider. Access to fishing and the caves requires a strenuous hike down a steep ridge (no pier), so take plenty of water and snacks. The joy can be in the journey, arrival, and exploring the area, taking in the rugged beauty in every direction.

Casper Area

Water sports are the major attraction here, with the exception of the Casper Mountain area south of Casper. It offers some pine-forested camping that hints of the Buffalo and Sheridan areas without the snowcapped mountains. Should you decide to investigate this area, a longer stay might be advised as access can take a considerable amount of time. There are reservoirs west and east of Casper, primarily along the North Platte River. They are under various management, including County and Wyoming State Parks, each with its own set of fees and regulations. Pay special attention to the reservation process. Also be advised that outside of any city of size, internet connectivity is very weak to nonexistent. It would be best to research this area while in a good internet area before embarking.

Wind can be brutal with no mercy here and without warning. Be careful about leaving camper awnings out if you should decide to tour some of the local attractions. The closer winter gets, the more abundant the wind, and summer heat can put a strain on air conditioners so pick your spots with care.

This enchanting place is waiting for its next tenant.

#		Yurts	Group sites	Tents	RV sites	Total # of sites	Hookups	Toilets	Showers	Drinking water	Dump station	Phone	Handicap	Recreation	Fee	Season	Can reserve	Stay limit	Picnic Area
1	Campbell Creek				6	6		V		X				FHiWPi	$	6/1–10/15		14	X
2	Curtis Gulch				6	6		V		X				FHiMWPi	$	6/1–10/15		14	X
3	Esterbrook				11	11		V		X			Y	HiBiWPi	$	5/15–10/15		14	X
4	Friend Park			3	8	11		V		X				FHiBiOhvWPi	$	5/15–10/15		14	X
5	Ayres Natural Bridge Park				10	10		V		X				HiPh	None	4/15–10/15		3	X
6	Rim				8	8		V					Y	HiPi	$	6/1–10/30		14	X
7	Lodgepole				15	15		V		X			Y	HiPi	$	6/1–10/30		14	X
8	Pete's Draw (Trapper's Route)				7	7		V					Y	FBoHiSWPi	$	6/1–10/30		14	X
	Natrona County Campgrounds																		
	Alcova Reservoir																		
9	Black Beach				20	20		V					Y	FBoWsHiPi	$$	5/1–10/30		10	X
10	Cottonwood Creek					Mult		V					Y	FBoWsHiPhBr	$$	5/1–10/30		10	X
11	Fremont Canyon					Mult		V					Y	FBoWsHiPhBr	$$	Year-round		10	X
12	Westside					Mult		V						FWsPi	$$	5/1–10/30		10	X
13	RV Park				22	22	All	Fl	X	X	X		Y	FBWs	$$$$	All season		10	X
14	Okie Beach				36	36		V					Y	FWsB	$	5/1–10/30		10	
15	Gray Reef Dam				8	8		V					Y	FBoFpBr	$$	Year-round		10	
	Casper Mountain																		
16	Skunk Hollow				10	10		V						HiBi	$	5/1–9/30		10	
17	Elkhorn Springs				6	6		V						HiBi	$	5/1–10/30		10	
18	Beartrap Meadows				29	29		V						HiB	$	5/1–10/30		10	
19	Deer Haven				11	11		V						HiBi	$	5/1–10/30		10	

Bi = biking, Bo = boating, Br = boat ramp, F = fishing, Fl = flush toilet, Fp = fishing pier, Hi = hiking, M = mountain biking, Mult = multiple primitive sites, Ohv = off highway vehicle, Ph = photography, Pi = picnicking, S = swimming, V = vault toilet, W = wildlife viewing, Ws = water sports

#		Yurts	Group sites	Tents	RV sites	Total # of sites	Hookups	Toilets	Showers	Drinking water	Dump station	Phone	Handicap	Recreation	Fee	Season	Can reserve	Stay limit	Picnic Area
Pathfinder Reservoir																			
20	Bishops Point					Mult		V					Y	FBoWsPi	$$	Year-round	Y	10	X
21	Weiss					Mult		V						FHiS	$$	Year-round		10	
22	Sage					Mult		V						FS	$$	Year-round		10	
23	Diabase					Mult		V						FBoWsBr	$$	Year-round		10	
Wyoming State Parks																			
Glendo State Park																			
24	Bennett Hill				44	44		V		X			Y	FBoHiWsPi	$$–$$$$	5/1–9/30		14	X
25	Waters Point				10	10		V					Y	FS	$$–$$$$	5/1–9/30		14	
26	Red Hills				22	22		V						HiS	$$–$$$$	5/1–9/30		14	
27	Cotter Bay				6	6		V					Y	FHiM	$$–$$$$	5/1–9/30		14	
28	Custer Cove				20	20		V					Y	FHiWs	$$–$$$$	5/1–9/30		14	
29	Soldier Rock				12	12		V						FHi	$$–$$$$	5/1–9/30		14	
30	Reno Cove				22	22		V		X			Y	FBoWs	$$–$$$$	5/1–9/30		14	
31	Mule Hill				13	13		V					Y	F	$$–$$$$	5/1–9/30		14	
32	Whiskey Gulch				29	29		V		X			Y	FBoWsHi	$$–$$$$	5/1–9/30		14	
33	Sagebrush				20	20		V		X			Y	FBoWs	$$–$$$$	5/1–9/30		14	
34	Shelter Point				26	26		V						FBoS	$$–$$$$	5/1–9/30		14	
35	Two Moon	3			87	90		V		X			Y	HiBiPi	$$–$$$$	Year-round		14	X
36	Sandy Beach Dune		7	16	51	74		V		X			Y	HiBiS	$$–$$$$	5/1–9/30		14	
37	Sandy Beach Willow		1	10	60	71		V		X			Y	HiBiS	$$–$$$$	5/1–9/30		14	
38	Cottonwood				14	14		V		X			Y	FHiMS	$$–$$$$	5/1–9/30		14	

Bi = biking, Bo = boating, Br = boat ramp, F = fishing, Fl = flush toilet, Fp = fishing pier, Hi = hiking, M = mountain biking , Mult = multiple primitive sites, Ohv = off highway vehicle, Ph = photography, Pi = picnicking, S = swimming, V = vault toilet, W = wildlife viewing, Ws = water sports

#	Name	Yurts	Group sites	Tents	RV sites	Total # of sites	Hookups	Toilets	Showers	Drinking water	Dump station	Phone	Handicap	Recreation	Fee	Season	Can reserve	Stay limit	Picnic Area
39	Indian Point				21	21		V						FBoMHiBr	$$-$$$$	5/1–9/30		14	
40	Broken Arrow				20	20		V						FHiM	$$-$$$$	5/1–9/30		14	
41	Elkhorn				9	9		V					Y	FBoBr	$$-$$$$	5/1–9/30		14	
	Guernsey State Park																		
42	Lower Spotted Tail				11	11		V		X				HiM	$$-$$$$	5/1–9/30		14	
43	Upper Spotted Tail				7	7		V		X				HiM	$$-$$$$	5/1–9/30		14	
44	Red Cloud				4	4		V		X				HiBiPi	$$-$$$$	5/1–9/30		14	X
45	Black Canyon Cove		1			1								HiMFPi	$$-$$$$	5/1–9/30		14	X
46	Black Canyon Point				4	4		V					Y	HiMPi	$$-$$$$	5/1–9/30		14	X
47	Fish Canyon				12	12		V		X			Y	HiM	$$-$$$$	5/1–9/30		14	
48	Fish Canyon Cove				5	5		V		X				FHiBi	$$-$$$$	5/1–9/30		14	
49	Deadman's Cove				1	1								FHiBi	$$-$$$$	5/1–9/30		14	
50	Long Canyon East				21	21		V		X			Y	FHiBi	$$-$$$$	5/1–9/30		14	X
51	Long Canyon West		2	3	5	5		V		X			Y	FBoPi	$$-$$$$	5/1–9/30		14	X
52	Skyline				19	19		V		X				HiM	$$-$$$$	5/1–9/30		14	
53	Newell Bay				3	3								FHiM	$$-$$$$	5/1–9/30		14	
54	Davis Bay				4	4							Y	FHiM	$$-$$$$	5/1–9/30		14	
55	Sandy Beach		1	16	36	53	X	V		X			Y	FBoWs	$$-$$$$	5/1–9/30		14	X
56	Cottonwood			4	5	9		V						FPi	$$-$$$$	5/1–9/30		14	X
57	Sandy Point			4	36	40	X	V		X			Y	FWsPi	$$-$$$$	5/1–9/30		14	X
58	Sandy Cove				12	12		V					Y	FWsPi	$$-$$$$	5/1–9/30		14	X

Bi = biking, Bo = boating, Br = boat ramp, F = fishing, Fl = flush toilet, Fp = fishing pier, Hi = hiking, M = mountain biking , Mult = multiple primitive sites, Ohv = off highway vehicle, Ph = photography, Pi = picnicking, S = swimming, V = vault toilet, W = wildlife viewing, Ws = water sports

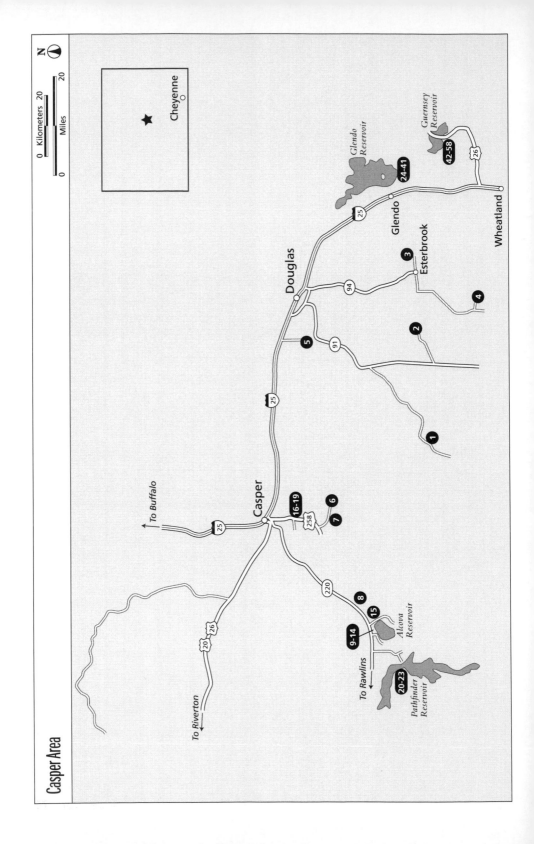

Casper Area

1 Campbell Creek

Location: 35 miles southwest of Douglas
GPS: N42 27.32' / W105 50.16'
Facilities and amenities: Vault toilet, fire rings, trash receptacles, picnic tables, drinking water
Elevation: 7,912 feet
Road conditions: Gravel
Hookups: None
Sites: 6 basic sites
Maximum RV length: 22 feet long
Season: June through mid-Oct, weather permitting
Fees: $ per night, Golden Age and Access Passport holders half price
Maximum stay: 14 days
Management: Medicine Bow National Forest, Douglas Ranger District, (307) 358-4690
Reservations: First-come, first-served
Pets: Pets must be on a leash and under control at all times.
Quiet hours: 10 p.m. to 6 a.m. (turn off generators)
ADA compliance: No
Activities: Fishing, hiking, wildlife viewing, picnicking
Finding the campground: Take WY 91 southwest out of Douglas for 20 miles and continue on CR 24 southwest for 13 miles.
About the campground: Campbell Creek bounces its way through the campground with fir and pine trees snuggled up to it. This is a fairly small campground with tight corners and challenging leveling options. There's plenty of shade, some coming from the most unique rock formations in the area. For those who prefer a more "primitive" type of camping, this is an excellent place to settle in. When the weather drops enough in temperature, the water and trash services will cease and no fee will be collected (usually from mid-Oct to mid-May). The vault toilet will be unlocked, but access to service may be delayed, so toilet paper may run short.

2 Curtis Gulch

Location: 38 miles southwest of Douglas
GPS: N42 24.45' / W105 37.46'
Facilities and amenities: Vault toilet, fire rings, trash receptacles, picnic tables, drinking water
Elevation: 6,626 feet
Road conditions: Good gravel changing to improved dirt in the campground
Hookups: None
Sites: 6 basic sites
Maximum RV length: 22 feet long
Season: June through mid-Oct, weather permitting: *Note:* Camping is allowed with no fee and with no amenities except the unlocked wheelchair-accessible vault toilet during the winter.
Fees: $ per night, Golden Age and Access Passport holders half price
Maximum stay: 14 days

Management: Medicine Bow National Forest, Douglas Ranger District, (307) 358-4690

Reservations: First-come, first-served

Pets: Pets must be on a leash and under control at all times.

Quiet hours: 10 p.m. to 6 a.m. (turn off generators)

ADA compliance: No

Activities: Fishing, hiking, mountain biking, wildlife viewing, picnicking

Finding the campground: Take WY 91 southwest for 20 miles and continue on CR 16 for 14 miles. Then take FR 658 east for 4 miles.

About the campground: This camping area is a wonderful place to relax during the heat of summer. The narrow canyon and steep side walls combined with mature ponderosa pine, aspen trees, and an assortment of willow brush and other evergreens offer an overabundance of shade. When the sun disappears in the afternoon, campfires are a welcome place to warm up and roast marshmallows. A shovel and water bucket are required tools when camping here. No doubt they are intended for stopping a campfire from getting out of control or at the very least making sure every campfire is dead out before retreating for your warm sleeping bag. La Bonte Creek wanders by on its way out of the mountains, inviting anglers, while nearby trails beckon to ATVs and mountain bikes alike.

3 Esterbrook

Location: 38 miles south of Douglas

GPS: N42 25.34' / W105 19.30'

Facilities and amenities: Vault toilet, fire rings, trash receptacles, picnic tables, drinking water

Elevation: 6,322 feet

Road conditions: Paved to campground entrance, gravel in the campground

Hookups: None

Sites: 11 basic sites

Maximum RV length: 30 feet long

Season: Mid-May through mid-Oct. *Note:* Camping is allowed with no fee and with no amenities except the unlocked wheelchair-accessible vault toilet during the winter.

Fees: $ per night, Golden Age and Access Passport holders half price

Maximum stay: 14 days

Management: Medicine Bow National Forest, Douglas Ranger District, (307) 358-4690

Reservations: First-come, first-served

Pets: Pets must be on a leash and under control at all times.

Quiet hours: 10 p.m. to 6 a.m. (turn off generators)

ADA compliance: Yes

Activities: Hiking, biking, wildlife viewing, picnicking

Finding the campground: Take WY 94 south out of Douglas for 16.4 miles. Bear left at the Y intersection and continue on CR 5/Esterbrook Road for 10.8 miles. At the Esterbrook Work Center, continue on FR 633, bearing left at 0.2 mile to stay on FR 633. Continue on FR 633 for 3 miles.

About the campground: Mature pine trees dominate this spacious campground with unmanicured grasses in between. Granite pops out of the grasses at various places, presenting a most interesting set of minerals to investigate. A hand pump provides drinking water, though there is a set of stairs required to access it, adding to the physical output. There is access to the Sunset Ridge Trail at two points within the campground. In addition, there is an OHV trailhead nearby. However, OHVs must not be operated in the campground and must remain loaded at all times while in the campground.

4 Friend Park

Location: 49 miles south of Douglas
GPS: N42 15.35' / W105 29.14'
Facilities and amenities: Vault toilets, fire rings, trash receptacles, picnic tables, drinking water
Elevation: 7,529 feet
Road conditions: There is more gravel (with various rough to very rough places) than pavement. On good weather days with little traffic, travel time is 1 1/2 hours from Douglas.
Hookups: None
Sites: 8 basic sites, 3 tents-only
Maximum RV length: 20 feet long
Season: Mid-May through mid-Oct
Fees: $ per night, Golden Age and Access Passport holders half price
Maximum stay: 14 days
Management: Medicine Bow National Forest, Laramie Ranger District, (307) 745-2300
Reservations: First-come, first-served
Pets: Pets must be leashed.
Quiet hours: 10 p.m. to 6 a.m. (turn off generators)
ADA compliance: No
Activities: Fishing, hiking, biking, OHV, wildlife viewing, picnicking
Finding the campground: Take WY 94 south out of Douglas for 17 miles (where the pavement ends) and continue onto Esterbrook Road/CR 5 for another 11 miles south. Turn right (west) on Esterbrook Road/CR 5 southwest and continue for 15 miles. Turn left (south) onto FR 671 and travel 2 miles, then turn left (east) onto FR 661 and travel 1 mile to the campground.
About the campground: Some of the lodgepole pines on-site shade more than one camping site. Larger RVs have been known to utilize this campground, but not without some serious effort with the long trip and some leveling challenges. The walk-in tent sites offer a greater separation from fellow campers, though new friends can be made as the campground fills up with those of like mind, making a memorable experience. The Laramie Peak Trail (OHV-motorized) and the Friend Park Trail (nonmotorized) are accessible from the campground. Stream fishing is available in some beaver ponds reportedly in the area, though they were not readily visible to us at the time of our visit. However, our attention was held with the 360-degree mountain scenery. Past fires have altered the tree types to more aspen, which are especially of photo quality in the fall. If you happen to be here when a substantial rain drops in, it would be advisable to stay a little longer before traveling. It's a lot easier driving on someone else's hardened ruts than to make your own.

5 Ayres Natural Bridge Park

Location: 30 miles west and south of Douglas
GPS: N42 44.02' / W105 36.69'
Facilities and amenities: Vault toilets, fire rings, barbecue grills, trash receptacles, picnic shelters with tables, drinking water
Elevation: 5,286 feet
Road conditions: Paved to the campground, then gravel
Hookups: None
Sites: 10 basic sites
Maximum RV length: 30 feet long
Season: Mid-Apr through mid-Oct, weather permitting
Fees: None
Maximum stay: 3 days
Management: Converse County, Ayres Natural Bridge Park, 448 Natural Bridge Rd., Douglas, WY 82633; (307) 358-3532
Reservations: First-come, first-served
Pets: No dogs are allowed.
Quiet hours: 10 p.m. to 6 a.m. (turn off generators)
ADA compliance: Yes
Activities: Hiking, photography
Finding the campground: Take I-25 for 37 miles east of Casper or 11 miles west of Douglas. At exit 15 take the Ayres Natural Bridge Road for 5 miles south.
About the campground: This quiet refuge really is not the best place to access with RVs, though some do make the trip. Rock cliffs hide this beautiful treasure with the natural bridge crossing over a clear-water stream.

6 Rim

Location: 33 miles south of Casper via the alternate "Circle Drive" route
GPS: N42 40.84' / W106 15.51'
Facilities and amenities: Double-vaulted toilet, fire rings, trash receptacles, level tent pads, picnic tables
Elevation: 8,289 feet
Road conditions: Gravel with some rough spots toward the end
Hookups: None
Sites: 8 basic sites
Maximum RV length: 20 feet long
Season: June–Oct, weather permitting
Fees: $ per night, $ per night per additional vehicle, Golden Age and Access Passport holders half price
Maximum stay: 14 days

Management: Bureau of Land Management, Casper Field Office, (307) 261-7600; casper_wymail@blm.gov

Reservations: First-come, first-served

Pets: Pets must be on a leash and not left unattended.

Quiet hours: 10 p.m. to 7 a.m.

ADA compliance: The campground is wheelchair accessible, though the primary access for both sites and vault toilet are packed gravel.

Activities: Hiking, picnicking

Finding the campground: Alternate route for large RVs: Start at the WY 257 intersection and travel west from Casper on US 220 for 10 miles. At WY 487 turn left (south) and travel 8.6 miles to Circle Drive/CR 505. Turn left (east) onto this gravel road and travel 9 miles. Turn right (south) onto the gravel BLM road and travel 4.5 miles to the Muddy Mountain Environmental Education Area. Upon entering the EEA, continue straight and travel 0.25 mile to the campground entrance on the left.

About the campground: Larger RVs, including towing units with travel trailers, will find a much gentler grade by taking the alternate "Circle" road, though it is more gravel and a greater distance of travel. The main Casper Mountain Road has some very steep and tight "hairpin" turns that can be nerve-testing going to or from the campground. There is no drinking water at this campground, but it is available at the nearby Lodgepole Campground, with the interpretation of "nearby" open to your point of view. The lodgepole pine trees offer shade but will take a little evaluation on positioning for the best options as days can become hot. Evenings are generally cooler to cold at times.

7 Lodgepole

Location: 32 miles south of Casper via the alternate "Circle Drive" route

GPS: N42 40.64' / W106 15.82'

Facilities and amenities: Vault toilets, fire rings, trash receptacles, picnic tables, drinking water

Elevation: 8,236 feet

Road conditions: Gravel

Hookups: None

Sites: 15 basic sites with level tent pads

Maximum RV length: 20 feet long

Season: June–Oct, weather permitting

Fees: $ per night, $3 per night per additional vehicle, Golden Age and Access Passport holders half price

Maximum stay: 14 days

Management: Bureau of Land Management, Casper Field Office, (307) 261-7600; casper_wymail@blm.gov

Reservations: First-come, first-served

Pets: Pets must be on a leash and not left unattended.

Quiet hours: 10 p.m. to 7 a.m.

ADA compliance: The campground is wheelchair accessible, though the primary access for both sites and vault toilet are packed gravel.

Activities: Hiking, picnicking

Finding the campground: Alternate route for large RVs: Start at the WY 257 intersection and travel west from Casper on US 220 for 10 miles. At WY 487 turn left (south) and travel 8.6 miles to Circle Drive/CR 505. Turn left (east) onto this gravel road and travel 9 miles. Turn right (south) onto the gravel BLM road and travel 4.5 miles to the Muddy Mountain Environmental Education Area. Upon entering the EEA, turn right and travel 0.2 mile to the campground entrance on the left.

About the campground: Larger RVs, including towing units with travel trailers, will find a much gentler grade by taking the alternate "Circle" road, though it is more gravel and a greater distance of travel. The main Casper Mountain Road has some very steep and tight "hairpin" turns that can be nerve-testing going to or from the campground. There are ADA-accessible trails linking the two campgrounds here. The pine trees offer shade, though some evaluation is in order as the afternoon heat can be intense. Sunshine seems to be more appreciated when present earlier in the day.

8 Pete's Draw (Trapper's Route)

Location: 33.5 miles west of Casper
GPS: N42 34.81' / W106 41.28'
Facilities and amenities: Vault toilets, table and shelters, fire rings, trash receptacles
Elevation: 5,320 feet
Road conditions: Gravel
Hookups: None
Sites: 7 basic sites
Maximum RV length: 40 feet long
Season: June–Oct, weather permitting
Fees: $ per night
Maximum stay: 14 days
Management: Bureau of Land Management, Casper Field Office, (307) 261-7600; casper_wymail@blm.gov
Reservations: First-come, first-served
Pets: Pets must be on a leash and not left unattended.
Quiet hours: 10 p.m. to 7 a.m.
ADA compliance: No
Activities: Fishing, boating, hiking, swimming, wildlife viewing, picnicking
Finding the campground: Take exit 302 off of I-25 and travel on US 20 and US 26 for 3.3 miles to WY 257. Travel on WY 257 for 7.7 miles to US 220. Follow the signs and ramp to the right and travel on US 220 for 20.5 miles and turn left onto CR 412. Travel for 2 miles. The campground is on the right.

About the campground: This campground is more about river access and is frequented by anglers and rafters. The shelters do provide shade but wind can be brutal at times. The day-use area offers a larger shelter than the ones found at the camping sites and offers adequate daytime parking. All in all it can be a pleasant place, but weather will dictate the quality. The paved road getting to the campground will have chuck-holes from time to time, and the gravel road in the campground is not one to get in a hurry on.

Natrona County Campgrounds

Overview

Pets:

- Dogs, cats, and other pets must be crated, caged, or on a controlled leash no longer than 10 feet.
- Pets are not allowed in public eating places, food stores, and buildings and on designated posted beach areas, with the exception of service animals.
- Pets must be attended at all times.
- Where hunting is permitted, hunting dogs must be under control at all times.
- Parcels of county parks may be closed for specified periods of time to domestic pets in order to protect wildlife or adjacent landowners' rights.
- Persons with pets will be responsible for proper removal and disposal of the animals' waste in an approved trash receptacle.

Quiet hours: 10 p.m. to 7 a.m. Generators may not be run during quiet hours with the exception of quiet-approved generators (decibel level below 60dB) required to maintain medical equipment to sustain or support life within a distance of 50 feet away.

Restrictions: Alcohol permits are required for gatherings of more than 10 adults where alcohol is present. These permits may be attained from the board.

Conduct:

- Visitors to any park shall conduct themselves in a lawful, peaceful, and orderly manner.
- No glass beverage containers are allowed in any county parks.
- All state statutes may be enforced within county parks.
- No person who is under the influence of intoxicating liquor or narcotics or hallucinatory drugs shall be permitted to create a disturbance to the orderly operation or enjoyment of the park or its visitors. No person who is under the influence of alcohol or any controlled substance to a degree that renders them a hazard to themselves or others shall be permitted in county parks.

⑨ Black Beach

Location: 34 miles southwest of Casper
GPS: N42 31.68' / W106 42.46'
Facilities and amenities: Vault toilets, fire rings, grills, trash receptacles, picnic shelters with tables, 2 boat ramps
Elevation: 5,523 feet
Road conditions: Gravel with improved dirt
Hookups: None
Sites: 20 primitive units
Maximum RV length: 40 feet long
Season: May–Oct, weather permitting
Fees: $$ per night
Maximum stay: 10 days
Management: Natrona County Parks & Recreation, Box 848, 538 SW Wyoming Blvd., Mills, WY 82604; (307) 235-9311; natronacounty-wy.gov
Reservations: First-come, first-served
Pets: Allowed with restrictions. See introduction to "Natrona County Campgrounds" above.
Quiet hours: 10 p.m. to 7 a.m.
ADA compliance: Yes
Activities: Fishing, boating, water sports, hiking
Finding the campground: Take WY 220 west out of Casper for about 30 miles from I-25 to the Alcova access road. Turn left and continue past Alcova for 3.5 miles to the Black Beach access. Turn right and travel 1.1 miles.
About the campground: There are some trees here, but the primary shade comes from the shelters over the picnic tables. The sun can be brutal, making a swim most appealing. Be sure to bring your camera as the scenic views here are well worth shooting some landscapes.

10 Cottonwood Creek

Location: 36 miles southwest of Casper
GPS: N42 31.29' / W106 44.60'
Facilities and amenities: Vault toilets, fire rings, picnic tables, group shelter, boat ramp
Elevation: 5,582 feet
Road conditions: Gravel
Hookups: None
Sites: Multiple primitive sites
Maximum RV length: 40 feet long
Season: May–Oct, weather permitting

Fees: $$ per night
Maximum stay: 10 days
Management: Natrona County Parks & Recreation, Box 848, 538 SW Wyoming Blvd., Mills, WY 82604; (307) 235-9311; natronacounty-wy.gov
Reservations: First-come, first-served
Pets: Allowed with restrictions. See introduction to "Natrona County Campgrounds" above.
Quiet hours: 10 p.m. to 7 a.m.
ADA compliance: Yes
Activities: Fishing, boating, water sports, hiking, photography
Finding the campground: Take WY 220 west out of Casper for about 30 miles from I-25 to the Alcova access road. Turn left and continue past Alcova for 5 miles to the Cottonwood Creek access. Turn right and travel 1.2 miles.
About the campground: Cedar trees are present, but shade is limited. Shelters provide the most reliable way to avoid too much sun. Water sports are the primary interest here and also offer an excellent way to cool off. Take some time to study the geological features in the landscape, and don't forget your camera. There is an informational "Dinosaur Trail" available with an additional five camping sites nearby, compliments of the BLM.

11 Fremont Canyon

Location: 37 miles southwest of Casper
GPS: N42 31.19' / W106 46.54'
Facilities and amenities: Vault toilets, fire rings, picnic tables, trash receptacles, boat ramp, boat dock
Elevation: 5,536 feet
Road conditions: Paved to improved dirt
Hookups: None
Sites: Multiple primitive sites
Maximum RV length: 30 feet long
Season: All year
Fees: $$ per night
Maximum stay: 10 days
Management: Natrona County Parks & Recreation, Box 848, 538 SW Wyoming Blvd., Mills, WY 82604; (307) 235-9311; natronacounty-wy.gov
Reservations: First-come, first-served
Pets: Allowed with restrictions. See introduction to "Natrona County Campgrounds" above.
Quiet hours: 10 p.m. to 7 a.m.
ADA compliance: Yes
Activities: Fishing, boating, water sports, hiking, picnicking
Finding the campground: Take WY 220 west out of Casper for about 32 miles from I-25. Turn left onto Lakeshore Drive and travel 4.5 miles.
About the campground: This campground stretches out along the shoreline, though the access is short and steep. Trailers do make it, but it is intimidating. There are some unique canyon views, but if your interest is water sports–related, this is probably not the best choice.

12 Westside

Location: 36 miles southwest of Casper
GPS: N42 31.60' / W106 46.60'
Facilities and amenities: Vault toilets, fire rings, shelters with picnic tables, large group shelter, trash receptacles
Elevation: 5,523 feet
Road conditions: Paved to campground then improved dirt
Hookups: None
Sites: Multiple primitive sites
Maximum RV length: 40 feet long
Season: May–Oct, weather permitting
Fees: $$ per night
Maximum stay: 10 days
Management: Natrona County Parks & Recreation, Box 848, 538 SW Wyoming Blvd., Mills, WY 82604; (307) 235-9311; natronacounty-wy.gov
Reservations: First-come, first-served
Pets: Allowed with restrictions. See introduction to "Natrona County Campgrounds" above.
Quiet hours: 10 p.m. to 7 a.m.
ADA compliance: No
Activities: Fishing, water sports, picnicking
Finding the campground: Take WY 220 west out of Casper for about 32 miles from I-25. Turn left onto Lakeshore Drive and travel 4.3 miles. The campground is on the left.
About the campground: Leveling can be difficult at some of the sites and shade is in short supply. Trees are in the area, but not many where their shade can be appreciated. As with the other camping areas, the primary appeal is the water sports.

13 RV Park

Location: 36 miles southwest of Casper
GPS: N42 31.74' / W106 46.73'
Facilities and amenities: Shelter, bathhouse, trash receptacle, drinking water
Elevation: 5,522 feet
Road conditions: Paved and gravel
Hookups: Water, electric, sewer
Sites: 22 basic sites
Maximum RV length: 40 feet long
Season: Year-round
Fees: $$$$ per night
Maximum stay: 10 days
Management: Natrona County Parks & Recreation, Box 848, 538 SW Wyoming Blvd., Mills, WY 82604; (307) 235-9311; natronacounty-wy.gov

Reservations: https://secure.rec1.com/WY/natrona-county-wy/catalog
Pets: Allowed with restrictions. See introduction to "Natrona County Campgrounds" above.
Quiet hours: 10 p.m. to 7 a.m.
ADA compliance: Yes
Activities: Fishing, boating, water sports
Finding the campground: Take WY 220 west out of Casper for about 32 miles from I-25. Turn left onto Lakeshore Drive and travel 4.3 miles. The RV park is on the right.
About the campground: There are a lot of activities available in the area, but all require some travel. This a good place to set up a sort of base camp. Shade is not abundant, but the 50-amp hookup will keep air conditioners cooling things off. Two of the RV sites are located in the adjacent trailer park.

14 Okie Beach

Location: 34 miles southwest of Casper
GPS: N42 32.02' / W106 45.59'
Facilities and amenities: Vault toilets, fire rings, picnic tables, trash receptacle, 5 boat docks
Elevation: 5,519 feet
Road conditions: Paved to improved dirt
Hookups: None
Sites: 36 primitive sites
Maximum RV length: 40 feet long
Season: May–Oct, weather permitting
Fees: $ per night
Maximum stay: 10 days
Management: Natrona County Parks & Recreation, Box 848, 538 SW Wyoming Blvd., Mills, WY 82604; (307) 235-9311; natronacounty-wy.gov
Reservations: https://secure.rec1.com/WY/natrona-county-wy/catalog
Pets: Allowed with restrictions. See introduction to "Natrona County Campgrounds" above.
Quiet hours: 10 p.m. to 7 a.m.
ADA compliance: Yes
Activities: Boating, water sports, fishing
Finding the campground: Take WY 220 west out of Casper for about 32 miles from I-25. Turn left onto Lakeshore Drive and travel 2.4 miles. The campground is on the left.
About the campground: There are some trees but in light of the five docks and a boat ramp, shade is not on the list that makes this a popular place. Summer nights can stay warm but not unbearable, but that could be disputed based on individual opinion.

15 Gray Reef Dam

Location: 30 miles southwest of Casper
GPS: N42 34.00' / W106 42.19'
Facilities and amenities: Vault toilet, fire rings, trash receptacle, picnic shelters with tables, fishing pier, boat ramp
Elevation: 5,323 feet
Road conditions: Gravel
Hookups: None
Sites: 8 basic sites plus dispersed sites
Maximum RV length: 40 feet long
Season: Year-round dependent upon weather
Fees: $$ per night
Maximum stay: 10 days
Management: Natrona County Parks & Recreation, Box 848, 538 SW Wyoming Blvd., Mills, WY 82604; (307) 235-9311; natronacounty-wy.gov
Reservations: First-come, first-served
Pets: Allowed with restrictions. See introduction to "Natrona County Campgrounds" above.
Quiet hours: 10 p.m. to 7 a.m.
ADA compliance: Yes
Activities: Fishing, boating
Finding the campground: Take US 220 west out of Casper for about 29 miles. At the sign turn left (south) onto CR 412 and travel for 1 mile on this paved road. The campground is on the right.
About the campground: Fly-fishing is the most popular choice for anglers that frequent this area, though it is not the only option. Wheelchair access is better than at most sites that offer fishing activities, where it would otherwise only be a passing thought. The quality of fishing changes with the flow of water, which can change daily as regulated by the Bureau of Reclamation.

Brown, rainbow, and cutthroat trout are available to sample the flies presented to them, but they are not the only fish that share these waters. Walleye are present for those who prefer their special type of taste when cooked without the thrill of resistance when caught.

When it rains puddles can form within the camping area, causing some grief and difficult driving. Taking extra water and other desired items will provide an opportunity to stay a little longer and enjoy watching for wildlife and blue sky while it dries out. Typically, most days are sunny and can be very relentless without some sort of shade. But all is forgiven when the sun sets and the night sky lights up with no highway noise and the complaining roar of the escaping water from the captivity of the dam.

Casper Mountain

The main Casper Mountain access road has a steep climb with a hairpin corner that is not "user-friendly" for large RVs or trailers. An alternative route is utilized for directions in an effort to allow visitors to avoid this area. This will no doubt be a relief to both travelers and residents alike, though it does involve travel on a gravel road with more total mileage to arrive.

16 Skunk Hollow

Location: 7 miles south of Casper
GPS: N42 44.29' / W106 18.99'
Facilities and amenities: Vault toilet, fire rings, trash receptacles, picnic tables
Elevation: 7,797 feet
Road conditions: Gravel
Hookups: None
Sites: 10 primitive sites
Maximum RV length: 30 feet long
Season: May–Sept, weather permitting
Fees: $ per night
Maximum stay: 10 days
Management: Natrona County Parks & Recreation, Box 848, 538 SW Wyoming Blvd., Mills, WY 82604; (307) 235-9311; natronacounty-wy.gov
Reservations: https://secure.rec1.com/WY/natrona-county-wy/catalog
Pets: Allowed with restrictions. See introduction to "Natrona County Campgrounds" above.
Quiet hours: 10 p.m. to 7 a.m.
ADA compliance: No
Activities: Hiking, biking
Finding the campground: Take WY 258 from either I-25 exit 185 in the east or WY 220 from the west. WY 251 intersects WY 258 just south of the main part of Casper, roughly halfway between. Turn onto WY 251 and travel south for 7 miles.

Alternate route for large RVs: Take WY 220 west out of Casper toward Alcova. At WY 487 turn left (south) and travel 8.6 miles to Circle Drive/CR 505. Turn left (east) onto this gravel road, travel 9 miles, and turn left (north) at the intersection to stay on CR 505. Continue going north for 4 miles.

About the campground: This campground has a one-way loop with a lot of space between camping units. The lodgepole pine are abundant with welcome shade on a hot summer day.

17 Elkhorn Springs

Location: 7 miles south of Casper
GPS: N42 44.29' / W106 18.99'
Facilities and amenities: Vault toilet, fire rings, picnic tables
Elevation: 7,797 feet
Road conditions: Gravel
Hookups: None
Sites: 6 basic sites
Maximum RV length: 20 feet long
Season: Memorial Day through Oct, weather permitting
Fee: $ per night
Maximum stay: 10 days
Management: Natrona County Parks & Recreation, Box 848, 538 SW Wyoming Blvd., Mills, WY 82604; (307) 235-9311; natronacounty-wy.gov
Reservations: https://secure.rec1.com/WY/natrona-county-wy/catalog
Pets: Allowed with restrictions. See introduction to "Natrona County Campgrounds" above.
Quiet hours: 10 p.m. to 7 a.m.
ADA compliance: No
Activities: Hiking, biking
Finding the campground: Take WY 258 from either I-25 exit 185 in the east or WY 220 from the west. WY 251 intersects WY 258 just south of the main part of Casper, roughly halfway between. Turn onto WY 251 and travel south for 7 miles.
About the campground: This campground could almost be considered an extension of the Skunk Hollow camping area with closer sites and no one-way access road. In fact, the vault toilet is shared by both.

18 Beartrap Meadows

Location: 7.2 miles south of Casper
GPS: N42 43.98' / W106 18.78'
Facilities and amenities: Vault toilets, fire rings, picnic tables, trash receptacles
Elevation: 7,875 feet
Road conditions: Gravel
Hookups: None
Sites: 29 primitive sites
Maximum RV length: 40 feet long
Season: Memorial Day through Oct
Fee: $ per night
Maximum stay: 10 days
Management: Natrona County Parks & Recreation, Box 848, 538 SW Wyoming Blvd., Mills, WY 82604; (307) 235-9311; natronacounty-wy.gov

Reservations: Must be made online at https://secure.rec1.com/WY/natrona-county-wy/catalog
Pets: Allowed with restrictions. See introduction to "Natrona County Campgrounds" above.
Quiet hours: 10 p.m. to 7 a.m.
ADA compliance: No
Activities: Hiking, biking
Finding the campground: Take WY 258 from either I-25 exit 185 in the east or WY 220 from the west. WY 251 intersects WY 258 just south of the main part of Casper, roughly halfway between. Turn onto WY 251 and travel south for 7.2 miles. The campground is on the right.
About the campground: Mature ponderosa pine trees are clustered at various places with open grassy areas in between. There are private cabins in the area with some confusion on which roads are private or not. This is a popular place for weddings and other group gatherings.

19 Deer Haven

Location: 7.2 miles south of Casper
GPS: N42 43.98' / W106 18.78'
Facilities and amenities: Vault toilet, fire rings, picnic tables, trash receptacle
Elevation: 7,883 feet
Road conditions: Gravel
Hookups: None
Sites: 11 primitive sites
Maximum RV length: 30 feet long
Season: May–Oct
Fees: $ per night
Maximum stay: 10 days
Management: Natrona County Parks & Recreation, Box 848, 538 SW Wyoming Blvd., Mills, WY 82604; (307) 235-9311; natronacounty-wy.gov
Reservations: Must be made online at https://secure.rec1.com/WY/natrona-county-wy/catalog
Pets: Allowed with restrictions. See introduction to "Natrona County Campgrounds" above.
Quiet hours: 10 p.m. to 7 a.m.
ADA compliance: No
Activities: Hiking, biking
Finding the campground: Take WY 258 from either I-25 exit 185 in the east or WY 220 from the west. WY 251 intersects WY 258 just south of the main part of Casper, roughly halfway between. Turn onto WY 251 and travel south for 7.2 miles. The campground is on the left.
About the campground: The camping units are closer here, but the pine trees help to fill some of the gap. Road noise may be an issue at times, with hopes that as the sun goes down so does the volume on traffic.

20 Bishops Point

Location: 44 miles southwest of Casper
GPS: N42 29.82' / W106 54.38'
Facilities and amenities: Vault toilets, fire rings, picnic tables (some with shelters), group shelter, trash receptacle, boat ramps and dock
Elevation: 5,886 feet
Road conditions: Gravel
Hookups: None
Sites: Multiple primitive sites
Maximum RV length: 50 feet long
Season: All year, weather permitting
Fees: $$ per night
Maximum stay: 10 days
Management: Natrona County Parks & Recreation, Box 848, 538 SW Wyoming Blvd., Mills, WY 82604; (307) 235-9311; natronacounty-wy.gov
Reservations: First-come, first-served
Pets: Allowed with restrictions. See introduction to "Natrona County Campgrounds" above.
Quiet hours: 10 p.m. to 7 a.m.
ADA compliance: Yes
Activities: Boating, fishing, water sports, picnicking
Finding the campground: Take WY 220 west out of Casper for about 36 miles from I-25 to the Pathfinder access road. Turn to the left onto this paved road and travel 3.6 miles to the gravel Bishops Point Road. Turn right and travel 4 miles.
About the campground: Boating was definitely the focus when this campground was constructed. With three boat ramps and a dock combined with the camping units lined up along the shore, there is no room to think otherwise. It can get really windy, with no shortage of boat-generated noise of various volumes. At times the toilet facilities can be overrun.

21 Weiss

Location: 40.7 miles southwest of Casper
GPS: N42 28.17' / W106 51.57'
Facilities and amenities: Vault toilets, fire rings, picnic tables with shelters, trash receptacle
Elevation: 5,866 feet
Road conditions: Gravel
Hookups: None
Sites: Multiple primitive sites
Maximum RV length: 40 feet long

Season: All year, weather permitting

Fees: $$ per night

Maximum stay: 10 days

Management: Natrona County Parks & Recreation, Box 848, 538 SW Wyoming Blvd., Mills, WY 82604; (307) 235-9311; natronacounty-wy.gov

Reservations: First-come, first-served

Pets: Allowed with restrictions. See introduction to "Natrona County Campgrounds" above.

Quiet hours: 10 p.m. to 7 a.m.

ADA compliance: No

Activities: Fishing, hiking, swimming

Finding the campground: Take WY 220 west out of Casper for about 36 miles from I-25 to the Pathfinder access road. Turn to the left onto this paved-turning-to-gravel road and travel 6.7 miles.

About the campground: Granite outcrops combine with the sandy desert with the confined waters of the Pathfinder Reservoir here. Wind and sunshine can create difficult times for boaters and campers alike, but conditions are not always unbearable. For those who persevere, a pleasant memory can be created.

22 Sage

Location: 41 miles southwest of Casper

GPS: N42 28.29' / W106 51.86'

Facilities and amenities: Vault toilets, fire rings, shelters with picnic tables, trash receptacle

Elevation: 5,980 feet

Road conditions: Gravel

Hookups: None

Sites: Multiple primitive sites

Maximum RV length: 40 feet long

Season: All year, weather permitting

Fees: $$ per night

Maximum stay: 10 days

Management: Natrona County Parks & Recreation, Box 848, 538 SW Wyoming Blvd., Mills, WY 82604; (307) 235-9311; natronacounty-wy.gov

Reservations: First-come, first-served

Pets: Allowed with restrictions. See introduction to "Natrona County Campgrounds" above.

Quiet hours: 10 p.m. to 7 a.m.

ADA compliance: No

Activities: Fishing, swimming

Finding the campground: Take WY 220 west out of Casper for about 36 miles from I-25 to the Pathfinder access road. Turn to the left onto this paved-turning-to-gravel road and travel 7 miles.

About the campground: There are trees here, but don't count on them for shade of any length. Wind and sunshine, like the previous site, are a reality to deal with. The wind does not blow all of the time but most of it. Mornings usually start out with the least amount of wind, with a steady increase in the late afternoon.

23 Diabase

Location: 44 miles southwest of Casper
GPS: N42 28.13' / W106 52.24'
Facilities and amenities: Vault toilets, fire rings, picnic tables with shelters, group shelter, boat ramp, dock, marina, trash receptacles
Elevation: 5,867 feet
Road conditions: Gravel
Hookups: None
Sites: Multiple primitive sites
Maximum RV length: 40 feet long
Season: All year
Fees: $$ per night
Maximum stay: 10 days
Management: Natrona County Parks & Recreation, Box 848, 538 SW Wyoming Blvd., Mills, WY 82604; (307) 235-9311; natronacounty-wy.gov
Reservations: First-come, first-served
Pets: Allowed with restrictions. See introduction to "Natrona County Campgrounds" above.
Quiet hours: 10 p.m. to 7 a.m.
ADA compliance: No
Activities: Boating, fishing, water sports
Finding the campground: Take WY 220 west out of Casper for about 36 miles from I-25 to the Pathfinder access road. Turn to the left onto this paved-turning-to-gravel road and travel 7.7 miles.
About the campground: The marina is open seasonally. Ice fishing is a popular activity when conditions are right, but depending on whether or not the marina or other amenities are open, it is uncertain. A lot of services have been affected since COVID-19 that have not recovered as of this writing.

Glendo State Park

Overview

Pets:

- All pets must be in a vehicle or on a leash no longer than 10 feet and physically controlled at all times.
- Pets shall not be left unattended for any time greater than 1 hour.
- Persons with pets on lawns, picnic areas, and camping areas will be responsible for proper removal of the animals' waste.
- Parcels of parkland may be closed permanently or for a specified period of time to domestic pets in order to protect wildlife or adjacent landowner rights.

Quiet hours: 10 p.m. to 6 a.m. All generators and electronic devices or any actions that may disturb the peace are prohibited during these hours.

Conduct:

- Glass beverage containers are prohibited outside vehicles and all camping units on parkland except on established commercial premises and designated historic sites.
- Draining or dumping refuse or waste, including gray water, from any source, except in places or receptacles provided for such use, is prohibited.

24 Bennett Hill

Location: 3 miles north and east of Glendo
GPS: N42 30.97' / W104 59.41'
Facilities and amenities: Vault toilets, fire rings, picnic tables, trash dumpsters, drinking water, picnic area, group picnic shelter, boat ramp
Elevation: 4,764 feet
Road conditions: Gravel
Hookups: Electricity and water available
Sites: 44 basic sites
Maximum RV length: NA
Season: May–Sept
Fees: $$ resident, $$$$ nonresident
Maximum stay: 14 days
Management: Glendo State Park, 397 Glendo Park Rd., Glendo, WY 82213; (307) 735-4433
Reservations: Online at wyomingstateparks.reserveamerica.com or by phone at (877) 996-7275
Pets: Allowed with restrictions. See introduction to "Glendo State Park" above.
Quiet hours: 10 p.m. to 6 a.m. Note the special restrictions in the area description.
ADA compliance: Yes

Activities: Fishing, boating, hiking, water sports, picnicking

Finding the campground: Leave I-25 at Glendo State Park/exit 111 and travel east into the town of Glendo. After crossing the railroad tracks (be aware the train will not sound a horn at this crossing), travel to North Yellowstone Highway/WY 319 (the second street) and turn left. Travel about 1 mile and turn right onto the paved Lakeshore Drive. The campground entrance is 1.8 miles away on the left. *Note:* The pavement of Lakeshore Drive changes to gravel at this point.

About the campground: There is plenty of space between camping units in the wide-open spaces in the prominent prairie, with units getting a little closer in the cottonwood trees closer to the shoreline. Fishing from the shore will take a little work finding an adequate access point due to the fluctuating water level, trees, and brush. Boating is by far the preferred choice. Shade is limited and the best sites are quickly filled. There are fenced group sites that will accommodate up to three units, an appealing aspect for get-togethers with close friends and family.

25 Waters Point

Location: 4 miles north and east of Glendo

GPS: N42 30.77' / W104 58.43'

Facilities and amenities: Vault toilet, fire rings, picnic tables, trash dumpsters

Elevation: 4,643 feet

Road conditions: Gravel to dirt (2 parallel ruts)

Hookups: None

Sites: 10 basic sites

Maximum RV length: 30 feet long

Season: May–Sept

Fees: $$ resident, $$$$ nonresident

Maximum stay: 14 days

Management: Glendo State Park, 397 Glendo Park Rd., Glendo, WY 82213; (307) 735-4433

Reservations: First-come, first-served

Pets: Allowed with restrictions. See introduction to "Glendo State Park" above.

Quiet hours: 10 p.m. to 6 a.m. Note the special restrictions in the area description.

ADA compliance: Yes

Activities: Fishing, swimming

Finding the campground: Leave I-25 at Glendo State Park/exit 111 and travel east into the town of Glendo. After crossing the railroad tracks (be aware the train will not sound a horn at this crossing), travel to North Yellowstone Highway/WY 319 (the second street) and turn left. Travel about 1 mile and turn right onto the paved Lakeshore Drive. The campground entrance is 2.8 miles farther on the left.

About the campground: There are two beaches available at this campground, welcome places to cool off when the unrelenting sun finds very little to nonexistent resipiscence due to the lack of trees. The campground road is considered undeveloped and as such can be a real big problem if rain or snow drops in to offer a drink to the local vegetation. Smaller RVs, tents, and four-wheel drive are recommended. Be sure to bring plenty of water, sunscreen, and extra supplies should you want to wait for things to dry out, if the weather offers the opportunity to extend your stay.

26 Red Hills

Location: 4.3 miles north and east of Glendo
GPS: N42 30.24' / W104 57.87'
Facilities and amenities: Vault toilet, fire rings, picnic tables
Elevation: 4,693 feet
Road conditions: Gravel
Hookups: None
Sites: 22 basic sites
Maximum RV length: 30 feet long
Season: May–Sept
Fees: $$ resident, $$$$ nonresident
Maximum stay: 14 days
Management: Glendo State Park, 397 Glendo Park Rd., Glendo, WY 82213; (307) 735-4433
Reservations: Online at wyomingstateparks.reserveamerica.com or by phone at (877) 996-7275
Pets: Allowed with restrictions. See introduction to "Glendo State Park" above.
Quiet hours: 10 p.m. to 6 a.m. Note the special restrictions in the area description.
ADA compliance: No
Activities: Hiking, swimming
Finding the campground: Leave I-25 at Glendo State Park/exit 111 and travel east into the town of Glendo. After crossing the railroad tracks (be aware the train will not sound a horn at this crossing), travel to North Yellowstone Highway/WY 319 (the second street) and turn left. Travel about 1 mile and turn right onto the paved Lakeshore Drive. The campground entrance is 3.1 miles away on the left. It is about 0.5 mile to the camping pull-through sites.
About the campground: The access road starts from a wide-open prairie sort of setting, then drops into a pine forest mixed with some juniper. The farther downhill you go toward the reservoir, the more cottonwood trees become prevalent. Access to the shoreline is difficult, though this could be a pleasant place to enjoy wind whispering in the pine trees. There is only one vault toilet, pretty much at the end of the camping area, and that is also the closest one will get to the water. The camping units here will likely fill quickly. There is a group camping area with a sand and gravel shoreline that is accessed from the campground situated some distance from the main camping area.

27 Colter Bay

Location: 3 miles southeast of Glendo
GPS: N42 29.13' / W104 59.53'
Facilities and amenities: Vault toilet, fire rings, picnic tables
Elevation: 4,652 feet
Road conditions: Improved dirt
Hookups: None
Sites: 6 basic sites

Maximum RV length: 20 feet long

Season: May–Sept

Fees: $$ resident, $$$$ nonresident

Maximum stay: 14 days

Management: Glendo State Park, 397 Glendo Park Rd., Glendo, WY 82213; (307) 735-4433

Reservations: First-come, first-served

Pets: Allowed with restrictions. See introduction to "Glendo State Park" above.

Quiet hours: 10 p.m. to 6 a.m. Note the special restrictions in the area description.

ADA compliance: Yes

Activities: Fishing, hiking, mountain biking

Finding the campground: Leave I-25 at Glendo State Park/exit 111 and travel east into the town of Glendo. After crossing the railroad tracks (be aware the train will not sound a horn at this crossing), travel to North Yellowstone Highway/WY 319 (the second street) and turn right. Travel 2 blocks and turn left onto C Street to the intersection. Turn right onto South Lincoln Avenue/Glendo Park Road and travel about 1.5 miles to Lakeshore Drive. Turn left onto this paved road and drive 1 mile. The campground access road is on the right side of the road.

About the campground: A grove of cottonwood trees houses these camping units. This is a popular area when the water is high, typically not past the end of July. After that, popularity diminishes, offering a unique place to settle in with little company.

28 Custer Cove

Location: 3.5 miles southeast of Glendo

GPS: N42 29.21' / W104 58.90'

Facilities and amenities: Vault toilet, fire rings, picnic tables, trash receptacles

Elevation: 4,685 feet

Road conditions: Gravel

Hookups: None

Sites: 20 basic units

Maximum RV length: 60 feet long

Season: May–Sept

Fees: $$ resident, $$$$ nonresident

Maximum stay: 14 days

Management: Glendo State Park, 397 Glendo Park Rd., Glendo, WY 82213; (307) 735-4433

Reservations: Online at wyomingstateparks.reserveamerica.com or by phone at (877) 996-7275

Pets: Allowed with restrictions. See introduction to "Glendo State Park" above.

Quiet hours: 10 p.m. to 6 a.m. Note the special restrictions in the area description.

ADA compliance: Yes

Activities: Water sports, fishing, hiking

Finding the campground: Leave I-25 at Glendo State Park/exit 111 and travel east into the town of Glendo. After crossing the railroad tracks (be aware the train will not sound a horn at this crossing), travel to North Yellowstone Highway/WY 319 (the second street) and turn right. Travel 2 blocks and turn left onto C Street to the intersection. Turn right onto South Lincoln Avenue/Glendo

Park Road and travel about 1.5 miles to Lakeshore Drive. Turn left onto this paved road and drive 2 miles. The campground access road is on the right side of the road.

About the campground: Pine trees and cedar share this camping area with the typical cottonwood that find the shoreline more to their liking, probably due to their need for more water. Swimming is a popular activity here and as such tends to attract a younger group of campers. With shade being plentiful, older campers can find some pleasant times tending a campfire or other related "chores" out of the office or just plain not at work. Pull-throughs accommodate the larger RVs, but the back-in sites are more suitable for smaller units and/or tents.

29 Soldier Rock

Location: 4 miles southeast of Glendo
GPS: N42 29.43' / W104 58.50'
Facilities and amenities: Vault toilet, fire rings, picnic tables
Elevation: 4,674 feet
Road conditions: Improved dirt, 4-wheel drive recommended
Hookups: None
Sites: 12 basic sites
Maximum RV length: 20 feet long
Season: May–Sept
Fees: $$ resident, $$$$ nonresident
Maximum stay: 14 days
Management: Glendo State Park, 397 Glendo Park Rd., Glendo, WY 82213; (307) 735-4433
Reservations: Online at wyomingstateparks.reserveamerica.com or by phone at (877) 996-7275
Pets: Allowed with restrictions. See introduction to "Glendo State Park" above.
Quiet hours: 10 p.m. to 6 a.m. Note the special restrictions in the area description.
ADA compliance: No
Activities: Fishing, hiking
Finding the campground: Leave I-25 at Glendo State Park/exit 111 and travel east into the town of Glendo. After crossing the railroad tracks (be aware the train will not sound a horn at this crossing), travel to North Yellowstone Highway/WY 319 (the second street) and turn right. Travel 2 blocks and turn left onto C Street to the intersection. Turn right onto South Lincoln Avenue/Glendo Park Road and travel about 1.5 miles to Lakeshore Drive. Turn left onto this paved road and drive 2.5 miles. This is the first of three campground access roads all on the right side of the road.

About the campground: Pine trees dominate the area along the road at the access areas, most of which are directly off the paved Lakeshore Drive. The poorly developed narrow roads do not make access a pleasant trip in or out. However, once everything is in place and everyone is engaged in their own pursuit of choice, all is forgiven.

30 Reno Cove

Location: 4.5 miles southeast of Glendo
GPS: N42 29.75' / W104 58.40'
Facilities and amenities: Vault toilets, fire rings, picnic tables, trash dumpsters, boat ramp, drinking water
Elevation: 4,765 feet
Road conditions: Gravel
Hookups: Electric
Sites: 22 basic sites
Maximum RV length: 60 feet long
Season: May–Sept
Fees: $$ resident, $$$$ nonresident
Maximum stay: 14 days
Management: Glendo State Park, 397 Glendo Park Rd., Glendo, WY 82213; (307) 735-4433
Reservations: Online at wyomingstateparks.reserveamerica.com or by phone at (877) 996-7275
Pets: Allowed with restrictions. See introduction to "Glendo State Park" above.
Quiet hours: 10 p.m. to 6 a.m. Note the special restrictions in the area description.
ADA compliance: Yes
Activities: Fishing, boating, water sports
Finding the campground: Leave I-25 at Glendo State Park/exit 111 and travel east into the town of Glendo. After crossing the railroad tracks (be aware the train will not sound a horn at this crossing), travel to North Yellowstone Highway/WY 319 (the second street) and turn right. Travel 2 blocks and turn left onto C Street to the intersection. Turn right onto South Lincoln Avenue/Glendo Park Road and travel about 1.5 miles to Lakeshore Drive. Turn left onto this paved road and drive 3 miles. The campground access road is on the right side of the road. *Note:* The pavement of Lakeshore Drive goes to gravel at this point.
About the campground: Ponderosa pine don't offer much shade but are pleasant on the eyes and tend to offer a special sort of music with the right breeze. The first camping area is a short distance off of Lakeshore Drive, with eleven units that have electric hookups. The remaining units are some distance away, much closer to the boat ramp and reservoir access.

31 Mule Hill

Location: 1.75 miles southeast of Glendo
GPS: N42 28.92' / W105 0.30'
Facilities and amenities: Vault toilet, fire rings, picnic tables
Elevation: 4,653 feet
Road conditions: Gravel
Hookups: None
Sites: 13 basic sites
Maximum RV length: 30 feet long
Season: May–Sept

Fees: $$ resident, $$$$ nonresident
Maximum stay: 14 days
Management: Glendo State Park, 397 Glendo Park Rd., Glendo, WY 82213; (307) 735-4433
Reservations: Online at wyomingstateparks.reserveamerica.com or by phone at (877) 996-7275
Pets: Allowed with restrictions. See introduction to "Glendo State Park" above.
Quiet hours: 10 p.m. to 6 a.m. Note the special restrictions in the area description.
ADA compliance: Yes
Activities: Fishing
Finding the campground: Leave I-25 at Glendo State Park/exit 111 and travel east into the town of Glendo. After crossing the railroad tracks (be aware the train will not sound a horn at this crossing), travel to North Yellowstone Highway/WY 319 (the second street) and turn right. Travel 2 blocks, turn left onto C Street, and travel to the next intersection. Turn right onto South Lincoln Avenue/Glendo Park Road and travel 1.75 miles. A short distance past the fee booth, the campground access is on the left.
About the campground: There are back-in sites, some pull-throughs, and one group area that will accommodate three units. Shade can be found in the cottonwood grove where the back-in sites are located. The other units have limited to no shade. If access to the reservoir water is important, May through mid-July is typically the best.

32 Whiskey Gulch

Location: 2.5 miles southeast of Glendo
GPS: N42 28.57' / W104 59.78'
Facilities and amenities: Vault toilets, fire rings, picnic tables, trash dumpsters, group shelters, boat ramp, drinking water
Elevation: 4,676 feet
Road conditions: Gravel
Hookups: None
Sites: 29 basic sites
Maximum RV length: 35 feet long
Season: May–Sept
Fees: $$ resident, $$$$ nonresident
Maximum stay: 14 days
Management: Glendo State Park, 397 Glendo Park Rd., Glendo, WY 82213; (307) 735-4433
Reservations: Online at wyomingstateparks.reserveamerica.com or by phone at (877) 996-7275
Pets: Allowed with restrictions. See introduction to "Glendo State Park" above.
Quiet hours: 10 p.m. to 6 a.m. Note the special restrictions in the area description.
ADA compliance: Yes
Activities: Boating, fishing, water sports, hiking
Finding the campground: Leave I-25 at Glendo State Park/exit 111 and travel east into the town of Glendo. After crossing the railroad tracks (be aware the train will not sound a horn at this crossing), travel to North Yellowstone Highway/WY 319 (the second street) and turn right. Travel 2 blocks, turn left onto C Street, and travel to the next intersection. Turn right onto South Lincoln Avenue/Glendo Park Road and travel about 2.5 miles. The campground access is on the left.

About the campground: The ease and year-round access to water make this a very popular spot. Cottonwood trees dominate the shoreline and offer some special recreation for canoeing and other small watercraft exploration and fishing. Two group shelters, one of which can be reserved, offer a convenient place for gatherings of family and friends. For obvious reasons the peak season is during the warmer part of the year.

33 Sagebrush

Location: 4 miles southeast of Glendo
GPS: N42 28.26' / W104 59.19'
Facilities and amenities: Vault toilets, fire rings, picnic tables, trash dumpsters, group shelter, drinking water
Elevation: 4,654 feet
Road conditions: Gravel
Hookups: None
Sites: 20 basic sites
Maximum RV length: 40 feet long
Season: May–Sept
Fees: $$ resident, $$$$ nonresident
Maximum stay: 14 days
Management: Glendo State Park, 397 Glendo Park Rd., Glendo, WY 82213; (307) 735-4433
Reservations: Online at wyomingstateparks.reserveamerica.com or by phone at (877) 996-7275
Pets: Allowed with restrictions. See introduction to "Glendo State Park" above.
Quiet hours: 10 p.m. to 6 a.m. Note the special restrictions in the area description.
ADA compliance: Yes
Activities: Boating, water sports, fishing
Finding the campground: Leave I-25 at Glendo State Park/exit 111 and travel east into the town of Glendo. After crossing the railroad tracks (be aware the train will not sound a horn at this crossing), travel to North Yellowstone Highway/WY 319 (the second street) and turn right. Travel 2 blocks, turn left onto C Street, and travel to the next intersection. Turn right onto South Lincoln Avenue/Glendo Park Road and travel about 3.5 miles to the Whiskey Gulch Boat Ramp access road. Turn to the left and travel 0.5 mile. The pavement will turn to gravel at the Sagebrush access road. The four separate Sagebrush camping areas are also accessible from the east via the Shelter Point intersection.
About the campground: This campground settles in between Whiskey Gulch and Shelter Point Campgrounds in a lower elevation. There are cottonwood trees in the area, but none that provide shade for camping units. The Whiskey Gulch boat ramp is conveniently just west of Sagebrush Campground. As with the other campgrounds in this park, water recreation is the major attraction. When the prime shaded spots are all taken, this could be a welcome spot. Anglers may have a more specific point of view should special fishing spots be easier to access from a particular boat ramp, not to mention the ease or lack thereof with respect to launching or loading their boat.

34 Shelter Point

Location: 2.5 miles southeast of Glendo
GPS: N42 28.17' / W104 58.57'
Facilities and amenities: Vault toilets, fire rings, picnic tables, group shelters
Elevation: 4,679 feet
Road conditions: Gravel
Hookups: None
Sites: 26 basic sites
Maximum RV length: 60 feet long
Season: May–Sept
Fees: $$ resident, $$$$ nonresident
Maximum stay: 14 days
Management: Glendo State Park, 397 Glendo Park Rd., Glendo, WY 82213; (307) 735-4433
Reservations: Online at wyomingstateparks.reserveamerica.com or by phone at (877) 996-7275
Pets: Allowed with restrictions. See introduction to "Glendo State Park" above.
Quiet hours: 10 p.m. to 6 a.m. Note the special restrictions in the area description.
ADA compliance: No
Activities: Fishing, swimming, boating
Finding the campground: Leave I-25 at Glendo State Park/exit 111 and travel east into the town of Glendo. After crossing the railroad tracks (be aware the train will not sound a horn at this crossing), travel to North Yellowstone Highway/WY 319 (the second street) and turn right. Travel 2 blocks, turn left onto C Street, and travel to the next intersection. Turn right onto South Lincoln Avenue/Glendo Park Road and travel 4 miles. The campground access road is on the left.
About the campground: The large camping units on this wide-open point are far enough away from each other that they can be seen but not heard. There is no shade here, but the night sky is unobstructed for stargazers. The marina is across the bay and is utilized by most of the campers staying here. There is also a popular small sandy beach on the south side inviting those who need to cool off or who find the fishing a little too slow.

35 Two Moon

Location: 4.8 miles southeast of Glendo
GPS: N42 28.16' / W104 57.59'
Facilities and amenities: Vault toilets, fire rings, picnic tables, trash dumpsters, drinking water
Elevation: 4,800 feet
Road conditions: Paved
Hookups: Electric
Sites: 87 basic sites, 3 yurts
Maximum RV length: 27 feet long
Season: Year-round
Fees: $$ resident, $$$$ nonresident

Maximum stay: 14 days
Management: Glendo State Park, 397 Glendo Park Rd., Glendo, WY 82213; (307) 735-4433
Reservations: Online at wyomingstateparks.reserveamerica.com or by phone at (877) 996-7275
Pets: Allowed with restrictions. See introduction to "Glendo State Park" above.
Quiet hours: 10 p.m. to 6 a.m. Note the special restrictions in the area description.
ADA compliance: Yes
Activities: Hiking, biking, picnicking
Finding the campground: Leave I-25 at Glendo State Park/exit 111 and travel east into the town of Glendo. After crossing the railroad tracks (be aware the train will not sound a horn at this crossing), travel to North Yellowstone Highway/WY 319 (the second street) and turn right. Travel 2 blocks, turn left onto C Street, and travel to the next intersection. Turn right onto South Lincoln Avenue/Glendo Park Road and travel 4.8 miles to the first of three access roads.
About the campground: A boat launch is available at the marina, and trails offer another form of access to the reservoir without dealing with traffic. This old campground has been well maintained and does not show its age. It snuggles into a ponderosa pine forest with a few cedars hiding in the shadows at various places. There is room for larger RVs at the first entrance and on the outskirts of the campground in different places, but the majority of camping areas do not work for longer units. Even if it could fit, finding a way past the trees standing guard in the narrow, twisting, turning access would produce "racing stripes" from scraping as the RV goes by.

36 Sandy Beach Dune

Location: 15 miles northeast of Glendo
GPS: N42 31.30' / W104 56.35'
Facilities and amenities: Vault toilets, fire rings, picnic tables, trash receptacles, drinking water
Elevation: 4,642 feet
Road conditions: Gravel to sandy
Hookups: Electric
Sites: 16 for tents only, 51 basic sites including 7 group sites
Maximum RV length: 40 feet long
Season: May–Sept
Fees: $$ resident, $$$$ nonresident
Maximum stay: 14 days
Management: Glendo State Park, 397 Glendo Park Rd., Glendo, WY 82213; (307) 735-4433
Reservations: Online at wyomingstateparks.reserveamerica.com or by phone at (877) 996-7275
Pets: Allowed with restrictions. See introduction to "Glendo State Park" above.
Quiet hours: 10 p.m. to 6 a.m. Note the special restrictions in the area description.
ADA compliance: Yes
Activities: Swimming, hiking, biking
Finding the campground: Leave I-25 at Glendo State Park/exit 111 and travel east into the town of Glendo. After crossing the railroad tracks (be aware the train will not sound a horn at this crossing), travel to North Yellowstone Highway/WY 319 (the second street) and turn right. Travel 2 blocks, turn left onto C Street, and travel to the next intersection. Turn right onto South Lincoln

Avenue/Glendo Park Road and travel (across the dam) 15 miles to the fee booth. The Dune Campground will be to the left after passing the guard shack.

About the campground: The cottonwood forest occupying this sandy portion of the reservoir offers shade and excellent access to swimming and other related water sports, making it a very popular destination in the heat of the summer. There are forty-eight sites that are very sandy, and smaller camping units and four-wheel drives are recommended. As of our visit, numerous deep ruts left evidence of those that took longer to make their way home than anticipated.

37 Sandy Beach Willow

Location: 15 miles northeast of Glendo
GPS: N42 31.32' / W104 56.35'
Facilities and amenities: Vault toilets, fire rings, picnic tables, trash receptacles, drinking water
Elevation: 4,641 feet
Road conditions: Gravel to sandy
Hookups: None
Sites: 10 for tents only, 60 basic sites including 1 group site
Maximum RV length: 40 feet long
Season: May–Sept
Fees: $$ resident, $$$$ nonresident
Maximum stay: 14 days
Management: Glendo State Park, 397 Glendo Park Rd., Glendo, WY 82213; (307) 735-4433
Reservations: Online at wyomingstateparks.reserveamerica.com or by phone at (877) 996-7275
Pets: Allowed with restrictions. See introduction to "Glendo State Park" above.
Quiet hours: 10 p.m. to 6 a.m. Note the special restrictions in the area description.
ADA compliance: Yes
Activities: Swimming, hiking, biking
Finding the campground: Leave I-25 at Glendo State Park/exit 111 and travel east into the town of Glendo. After crossing the railroad tracks (be aware the train will not sound a horn at this crossing), travel to North Yellowstone Highway/WY 319 (the second street) and turn right. Travel 2 blocks, turn left onto C Street, and travel to the next intersection. Turn right onto South Lincoln Avenue/Glendo Park Road and travel 15 miles. The campground is to the right after passing the guard shack.
About the campground: Back-in sites are found at the first right turn and have the greatest distance to the water and are best suited for larger units. Like the other camping units in the Dune Campground, the closer one gets to the water, the sandier conditions create a nasty situation for traction. Smaller camping units and four-wheel drive (not to mention shovels) are recommended.

38 Cottonwood

Location: 15.5 miles northeast of Glendo
GPS: N42 31.72' / W104 56.52'
Facilities and amenities: Vault toilet, fire rings, picnic tables, drinking water
Elevation: 4,656 feet
Road conditions: Gravel
Hookups: None
Sites: 14 basic sites
Maximum RV length: 40 feet long
Season: May–Sept
Fees: $$ resident, $$$$ nonresident
Maximum stay: 14 days
Management: Glendo State Park, 397 Glendo Park Rd., Glendo, WY 82213; (307) 735-4433
Reservations: Online at wyomingstateparks.reserveamerica.com or by phone at (877) 996-7275
Pets: Allowed with restrictions. See introduction to "Glendo State Park" above.
Quiet hours: 10 p.m. to 6 a.m. Note the special restrictions in the area description.
ADA compliance: Yes
Activities: Fishing, swimming, hiking, mountain biking
Finding the campground: Leave I-25 at Glendo State Park/exit 111 and travel east into the town of Glendo. After crossing the railroad tracks (be aware the train will not sound a horn at this crossing), travel to North Yellowstone Highway/WY 319 (the second street) and turn right. Travel 2 blocks, turn left onto C Street, and travel to the next intersection. Turn right onto South Lincoln Avenue/Glendo Park Road and travel 15 miles. Turn to the right onto the gravel road and travel 0.6 mile. The campground access road is on the left.
About the campground: Cottonwood trees still occupy the shoreline and then work their way uphill as the ground rises. As the summer moves toward fall, the shoreline typically moves farther away from the camping units much faster than in the Dune and Willow areas. This campground is spread out over a sizable distance, with the vault toilet and water at the first access road.

39 Indian Point

Location: 17.9 miles northwest of Glendo
GPS: N42 32.18' / W104 57.33'
Facilities and amenities: Vault toilets, fire rings, picnic tables, boat ramp available
Elevation: 4,642 feet
Road conditions: Improved dirt to 2-track
Hookups: None
Sites: 21 basic sites
Maximum RV length: 20 feet long
Season: May–Sept
Fees: $$ resident, $$$$ nonresident

Maximum stay: 14 days

Management: Glendo State Park, 397 Glendo Park Rd., Glendo, WY 82213; (307) 735-4433

Reservations: Online at wyomingstateparks.reserveamerica.com or by phone at (877) 996-7275

Pets: Allowed with restrictions. See introduction to "Glendo State Park" above.

Quiet hours: 10 p.m. to 6 a.m. Note the special restrictions in the area description.

ADA compliance: No

Activities: Boating, fishing, mountain biking, hiking

Finding the campground: Leave I-25 at Glendo State Park/exit 111 and travel east into the town of Glendo. After crossing the railroad tracks (be aware the train will not sound a horn at this crossing), travel to North Yellowstone Highway/WY 319 (the second street) and turn right. Travel 2 blocks, turn left onto C Street, and travel to the next intersection. Turn right onto South Lincoln Avenue/Glendo Park Road and travel 15 miles. Turn to the right onto the gravel road and travel 2.9 miles. The campground is on the left.

About the campground: The nearby boat ramp is likely the major attraction as campers can spend time on the water or in a rather isolated camping spot in between. The cottonwood trees are present at various locations but offer no real source of shade with respect to the camping site. The units are spread out into three separate areas, increasing the solitude as well.

40 Broken Arrow

Location: 18.4 miles northwest of Glendo

GPS: N42 32.45' / W104 57.47'

Facilities and amenities: Vault toilet, fire rings, picnic tables

Elevation: 4,648 feet

Road conditions: Improved dirt to sand (impassable when wet)

Hookups: None

Sites: 20 basic sites

Maximum RV length: 20 feet long

Season: May–Sept

Fees: $$ resident, $$$$ nonresident

Maximum stay: 14 days

Management: Glendo State Park, 397 Glendo Park Rd., Glendo, WY 82213; (307) 735-4433

Reservations: Online at wyomingstateparks.reserveamerica.com or by phone at (877) 996-7275

Pets: Allowed with restrictions. See introduction to "Glendo State Park" above.

Quiet hours: 10 p.m. to 6 a.m. Note the special restrictions in the area description.

ADA compliance: No

Activities: Fishing, hiking, mountain biking

Finding the campground: Leave I-25 at Glendo State Park/exit 111 and travel east into the town of Glendo. After crossing the railroad tracks (be aware the train will not sound a horn at this crossing), travel to North Yellowstone Highway/WY 319 (the second street) and turn right. Travel 2 blocks, turn left onto C Street, and travel to the next intersection. Turn right onto South Lincoln Avenue/Glendo Park Road and travel 15 miles. Turn to the right onto the gravel road and travel 3.4 miles. The campground is on the left.

About the campground: The camping units circle along the edge of a relatively flat meadow with a partial cottonwood forest boundary. Shade is not available for the tables or those parked in the area. However, the trees are not too far away for those who want to take a short hike to the water, which will get farther away as summer moves toward fall. This is a good place for those who would like to share time with family and friends as a group. Should it rain or snow, getting in or out will be difficult to impossible. Plan accordingly.

41 Elkhorn

Location: 4 miles north of Glendo
GPS: N42 33.54' / W105 1.87'
Facilities and amenities: Vault toilet, fire rings, picnic tables, boat ramp
Elevation: 4,647 feet
Road conditions: Gravel
Hookups: None
Sites: 9 basic sites
Maximum RV length: 40 feet long
Season: May–Sept
Fees: $$ resident, $$$$ nonresident
Maximum stay: 14 days
Management: Glendo State Park, 397 Glendo Park Rd., Glendo, WY 82213; (307) 735-4433
Reservations: Online at wyomingstateparks.reserveamerica.com or by phone at (877) 996-7275
Pets: Allowed with restrictions. See introduction to "Glendo State Park" above.
Quiet hours: 10 p.m. to 6 a.m. Note the special restrictions in the area description.
ADA compliance: Yes
Activities: Fishing, boating
Finding the campground: Leave I-25 at Glendo State Park/exit 111 and travel east into the town of Glendo. After crossing the railroad tracks (be aware the train will not sound a horn at this crossing), travel to North Yellowstone Highway/WY 319 (the second street) and turn left. Travel 3.5 miles to the access road. Turn right and travel another 0.5 mile to the first camping units.
About the campground: This can be a very pleasant place to stay, with shade from the cottonwood trees predominating in the afternoon, the hottest part of the day. However, weather will have a definite effect on availability as the water level of the reservoir may have the camping units under water. On the flip side, later in the summer the water is too far away to put a boat in, though it would be a fair bet that you might be the only camper in the place when the water is that low.

Guernsey State Park

Campgrounds are organized from the south entrance, otherwise understood to be the main entrance. An RV dump is just past the fee booth. There is an east and a west side. There are 245 designated campsites in Guernsey State Park.

42 Lower Spotted Tail

Location: 1.7 miles northeast of the south gate fee booth
GPS: N42 17 58.9' / W104 45 51.2'
Facilities and amenities: Vault toilet, fire rings, picnic tables, trash receptacles, drinking water
Elevation: 4,462 feet
Road conditions: Paved to access, then gravel
Hookups: None
Sites: 11 basic sites
Maximum RV length: 40 feet long
Season: May–Sept
Fees: Day use: $ per day resident, $$ per day nonresident. Plus, camping fee: $$ per night resident, $$$$ per night nonresident
Maximum stay: 14 days
Management: Guernsey State Park, 2187 Lake Side Dr., Guernsey, WY 82214; (307) 836-2334
Reservations: Online at wyomingstateparks.reserveamerica.com or by phone at (877) 996-7275
Pets: All pets must be in a vehicle or on a leash no longer than 10 feet and physically controlled at all times.
Quiet hours: 10 p.m. to 6 a.m. (turn off generators)
ADA compliance: No
Activities: Hiking, mountain biking
Finding the campground: At exit 92 on I-25, take US 26 east for 15 miles. Turn left at the directional State Park sign onto WY 317 and travel 1.5 miles to the south gate fee booth. Travel on Lake Shore Drive for 1.7 miles. The campground is on the left.
About the campground: Pine trees offer shade when the colorful rocky cliffs towering above cast no shadows. The cool to cold water of the reservoir can be difficult to access but not impossible. The accommodations built in the past still maintain a solid status, as a testimony to their workmanship and building materials. Leveling campers may take some time depending upon which site is selected.

43 Upper Spotted Tail

Location: 2 miles north of the south gate fee booth
GPS: N42 18 1.8' / W104 45.47'
Facilities and amenities: Vault toilets, fire rings, picnic tables, trash receptacles, drinking water
Elevation: 4,477 feet
Road conditions: Gravel
Hookups: None
Sites: 7 basic sites
Maximum RV length: 30 feet long
Season: May–Sept
Fees: Day use: $ per day resident, $$ per day nonresident. Plus, camping fee: $$ per night resident, $$$$ per night nonresident
Maximum stay: 14 days
Management: Guernsey State Park, 2187 Lake Side Dr., Guernsey, WY 82214; (307) 836-2334
Reservations: First-come, first-served
Pets: All pets must be in a vehicle or on a leash no longer than 10 feet and physically controlled at all times.
Quiet hours: 10 p.m. to 6 a.m. (turn off generators)
ADA compliance: No
Activities: Hiking, mountain biking
Finding the campground: At exit 92 on I-25, take US 26 east for 15 miles. Turn left at the directional State Park sign onto WY 317 and travel 1.5 miles to the south gate fee booth. Travel on Lake Shore Drive for 2 miles. The campground is on the right.
About the campground: Pine trees are scattered out along this otherwise open sloping draw with treeless ridges in the background. Tent campers have a better selection of shade options than RVs. It is a pretty good distance to the reservoir, but the traffic noise will be reduced if not eliminated in this spot even during the day.

44 Red Cloud

Location: 2.3 miles north of the south gate fee booth
GPS: N42 18 13.3' / W104 45 55.2'
Facilities and amenities: Vault toilet, fire rings, picnic tables, picnic area, drinking water
Elevation: 4,422 feet
Road conditions: Steep access paved to gravel
Hookups: None
Sites: 4 basic sites
Maximum RV length: 20 feet long
Season: May–Sept
Fees: Day use: $ per day resident, $$ per day nonresident. Plus, camping fee: $$ per night resident, $$$$ per night nonresident.

Maximum stay: 14 days
Management: Guernsey State Park, 2187 Lake Side Dr., Guernsey, WY 82214; (307) 836-2334
Reservations: Online at wyomingstateparks.reserveamerica.com or by phone at (877) 996-7275
Pets: All pets must be in a vehicle or on a leash no longer than 10 feet and physically controlled at all times.
Quiet hours: 10 p.m. to 6 a.m. (turn off generators)
ADA compliance: No
Activities: Hiking, biking, picnicking
Finding the campground: At exit 92 on I-25, take US 26 east for 15 miles. Turn left at the directional State Park sign onto WY 317 and travel 1.5 miles to the south gate fee booth. Travel on Lake Shore Drive for 2.3 miles. The campground is on the left.
About the campground: The pine trees and camping units hug the shoreline and circle around the restroom and water spot. A very unique group shelter constructed of logs and complete with a large stone fireplace invites campers to unite and share the time together. This would also be a very good place for a smaller family reunion.

45 Black Canyon Cove

Location: 2.5 miles north of the south gate fee booth
GPS: N42 18 32.8' / W104 45 53.9'
Facilities and amenities: Fire rings, picnic tables
Elevation: 4,441 feet
Road conditions: Gravel
Hookups: None
Sites: 1 group site, maximum 20 persons
Maximum RV length: 45 feet long
Season: May–Sept
Fees: Day use: $ per day resident, $$ per day nonresident. Plus, camping fee: $$ per night resident, $$$$ per night nonresident.
Maximum stay: 14 days
Management: Guernsey State Park, 2187 Lake Side Dr., Guernsey, WY 82214; (307) 836-2334
Reservations: Online at wyomingstateparks.reserveamerica.com or by phone at (877) 996-7275
Pets: All pets must be in a vehicle or on a leash no longer than 10 feet and physically controlled at all times.
Quiet hours: 10 p.m. to 6 a.m. (turn off generators)
ADA compliance: No
Activities: Hiking, mountain biking, fishing, picnicking
Finding the campground: At exit 92 on I-25, take US 26 east for 15 miles. Turn left at the directional State Park sign onto WY 317 and travel 1.5 miles to the south gate fee booth. Travel on Lake Shore Drive for 2.5 miles. The campground is on the left.
About the campground: Reservoir access is easy, and the cottonwood trees offer shade with variations dependent upon your exact camper positioning.

46 Black Canyon Point

Location: 2.7 miles north of the south gate fee booth
GPS: N42 18 33.2' / W104 46 1.5'
Facilities and amenities: Vault toilet, fire rings, picnic tables, trash receptacles, group picnic shelter
Elevation: 4,513 feet
Road conditions: Gravel
Hookups: None
Sites: 4 basic sites
Maximum RV length: 45 feet long
Season: May–Sept
Fees: Day use: $ per day resident, $$ per day nonresident. Plus, camping fee: $$ per night resident, $$$$ per night nonresident
Maximum stay: 14 days
Management: Guernsey State Park, 2187 Lake Side Dr., Guernsey, WY 82214; (307) 836-2334
Reservations: Online at wyomingstateparks.reserveamerica.com or by phone at (877) 996-7275
Pets: All pets must be in a vehicle or on a leash no longer than 10 feet and physically controlled at all times.
Quiet hours: 10 p.m. to 6 a.m. (turn off generators)
ADA compliance: Yes
Activities: Hiking, mountain biking, picnicking
Finding the campground: At exit 92 on I-25, take US 26 east for 15 miles. Turn left at the directional State Park sign onto WY 317 and travel 1.5 miles to the south gate fee booth. Travel on Lake Shore Drive for 2.7 miles. The campground is on the left.
About the campground: The campground access tends to appear without enough room to react if oncoming traffic happens to be present. Be careful: If it does happen, it would be much better to pass this one by or go on up the road and turn around. At the time of our visit, the water pump was not functional. That may change by the time this book is in print, but it is uncertain.

47 Fish Canyon

Location: 3.2 miles north of the south gate fee booth
GPS: N42 18 56.7' / W104 45.49'
Facilities and amenities: Vault toilets, fire rings, picnic tables, trash receptacles, drinking water
Elevation: 4,424 feet
Road conditions: Gravel
Hookups: None
Sites: 12 basic sites
Maximum RV length: 40 feet long
Season: May–Sept

Fees: Day use: $ per day resident, $$ per day nonresident. Plus, camping fee: $$ per night resident, $$$$ per night nonresident

Maximum stay: 14 days

Management: Guernsey State Park, 2187 Lake Side Dr., Guernsey, WY 82214; (307) 836-2334

Reservations: Online at wyomingstateparks.reserveamerica.com or by phone at (877) 996-7275

Pets: All pets must be in a vehicle or on a leash no longer than 10 feet and physically controlled at all times.

Quiet hours: 10 p.m. to 6 a.m. (turn off generators)

ADA compliance: Yes

Activities: Hiking, mountain biking

Finding the campground: At exit 92 on I-25, take US 26 east for 15 miles. Turn left at the directional State Park sign onto WY 317 and travel 1.5 miles to the south gate fee booth. Travel on Lake Shore Drive for 3.2 miles. The campground is on the left.

About the campground: Cedar is scattered about, with grassy open areas in between and a lot of space between units. Tents have the best advantage with respect to shade. It's a very private sort of place but a considerable distance from the reservoir for those who like better access to the shoreline.

48 Fish Canyon Cove

Location: 3.25 miles north of the south gate fee booth

GPS: N42 18 54.4' / W104 45 51.6'

Facilities and amenities: Both the vault toilet and trash dumpsters are across the road; fire rings, picnic tables, drinking water

Elevation: 4,449 feet

Road conditions: Gravel

Hookups: None

Sites: 5 basic sites

Maximum RV length: 40 feet long

Season: May–Sept

Fees: Day use: $ per day resident, $$ per day nonresident. Plus, camping fee: $$ per night resident, $$$$ per night nonresident

Maximum stay: 14 days

Management: Guernsey State Park, 2187 Lake Side Dr., Guernsey, WY 82214; (307) 836-2334

Reservations: Online at wyomingstateparks.reserveamerica.com or by phone at (877) 996-7275

Pets: All pets must be in a vehicle or on a leash no longer than 10 feet and physically controlled at all times.

Quiet hours: 10 p.m. to 6 a.m. (turn off generators)

ADA compliance: No

Activities: Fishing, hiking, biking

Finding the campground: At exit 92 on I-25, take US 26 east for 15 miles. Turn left at the directional State Park sign onto WY 317 and travel 1.5 miles to the south gate fee booth. Travel on Lake Shore Drive for 3.25 miles. The campground is on the left.

About the campground: For anglers who like shore fishing, this is a tempting spot to see what the fish are biting. Cottonwood trees offer shade for those who arrive in time to select the best unit to set up in. A portable tent toilet could be a real benefit in this camping area. Several have been seen during the course of our campground visits, with no personal experience with them, good or bad.

49 Deadman's Cove

Location: 4.15 miles north of the south gate fee booth
GPS: N42 19 19.9' / W104 46 8.1'
Facilities and amenities: Fire ring, picnic table
Elevation: 4,459 feet
Road conditions: Gravel
Hookups: None
Sites: 1
Maximum RV length: 20 feet long
Season: May–Sept
Fees: Day use: $ per day resident, $$ per day nonresident. Plus, camping fee: $$ per night resident, $$$$ per night nonresident
Maximum stay: 14 days
Management: Guernsey State Park, 2187 Lake Side Dr., Guernsey, WY 82214; (307) 836-2334
Reservations: Online at wyomingstateparks.reserveamerica.com or by phone at (877) 996-7275
Pets: All pets must be in a vehicle or on a leash no longer than 10 feet and physically controlled at all times.
Quiet hours: 10 p.m. to 6 a.m. (turn off generators)
ADA compliance: No
Activities: Fishing, hiking
Finding the campground: At exit 92 on I-25, take US 26 east for 15 miles. Turn left at the directional State Park sign onto WY 317 and travel 1.5 miles to the south gate fee booth. Travel on Lake Shore Drive for 4.15 miles. The campground is on the left.
About the campground: Shade is an added benefit, with perhaps the greatest appeal being there are no "neighbors" so to speak. A longer RV might be installed here, but backing and leveling skills would be tested, especially if traffic is heavy as it would have to be backed in from the highway.

50 Long Canyon East

Location: 5.3 miles north of the south gate fee booth
GPS: N42 19 53.7' / W104 46 47.9'
Facilities and amenities: Vault toilets, fire rings, picnic tables, trash receptacles, group shelter, drinking water
Elevation: 4,647 feet

Road conditions: Gravel
Hookups: None
Sites: 21 basic sites
Maximum RV length: 45 feet long
Season: May–Sept
Fees: Day use: $ per day resident, $$ per day nonresident. Plus, camping fee: $$ per night resident, $$$$ per night nonresident
Maximum stay: 14 days
Management: Guernsey State Park, 2187 Lake Side Dr., Guernsey, WY 82214; (307) 836-2334
Reservations: Online at wyomingstateparks.reserveamerica.com or by phone at (877) 996-7275
Pets: All pets must be in a vehicle or on a leash no longer than 10 feet and physically controlled at all times.
Quiet hours: 10 p.m. to 6 a.m. (turn off generators)
ADA compliance: Yes
Activities: Fishing, hiking, picnicking
Finding the campground: At exit 92 on I-25, take US 26 east for 15 miles. Turn left at the directional State Park sign onto WY 317 and travel 1.5 miles to the south gate fee booth. Travel on Lake Shore Drive for 5.3 miles. The campground is on the left.
About the campground: Longer trailers do fit here, but it would be best to consider coming in from the north entrance. Trailers over 45 feet long are not permitted beyond this entrance toward the south. Cottonwood trees do provide shade at various spots, so it will take some evaluation on the available units to make a choice best suited to your desires.

51 Long Canyon West

Location: 5.3 miles north of the south gate fee booth
GPS: N42 19 51.4' / W104 46 54.6'
Facilities and amenities: Vault toilet, fire rings, picnic tables, trash dumpsters, drinking water
Elevation: 4,454 feet
Road conditions: Gravel
Hookups: None
Sites: 3 for tents, 1 accessible, 2 group
Maximum RV length: 45 feet long
Season: May–Sept
Fees: Day use: $ per day resident, $$ per day nonresident. Plus, camping fee: $$ per night resident, $$$$ per night nonresident
Maximum stay: 14 days
Management: Guernsey State Park, 2187 Lake Side Dr., Guernsey, WY 82214; (307) 836-2334
Reservations: Online at wyomingstateparks.reserveamerica.com or by phone at (877) 996-7275
Pets: All pets must be in a vehicle or on a leash no longer than 10 feet and physically controlled at all times.
Quiet hours: 10 p.m. to 6 a.m. (turn off generators)
ADA compliance: Yes
Activities: Fishing, boating, picnicking

Finding the campground: At exit 92 on I-25, take US 26 east for 15 miles. Turn left at the directional State Park sign onto WY 317 and travel 1.5 miles to the south gate fee booth. Travel on Lake Shore Drive for 5.3 miles. The campground is on the left.

About the campground: This might be a dead-end road, but when the weather's hot and the lake is calling, there is no shortage of boats making their way to the ramp behind a variety of vehicles. Typically, the dust and the noise attached with it sets into silence as darkness extends the shadows above the treetops.

52 Skyline

Location: 0.5 mile northwest of the south gate fee booth
GPS: N42 17 10.4' / W104 46 24.9'
Facilities and amenities: Vault toilet, fire rings, picnic tables, drinking water
Elevation: 4,606 feet
Road conditions: Gravel
Hookups: None
Sites: 19 basic sites
Maximum RV length: 40 feet long
Season: May–Sept
Fees: Day use: $ per day resident, $$ per day nonresident. Plus, camping fee: $$ per night resident, $$$$ per night nonresident.
Maximum stay: 14 days
Management: Guernsey State Park, 2187 Lake Side Dr., Guernsey, WY 82214; (307) 836-2334
Reservations: First-come, first-served
Pets: All pets must be in a vehicle or on a leash no longer than 10 feet and physically controlled at all times.
Quiet hours: 10 p.m. to 6 a.m. (turn off generators)
ADA compliance: No
Activities: Hiking, mountain biking
Finding the campground: At exit 92 on I-25, take US 26 east for 15 miles. Turn left at the directional State Park sign onto WY 317 and travel 1.5 miles to the south gate fee booth. Just past the fee booth at the entrance to the RV dump (on the right) turn left onto Skyline Drive and travel 0.5 mile. The campground is on the right.

About the campground: There are trees in sight on the rolling hills and in the camping area, but shade is only available when the camper happens to be opposite the sun's position. Water activities typical for a reservoir are not easily accessed from this campground. However, the noise associated with such sports are also absent. When the new moon allows the stars to show their stuff, this would be a very good place to stay up late.

53 Newell Bay

Location: 2.5 miles northwest of the south gate fee booth
GPS: N42 17 53.8' / W104 46.48'
Facilities and amenities: Vault toilet, fire rings, picnic tables
Elevation: 4,543 feet
Road conditions: Improved dirt
Hookups: None
Sites: 3 basic sites
Maximum RV length: 20 feet long
Season: May–Sept
Fees: Day use: $ per day resident, $$ per day nonresident. Plus, camping fee: $$ per night resident, $$$$ per night nonresident
Maximum stay: 14 days
Management: Guernsey State Park, 2187 Lake Side Dr., Guernsey, WY 82214; (307) 836-2334
Reservations: First-come, first-served
Pets: All pets must be in a vehicle or on a leash no longer than 10 feet and physically controlled at all times.
Quiet hours: 10 p.m. to 6 a.m. (turn off generators)
ADA compliance: No
Activities: Fishing, hiking, mountain biking
Finding the campground: At exit 92 on I-25, take US 26 east for 15 miles. Turn left at the directional State Park sign onto WY 317 and travel 1.5 miles to the south gate fee booth. Just past the fee booth at the entrance to the RV dump (on the right), turn left onto Skyline Drive and travel 1.6 miles to the access road (across the railroad tracks). Turn to the right onto the gravel road and travel 0.6 mile. The campground vault toilet is 0.3 mile at the three-way intersection.
About the campground: The single-lane access road to these camping sites dives downhill on a winding rocky ridge, with ponderosa pine increasing in number on the descent. Upon arrival at the vault toilet, a three-way intersection is about the only place with any width to turn around. The task doesn't end there as there is no small distance to back down another set of downhill turns. Unless the first site located at the intersection, also the closest one to the vault toilet and the farthest from the shoreline, is to your liking.

54 Davis Bay

Location: 2.7 miles northwest of the south gate fee booth
GPS: N42 18 25.2' / W104 47 11.9'
Facilities and amenities: Vault toilet, fire rings, picnic tables, trash receptacles
Elevation: 4,626 feet
Road conditions: Somewhat steep gravel access road
Hookups: None
Sites: 4 basic sites

Maximum RV length: 45 feet long

Season: May–Sept

Fees: Day use: $ per day resident, $$ per day nonresident. Plus, camping fee: $$ per night resident, $$$$ per night nonresident

Maximum stay: 14 days

Management: Guernsey State Park, 2187 Lake Side Dr., Guernsey, WY 82214; (307) 836-2334

Reservations: Online at wyomingstateparks.reserveamerica.com or by phone at (877) 996-7275

Pets: All pets must be in a vehicle or on a leash no longer than 10 feet and physically controlled at all times.

Quiet hours: 10 p.m. to 6 a.m. (turn off generators)

ADA compliance: Yes

Activities: Hiking, fishing, mountain biking

Finding the campground: At exit 92 on I-25, take US 26 east for 15 miles. Turn left at the directional State Park sign onto WY 317 and travel 1.5 miles to the south gate fee booth. Just past the fee booth at the entrance to the RV dump (on the right), turn left onto Skyline Drive and travel 2.7 miles to the access road (across the railroad tracks). Turn to the right onto the gravel road and travel 0.4 mile to the three-way-intersection.

About the campground: Ponderosa pine trees stand watch over the access in the beginning. Cottonwoods dominate the final stopping place after descending off of the upper ridge. It is a long walk uphill to the restroom, so as with other camping areas, a "portable tent toilet/shower" could make it possible to have more free time for recreational-type things. There are several choices of hiking trails waiting for your inspection.

55 Sandy Beach

Location: 3.6 miles northwest of the south gate fee booth (last access)

GPS: N42 18 21.6' / W104 48 6.1'

Facilities and amenities: Vault toilets, fire rings, picnic tables, trash receptacles, drinking water, boat ramp

Elevation: 4,484 feet

Road conditions: Gravel

Hookups: Electric and water

Sites: 16 for tents, 36 basic sites, 1 group site

Maximum RV length: 50 feet long

Season: May–Sept

Fees: Day use: $ per day resident, $$ per day nonresident. Plus, camping fee: $$ per night resident, $$$$ per night nonresident

Maximum stay: 14 days

Management: Guernsey State Park, 2187 Lake Side Dr., Guernsey, WY 82214; (307) 836-2334

Reservations: Online at wyomingstateparks.reserveamerica.com or by phone at (877) 996-7275

Pets: All pets must be in a vehicle or on a leash no longer than 10 feet and physically controlled at all times.

Quiet hours: 10 p.m. to 6 a.m. (turn off generators)

ADA compliance: Yes

Activities: Fishing, boating, water sports

Finding the campground: At exit 92 on I-25, take US 26 east for 15 miles. Turn left at the directional State Park sign onto WY 317 and travel 1.5 miles to the south gate fee booth. Just past the fee booth at the entrance to the RV dump (on the right), turn left onto Skyline Drive and travel 3.6 miles to the access road. The campground is on the right with a total of three access entries.

About the campground: This is a popular place, with young families representing the majority of those camping during our visit. Mature cottonwood trees line the shore, offering shade for picnic tables with a little overflow for camping trailers later in the day. Not all of the RV units have shade and of course those are usually the sites that fill up last. Reservations are recommended well in advance if water sports are your preference.

56 Cottonwood

Location: 4 miles northwest of the south gate fee booth

GPS: N42 18 23.5' / W104 48 37.9'

Facilities and amenities: Fire rings, picnic tables

Elevation: 4,469 feet

Road conditions: Gravel

Hookups: None

Sites: 4 for tents, 5 basic sites

Maximum RV length: 40 feet long

Season: May–Sept

Fees: Day use: $ per day resident, $$ per day nonresident. Plus, camping fee: $$ per night resident, $$$$ per night nonresident

Maximum stay: 14 days

Management: Guernsey State Park, 2187 Lake Side Dr., Guernsey, WY 82214; (307) 836-2334

Reservations: Online at wyomingstateparks.reserveamerica.com or by phone at (877) 996-7275

Pets: All pets must be in a vehicle or on a leash no longer than 10 feet and physically controlled at all times.

Quiet hours: 10 p.m. to 6 a.m. (turn off generators)

ADA compliance: No

Activities: Fishing, picnicking

Finding the campground: At exit 92 on I-25, take US 26 east for 15 miles. Turn left at the directional State Park sign onto WY 317 and travel 1.5 miles to the south gate fee booth. Just past the fee booth at the entrance to the RV dump (on the right), turn left onto Skyline Drive and travel 4 miles to the access road. The campground is on the right.

About the campground: There is no official public beach listed here, but signs are present advising campers "no pets on beach." This primitive camping area has plenty of shade provided by the mature cottonwood trees common to this shoreline. The hustle and bustle complete with all the noise associated with public beaches is lacking here, along with the missing restroom and other amenities, with the exception of the active railroad just across the road.

57 Sandy Point

Location: 4.1 miles northwest of the south gate fee booth (last access)
GPS: N42 18 23.7' / W104 48 44.5'
Facilities and amenities: Vault toilets, fire rings, picnic tables, trash receptacles, drinking water
Elevation: 4,488 feet
Road conditions: Gravel
Hookups: Electric and water
Sites: 4 for tents, 36 basic sites
Maximum RV length: 50 feet long
Season: May–Sept
Fees: Day use: $ per day resident, $$ per day nonresident. Plus, camping fee: $$ per night resident, $$$$ per night nonresident
Maximum stay: 14 days
Management: Guernsey State Park, 2187 Lake Side Dr., Guernsey, WY 82214; (307) 836-2334
Reservations: Online at wyomingstateparks.reserveamerica.com or by phone at (877) 996-7275
Pets: All pets must be in a vehicle or on a leash no longer than 10 feet and physically controlled at all times.
Quiet hours: 10 p.m. to 6 a.m. (turn off generators)
ADA compliance: Yes
Activities: Fishing, water sports, picnicking
Finding the campground: At exit 92 on I-25, take US 26 east for 15 miles. Turn left at the directional State Park sign onto WY 317 and travel 1.5 miles to the south gate fee booth. Just past the fee booth at the entrance to the RV dump (on the right), turn left onto Skyline Drive and travel 4.1 miles to the access road.
About the campground: There are a few cedar trees scattered around the camping area, though the dominant cottonwood maintains possession of the shoreline. Camping units with a possibility of shade fill first, leaving units with electric and water hookups unoccupied for a time. There is a boat ramp available at Sandy Beach, though it will be a little bit of a drive.

58 Sandy Cove

Location: 4.2 miles northwest of the south gate fee booth
GPS: N42 18 24.6' / W104 48 55.1'
Facilities and amenities: Vault toilet, fire rings, picnic tables
Elevation: 4,483 feet
Road conditions: Gravel
Hookups: None
Sites: 12 basic sites
Maximum RV length: 40 feet long
Season: May–Sept

Fees: Day use: $ per day resident, $$ per day nonresident. Plus, camping fee: $$ per night resident, $$$$ per night nonresident

Maximum stay: 14 days

Management: Guernsey State Park, 2187 Lake Side Dr., Guernsey, WY 82214; (307) 836-2334

Reservations: Online at wyomingstateparks.reserveamerica.com or by phone at (877) 996-7275

Pets: All pets must be in a vehicle or on a leash no longer than 10 feet and physically controlled at all times.

Quiet hours: 10 p.m. to 6 a.m. (turn off generators)

ADA compliance: Yes

Activities: Fishing, water sports, picnicking

Finding the campground: At exit 92 on I-25, take US 26 east for 15 miles. Turn left at the directional State Park sign onto WY 317 and travel 1.5 miles to the south gate fee booth. Just past the fee booth at the entrance to the RV dump (on the right), turn left onto Skyline Drive and travel 4.2 miles to the access road. This is pretty much the end of the road.

About the campground: Boating is not listed here though there is a boat ramp at Sandy Beach. Water sports are still the major attraction here. As with other campgrounds, the cottonwood trees offer shade, but when the sun is hot, the cold reservoir water functions with more appeal than air-conditioning.

Cody Area

History, high mountains, and two of the three Yellowstone National Park entrances from Wyoming are the highlights of this area. The Buffalo Bill Historic Center in Cody presents an overwhelming collection of historical artifacts for interpretation. Be prepared for the disappointment of inadequate time. Reportedly, some have spent a month investigating the displays and still did not see all of them.

The main highlight, of course, is Yellowstone National Park. And that means the campgrounds along the main route fill very quickly. Preplanning and a little extra time will allow campers to explore the out-of-the-way places listed in this book. Backtracking a portion of Chief Joseph's trail to the northeast entrance presents travelers with less traffic and scenic views missed by the majority of national park visitors.

Grizzly bears and other wildlife are frequently seen in this area, requiring proper safety measures. Keep in mind the *wild* in wildlife comes first, and this is their home. We as travelers are not always, if ever, welcome guests.

Some locally gathered firewood at Island Lake.

#		Group sites	Tents	RV sites	Total # of sites	Picnic area	Toilets	Hookups	Drinking water	Dump station	Handicap	Recreation	Fee	Season	Can reserve	Stay limit
1	Wood River			5	5		V					FHiMW	D	5/1-10/31		16
2	Brown Mountain			7	7		V					FHiMW	D	5/1-1/31		16
3	Jack Creek			4	4		V					FHiMWHuHr	D	Year-round		16
4	Dead Indian			10	10		V					FHiW	$	5/28-9/15		16
5	Hunter Peak			10	10		V		X			FBoMhrWCTh	$$	6/1-9/15	X	16
6	Lake Creek			6	6		V					FHiW	$	6/15-9/15		16
7	Crazy Creek			16	16		V					HiW	$	6/1-9/15		16
8	Colter (Montana)			18	18		V		X		X	Hi	$	6/15-9/1		16
9	Soda Butte (Montana)			27	27		V		X			HiFW	$$	6/1-9/1		16
10	Beartooth Lake			21	21		V		X			FBoHiWPh	$$	7/1-9/15		16
11	Island Lake			21	21		V		X			FBoHiWPh	$$	7/1-9/15		16
12	Wapiti			41	41		V	El	X			FHiW	$$	5/15-10/15	X	16
13	Elk Fork			13	13		V					FHiHrCW	$	Year-round		16
14	Clearwater	1	11		12		V					FHiW	$-$$$$$$	5/1-9/30	X	16
15	Rex Hale			30	30		V	El	X			FHiW	$$	5/15-9/15	X	16
16	Newton Creek			31	31		V		X			FHiW	$$	5/15-9/30		16
17	Eagle Creek			20	20		V		X		X	FHiW	$$	5/15-9/15		16
18	Three Mile			21	21		V		X			FHiW	$$	7/1-9/30		16
	Buffalo Bill State Park															
19	North Fork		6	60	66		V	El	X	X	X X	FHi	$-$$	5/1-9/30	X	14
20	Lake Shore		5	32	37		V	ElWa	X	X	X	FBoSBr	$-$$	Year-round	X	14

Bo = boating, Br = boat ramp, C = corral, D = donation, El = electric hookups, F = fishing, Hi = hiking, Hr = horseback riding, Hu = hunting, M = mountain biking, Ph = photography, S = swimming, Th = trailhead, V = vault toilet, W = wildlife viewing, Wa = water hookup

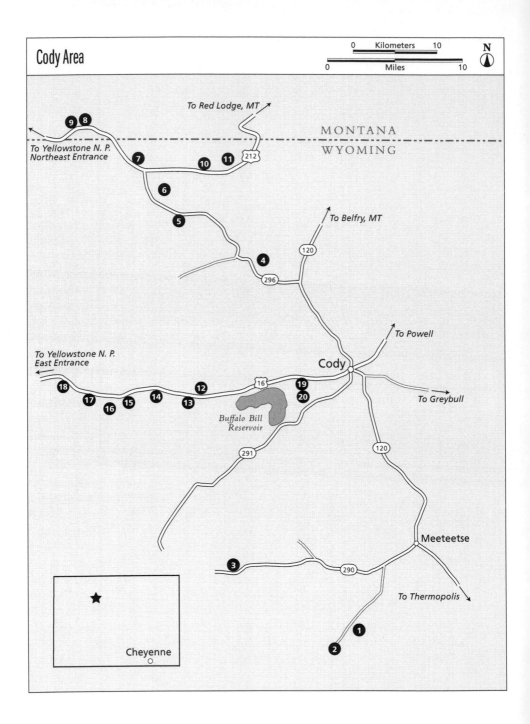

Cody Area

Kilometers
0   10

Miles
0   10

N

To Red Lodge, MT

MONTANA
WYOMING

To Yellowstone N. P.
Northeast Entrance

212

To Belfry, MT

120

296

To Powell

Cody

To Yellowstone N. P.
East Entrance

16

To Greybull

Buffalo Bill
Reservoir

291

120

Meeteetse

290

To Thermopolis

Cheyenne

1 Wood River

Location: 25 miles southwest of Meeteetse
GPS: N42 55.93' / W109 7.89'
Facilities and amenities: Vault toilet, fire rings, picnic tables
Elevation: 7,276 feet
Road conditions: Gravel
Hookups: None
Sites: 5 basic sites
Maximum RV length: 30-foot-long parking apron
Season: Mid-May through mid-Oct
Fees: Donation
Maximum stay: 16 days
Management: Shoshone National Forest, Greybull Ranger District, 203A Yellowstone Ave., Cody, WY 82414; (307) 527-6921 or (800) 517-0413
Reservations: First-come, first-served
Pets: Pets must be on a leash and under physical control at all times.
Quiet hours: Campers courtesy
ADA compliance: No
Activities: Fishing, hiking, mountain biking, wildlife viewing
Finding the campground: From Cody travel south on WY 120 for 32 miles to Meeteetse. Take WY 290 west of Meeteetse for 7 miles to Wood River Road (CR 4DT) and turn left. Travel down this paved-turning-to-gravel road for about 14 miles. The campground is on the left.
About the campground: Washakie Wilderness access keeps this campground very active. Evergreen trees shade the units, though just outside the campground, sagebrush takes over. Larger units do make the trip, but most are very familiar with the terrain. The Kirwin ghost town draws plenty of curious types. Some of the cars hosting the curious really do not belong on this backcountry road. So be cautious on your way into this place.

2 Brown Mountain

Location: 28 miles southwest of Meeteetse
GPS: N43 56.14' / W109 10.75'
Facilities and amenities: Vault toilet, fire rings, picnic tables, food storage
Elevation: 7,559 feet
Road conditions: Gravel
Hookups: None
Sites: 7 basic sites
Maximum RV length: 16 feet long
Season: Mid-May through mid-Oct
Fees: Donation
Maximum stay: 16 days

Management: Shoshone National Forest, Greybull Ranger District, 203A Yellowstone Ave., Cody, WY 82414; (307) 527-6921 or (800) 517-0413

Reservations: First-come, first-served

Pets: Pets must be on a leash and under physical control at all times.

Quiet hours: Campers courtesy

ADA compliance: No

Activities: Fishing, hiking, mountain biking, wildlife viewing

Finding the campground: From Cody take WY 120 south 32 miles to Meeteetse. Take WY 290 west of Meeteetse 7 miles to CR 4DT (Wood River Road). Turn left and travel for about 16 miles. This paved road will turn to gravel as it nears the national forest boundary. The campground access road is on the left.

About the campground: Douglas firs dominate the camping area, with a grassy field in between it and the main road. Tall, thick willow brush takes over before getting to the river. Shade is present, but a little evaluation can place your camper to maximize the value of this feature for comfort on a hot day. Wood River rages by with plenty of things to say. Horses and riders can become plentiful, with an accumulation of dust on dry days, which most are.

3 Jack Creek

Location: 28 miles west of Meeteetse

GPS: N44 6.60' / W109 21.13'

Facilities and amenities: Vault toilet, fire rings, picnic tables

Elevation: 7,571 feet

Road conditions: Improved dirt

Hookups: None

Sites: 4 basic sites

Maximum RV length: 32 feet long

Season: Open year-round

Fees: Donation

Maximum stay: 16 days

Management: Shoshone National Forest, Wapiti Ranger District, 203A Yellowstone Ave., Cody, WY 82414; (307) 527-6921 or (800) 517-0413

Reservations: First-come, first-served

Pets: Pets must be on a leash and under physical control at all times.

Quiet hours: Campers courtesy

ADA compliance: No

Activities: Fishing, hiking, mountain biking, wildlife viewing, hunting, horseback riding

Finding the campground: From Cody take WY 120 south 32 miles to Meeteetse. Turn left onto WY 290 west. Travel on this road (the pavement ends after about 11 miles) for approximately 19 miles to the campground and trailhead. Directional signs are few and far between, with more than one intersection. Most of them will designate the way to the trailhead. The road deteriorates from rough gravel to dry dirt (very muddy when wet) to huge boulder infestation.

About the campground: Aspen and willow trees shade what tables remain, and fire rings have been reduced in number as well. Firewood could take some traveling to find. Bear warning signs are posted for good reason. This remote camping area offers plenty for those wanting to escape civilization. Hunting season brings the majority of visitors, though they generally do not camp here. Snowcapped mountains in the background are better seen on the way in. Be sure to have plenty of supplies and warm clothes. If the weather turns bad, it could be some time before you get out. Keep in mind that when the sun goes down in this high mountain country, the heat goes with it. It might be desert, but it is a high-altitude desert. Days are hot and nights are cold.

4 Dead Indian

Location: 40 miles northwest of Cody
GPS: N44 45.18' / W109 25.02'
Facilities and amenities: Vault toilets, fire rings, picnic tables
Elevation: 6,013 feet
Road conditions: Gravel
Hookups: None
Sites: 10 basic sites
Maximum RV length: 32 feet long
Season: Last week of May through mid-Sept
Fees: $ per night, Golden Age and Access Passport holders half price
Maximum stay: 16 days
Management: Shoshone National Forest, Clarks Fork Ranger District, 808 Meadow Lane Ave., Cody, WY 82414; (307) 527-6921
Reservations: First-come, first-served
Pets: Pets must be on a leash.
Quiet hours: 10 p.m. to 6 a.m. (turn off generators)
ADA compliance: No
Activities: Fishing, hiking, wildlife viewing
Finding the campground: From Cody travel north on WY 120 for 16 miles. Turn left (west) on Chief Joseph Scenic Highway (WY 296). Travel west about 16 miles to the campground. This is a steep mountain road with hairpin switchbacks—it is no place to be in a hurry. The campground is on the right side.
About the campground: Dead Indian Creek divides the campground in two, and there are separate access roads. A mixture of trees, including spruce, cottonwood, and willow, stands alone in this highway loop near the raging waters of the creek. Most of the units are fairly level, though not all are the same length. A host occupies one of the sites in the campground. As you wind down the hairpin turns, keep an eye out for the bottom—the campground area can be spotted long before you get there. Keep your camera loaded and handy for the scenic views offered from any one of the pullouts. Traffic is very noisy during the day from every unit in the campground. Generally, as the sun sets so does the racket, and it is replaced with the unmuffled rampage of rock versus water, a most welcome change. Fill up your water jugs before you come. There is no drinking water here.

5 Hunter Peak

Location: 59 miles northwest of Cody
GPS: N44 53.17' / W109 39.33'
Facilities and amenities: Vault toilet, fire rings, picnic tables, drinking water, corral, trailhead
Elevation: 6,527 feet
Road conditions: Gravel
Hookups: None
Sites: 10 basic sites
Maximum RV length: 32 feet long
Season: End of May through mid-Sept
Fees: $$ per night, Golden Age and Access Passport holders half price
Maximum stay: 16 days
Management: Shoshone National Forest, Clarks Fork Ranger District, 808 Meadow Lane Ave., Cody, WY 82414; (307) 527-6921
Reservations: National Recreation Reservation Service toll-free at (877) 444-6777 or online at recreation.gov
Pets: Pets must be on a leash.
Quiet hours: 10 p.m. to 6 a.m. (turn off generators)
ADA compliance: No
Activities: Fishing, boating, mountain biking, horseback riding, wildlife viewing
Finding the campground: Take WY 120 north out of Cody for 17 miles. Turn left onto WY 296 and travel 42 miles. The campground is on the left side of the road.
About the campground: The parking spots are wider than at typical campgrounds, allowing towing units to unhook and then park beside the trailer. This can be quite convenient, though slide-outs will take some evaluation for placement. Granite outcrops pop up randomly, with a creek cruising past nearby. Spruce and pine dominate this cubbyhole along the Clarks Fork Yellowstone River. A few aspen appear at random areas with some grass between.

6 Lake Creek

Location: 63 miles northwest of Cody
GPS: N44 55.26' / W109 42.44'
Facilities and amenities: Vault toilet, fire rings, food-storage boxes, picnic tables
Elevation: 6,638 feet
Road conditions: Gravel
Hookups: None
Sites: 6 basic sites
Maximum RV length: 22 feet long
Season: Mid-June through mid-Sept
Fees: $ per night, Golden Age and Access Passport holders half price
Maximum stay: 16 days

Management: Shoshone National Forest, Clarks Fork Ranger District, 808 Meadow Lane Ave., Cody, WY 82414; (307) 527-6921

Reservations: First-come, first-served

Pets: Pets must be on a leash.

Quiet hours: 10 p.m. to 6 a.m. (turn off generators)

ADA compliance: No

Activities: Fishing, hiking, wildlife viewing

Finding the campground: Take WY 120 north out of Cody for 17 miles. Turn left onto WY 296 and travel 46 miles. The campground is on the right side of the road.

About the campground: The forest hides all but the first parking spot, which is also the most likely to suffer from traffic noise the most. A small loop toward the back nestles in under pine and spruce trees. Plenty of space between the sites provides a sense of privacy. The Clarks Fork Yellowstone River requires a bit of a hike across the road.

7 Crazy Creek

Location: 69 miles northwest of Cody

GPS: N44 56.53' / W109 46.37'

Facilities and amenities: Vault toilet, fire rings, picnic tables

Elevation: 6,924 feet

Road conditions: Gravel

Hookups: None

Sites: 16 basic sites

Maximum RV length: 28 feet long

Season: End of May through mid-Sept

Fees: $ per night, Golden Age and Access Passport holders half price

Maximum stay: 16 days

Management: Shoshone National Forest, Clarks Fork Ranger District, 808 Meadow Lane Ave., Cody, WY 82414; (307) 527-6921

Reservations: First-come, first-served

Pets: Pets must be on a leash.

Quiet hours: 10 p.m. to 6 a.m. (turn off generators)

ADA compliance: No

Activities: Hiking, wildlife viewing

Finding the campground: From Cody take WY 120 north for 16 miles. Turn left onto WY 296/Chief Joseph Scenic Highway. Proceed about 46 miles to the junction with US 212, turn left, and travel about 3.5 miles. The campground is on the right side of the road.

About the campground: The semi-level parking spots seem out of place in the granite outcrops. The pine forest shades picnic tables and parking alike, with a few spruce trees mingled within. Sagebrush takes over where the trees stop, offering a pleasant fragrance for those not allergic to them. A host is typically present, however, we did not see one upon our visit. Be sure to bring plenty of drinking water as none is available here. The river is accessible, though there is a steep hill for direct access. Sounds of crashing water from the Clarks Fork ride the breeze, adding to the whispering forest with increasing volume as traffic noise disappears with the setting sun.

8 Colter (Montana)

Location: 79 miles northwest of Cody
GPS: N45 1.62' / W109 53.70'
Facilities and amenities: Handicap-accessible vault toilets, fire rings, trash receptacles, picnic tables, drinking water
Elevation: 8,044 feet
Road conditions: Gravel; access road not suitable for vehicles longer than 48 feet
Hookups: None
Sites: 18 sites for hard-sided units only
Maximum RV length: 60 feet long
Season: Late June through Labor Day, weather permitting
Fees: $ per night, $ with Golden Age/Access or Interagency Senior/Access Pass Discount, $ per additional vehicle, Golden Age and Access Passport holders half price
Maximum stay: 16 days
Management: Custer Gallatin National Forest, Gardiner Office, PO Box 5, 805 Scott St., Gardiner, MT 59030; (406) 848-7375
Reservations: First-come, first-served
Pets: Pets must be on a leash.
Quiet hours: 10 p.m. to 6 a.m. (turn off generators)
ADA compliance: Yes
Activities: Hiking
Finding the campground: Take WY 120 north out of Cody for 17 miles. Turn left onto WY 296 and travel 47 miles. Turn left onto US 212 and travel 15 miles. The campground is on the right side of the road.
About the campground: There is no obvious evidence of the past fires that ravaged this campground. Lush grassy meadows filled spaces between maturing fir trees, offering shade and new life. The two loops circle about in an unusual manner. An inner, unmarked loop holds thirteen sites. Spruce trees inhabit the sites toward the back. Units have a lot of room in the outer loop, with a small draw hiding most from the upper sites. As of our visit, firewood was available at the information sign at the entrance. Numerous spigots provide refreshing drinking water.

9 Soda Butte (Montana)

Location: 80 miles northwest of Cody
GPS: N45 1.43' / W109 55.04'
Facilities and amenities: Vault toilets, fire rings, food storage, trash receptacles, picnic tables, drinking water
Elevation: 7,118 feet
Road conditions: Gravel
Hookups: None
Sites: 27 sites for hard-sided units only

Maximum RV length: 48 feet long. *Note:* The access road into the campground is not suitable for vehicles longer than this.

Season: Late June through Labor Day, weather permitting

Fees: $$ per night, $ per additional vehicle, Golden Age and Access Passport holders half price

Maximum stay: 16 days

Management: Custer Gallatin National Forest, Gardiner Office, PO Box 5, 805 Scott St., Gardiner, MT 59030; (406) 848-7375

Reservations: First-come, first-served

Pets: Pets must be on a leash.

Quiet hours: 10 p.m. to 6 a.m. (turn off generators)

ADA compliance: No

Activities: Hiking, fishing, wildlife viewing

Finding the campground: Take WY 120 north out of Cody for 17 miles. Turn left onto WY 296 and travel 47 miles. Turn left onto US 212 and travel 16 miles. The campground is on the left side of the road.

About the campground: Permanent campers reside in the old Cooke City Cemetery next to the access road. These campers were here long before any road wound its way to this remote spot. Tall pine and spruce trees share the meadows with camping units. Most of the parking areas are not level. Numerous water spigots are easily accessible, unlike firewood. Rugged mountains overlook the campground peeking through open spots. A turnaround allows trailers and longer RVs to scope out any available sites. The distance between units varies some, with most somewhat isolated. The grass and underbrush can get pretty tall in places, but it is a nice change from the dry and dusty desert camping we experienced making the journey.

10 Beartooth Lake

Location: 77 miles northwest of Cody

GPS: N44 56.51' / W109 35.78'

Facilities and amenities: Vault toilets, fire rings, food storage, picnic tables, trash receptacles, drinking water

Elevation: 8,940 feet

Road conditions: Gravel

Hookups: None

Sites: 21 basic sites

Maximum RV length: 32 feet long

Season: July through mid-Sept, weather permitting

Fees: $$ per night, Golden Age and Access Passport holders half price

Maximum stay: 16 days

Management: Shoshone National Forest, Clarks Fork Ranger District, 808 Meadow Lane Ave., Cody, WY 82414; (307) 527-6921

Reservations: First-come, first-served

Pets: Pets must be on a leash.

Quiet hours: 10 p.m. to 6 a.m. (turn off generators)

ADA compliance: No

Activities: Fishing, boating, hiking, wildlife viewing, photography

Finding the campground: From Cody take WY 120 north for 16 miles. Turn left onto WY 296, the Chief Joseph Scenic Highway. Travel about 46 miles to the junction with US 212. Turn right onto US 212 and travel about 8 miles. The campground is on the left.

About the campground: This has been and still is bear country. Make sure you understand and follow the rules. Moose have been seen in the willow swamp along the south side of the campground as well and can alter plans without asking permission. Stay alert and be aware of what you may need to do. Beartooth Lake sits peacefully under the dramatic colors of Beartooth Butte. Hikers can exercise a little to get a closer view of the waterfall revealed along the road. Spruce and pine trees grow thick enough to keep grass from growing between. Loop A holds six units. Loop B offers some pull-through in the nine spaces available. Loop C holds four shorter, sloping parking areas. Loop C accommodates tents best, though getting to a toilet from Loop C requires some footwork. The smaller pieces of firewood were picked up long ago. Deadfall can be found in places farther away—in areas you might consider driving to. A host is available.

11 Island Lake

Location: 80 miles northwest of Cody

GPS: N44 56.30' / W109 32.21'

Facilities and amenities: Vault toilets, fire rings, picnic tables, boat ramp, drinking water

Elevation: 9,544 feet

Road conditions: Gravel

Hookups: None

Sites: 21 basic sites

Maximum RV length: 32 feet long

Season: July through mid-Sept

Fees: $$ per night, Golden Age and Access Passport holders half price

Maximum stay: 16 days

Management: Shoshone National Forest, Clarks Fork Ranger District, 808 Meadow Lane Ave., Cody, WY 82414; (307) 527-6921

Reservations: First-come, first-served

Pets: Pets must be on a leash.

Quiet hours: 10 p.m. to 6 a.m. (turn off generators)

ADA compliance: No

Activities: Fishing, boating, hiking, wildlife viewing, photography

Finding the campground: From Cody take WY 120 north for 16 miles. Turn left onto WY 296, the Chief Joseph Scenic Highway. Travel about 46 miles to the junction with US 212. Turn right onto US 212 and travel about 20 miles. The campground will be on the left.

About the campground: Alpine meadows and the snowcapped Beartooth Mountains surround the granite outcrops this campground is perched on. White pine and spruce defiantly cling to the rock in all three loops. Loop A settles into southern exposure just out of sight of Island Lake. Loop B offers some of the more creative hideouts. One of the units perches tightly on top of a granite outcrop. Loop C grants some beautiful scenery with ice-cold Island Lake in front of the majestic mountains. As of our visit, this was a "pack-it-in, pack-it-out" campground. That may change as the road construction is completed in the future.

12 Wapiti

Location: 29 miles west of Cody
GPS: N44 27.87' / W109 37.46'
Facilities and amenities: Vault toilets, fire rings, picnic tables, trash receptacles, drinking water
Elevation: 5,960 feet
Road conditions: Gravel
Hookups: Electric (15 and 30 amp)
Sites: 41 basic units
Maximum RV length: 45 feet long
Season: Mid-May through mid-Oct, weather permitting
Fees: $$ per night with electricity, $$ per night with no electricity, Golden Age and Access Passport holders half price
Maximum stay: 16 days
Management: Shoshone National Forest, Wapiti Ranger District, 203A Yellowstone Ave., Cody, WY 82414; (307) 527-6921 or (800) 517-0413
Reservations: National Recreation Reservation Service toll-free at (877) 444-6777 or online at recreation.gov
Pets: Pets must be on a leash.
Quiet hours: 10 p.m. to 6 a.m. (turn off generators)
ADA compliance: Yes
Activities: Fishing, hiking, wildlife viewing
Finding the campground: Take US 14/16/20 for 29 miles west out of Cody. The campground is on the right side of the road.
About the campground: Cottonwood and cedar trees provide just the right amount of shade. Parking units stretch out along the south side of the North Fork Shoshone River with a lot of room between. A host is present at the campground. The sites closest to the river generally fill first. The traffic tends to die down after dark, though during daylight noise levels get high. As of late January 2023, the official government web page listed this campground as open. Recreation.gov also functioned for making reservations. Based upon this information, it is assumed the flood damage observed when we visited has been remedied.

13 Elk Fork

Location: 30 miles west of Cody
GPS: N44 27.89' / W109 37.62'
Facilities and amenities: Vault toilet, fire rings, picnic tables, trash receptacles, horse corrals
Elevation: 5,960 feet

Road conditions: Paved
Hookups: None
Sites: 13 basic units
Maximum RV length: 22 feet long
Season: Year-round (fee charged May–Sept)
Fees: $ per night, Golden Age and Access Passport holders half price
Maximum stay: 16 days
Management: Shoshone National Forest, Wapiti Ranger District, 203A Yellowstone Ave., Cody, WY 82414; (307) 527-6921 or (800) 517-0413
Reservations: First-come, first-served
Pets: Pets must be on a leash.
Quiet hours: 10 p.m. to 6 a.m. (Generators must be shut off during quiet hours.)
ADA compliance: No
Activities: Fishing, hiking, horseback riding, wildlife viewing
Finding the campground: Take US 14/16/20 for 30 miles west out of Cody. The campground is on the left side of the road.
About the campground: Cedar and cottonwood trees add shade to this narrow end of the draw. Not all of the paved parking spots accommodate long RVs. The corrals and adjacent trailhead keep this place active. A host is present, but firewood will take some effort to find. Be sure to bring plenty of water, and if your visit is in the early spring, don't forget the bug spray.

14 Clearwater

Location: 32 miles west of Cody
GPS: N44 27.75' / W109 40.11'
Facilities and amenities: Vault toilets, fire rings, picnic tables, trash receptacles
Elevation: 6,008 feet
Road conditions: Gravel
Hookups: None
Sites: 11 for tents, 1 group site
Maximum RV length: 30 feet long
Season: May–Sept, weather permitting
Fees: $ per night, $$$$$$ for group site, Golden Age and Access Passport holders half price
Maximum stay: 16 days
Management: Shoshone National Forest, Wapiti Ranger District, 203A Yellowstone Ave., Cody, WY 82414; (307) 527-6921 or (800) 517-0413
Reservations: National Recreation Reservation Service toll-free at (877) 444-6777 or online at recreation.gov
Pets: Pets must be on a leash.
Quiet hours: 10 p.m. to 6 a.m. (turn off generators)
ADA compliance: No
Activities: Fishing, hiking, wildlife viewing
Finding the campground: Take US 14/16/20 west out of Cody for 32 miles. The campground is on the left side of the road.

About the campground: If you are a tent camper, this would be a very good spot, especially if you prefer not to share a camping experience with the more dominant "tin teepee" campers. The tent sites are walk-in, with cedar, cottonwood, and willow trees providing a little shade in this desert-like setting. Numbered picnic tables match unit sites to avoid confusion. A host is present at the campground. Trout live in the river passing by, tempting any visiting anglers.

15 Rex Hale

Location: 32 miles west of Cody
GPS: N44 27.35' / W109 43.71'
Facilities and amenities: Vault toilet, fire rings, picnic tables, food storage, trash receptacles, drinking water
Elevation: 6,153 feet
Road conditions: Gravel
Hookups: Electric
Sites: 30 basic sites
Maximum RV length: 40 feet long
Season: Mid-May through mid-Sept
Fees: $$ per night with electricity, $$ per night without electricity, Golden Age and Access Passport holders half price
Maximum stay: 16 days
Management: Shoshone National Forest, Wapiti Ranger District, 203A Yellowstone Ave., Cody, WY 82414; (307) 527-6921 or (800) 517-0413
Reservations: National Recreation Reservation Service toll-free at (877) 444-6777 or online at recreation.gov
Pets: Pets must be on a leash.
Quiet hours: 10 p.m. to 6 a.m. (turn off generators)
ADA compliance: No
Activities: Fishing, hiking, wildlife viewing
Finding the campground: Take US 14/16/20 west out of Cody for 36 miles. The campground is on the left side of the road.
About the campground: The river provides some nighttime serenading in addition to challeng-ing anglers to attempt catching one of the cold-water trout. Should electricity be of value to your camping experience, reservations are recommended well in advance of your visit. It is a well-known feature. This a popular base camp for those who want to visit Yellowstone National Park.

16 Newton Creek

Location: 38 miles west of Cody
GPS: N44 27.23' / W109 45.56'
Facilities and amenities: Vault toilets, fire rings, picnic tables, food storage, trash receptacles, drinking water

Elevation: 6,238 feet
Road conditions: Gravel
Hookups: None
Sites: 31 basic sites (hard-sided campers only)
Maximum RV length: 40 feet long
Season: Mid-May through Sept
Fees: $$ per night, Golden Age and Access Passport holders half price
Maximum stay: 16 days
Management: Shoshone National Forest, Wapiti Ranger District, 203A Yellowstone Ave., Cody, WY 82414; (307) 527-6921 or (800) 517-0413
Reservations: First-come, first-served
Pets: Pets must be on a leash.
Quiet hours: 10 p.m. to 6 a.m. (turn off generators)
ADA compliance: No
Activities: Fishing, hiking, wildlife viewing
Finding the campground: Take US 14/16/20 west out of Cody for 38 miles. The campground is on the left side of the road
About the campground: Fir trees grant plenty of shade in this hollow. The parking spots follow along a high bank of the North Fork Shoshone River. Be especially careful of young children getting too close. The highway tends to squeeze the left loop tighter to the river. Precious few spots will accommodate RVs 40 feet long.

17 Eagle Creek

Location: 45 miles west of Cody
GPS: N44 28.34' / W109 53.30'
Facilities and amenities: Vault toilets, fire rings, picnic tables, food storage, trash receptacles, drinking water
Elevation: 6,467 feet
Road conditions: Gravel
Hookups: None
Sites: 20 basic sites (hard-sided campers only)
Maximum RV length: 40 feet long
Season: Mid-May through mid-Sept, weather permitting
Fees: $$ per night, Golden Age and Access Passport holders half price
Maximum stay: 16 days
Management: Shoshone National Forest, Wapiti Ranger District, 203A Yellowstone Ave., Cody, WY 82414; (307) 527-6921 or (800) 517-0413
Reservations: First-come, first-served
Pets: Pets must be on a leash.
Quiet hours: 10 p.m. to 6 a.m. (turn off generators)
ADA compliance: Yes
Activities: Fishing, hiking, wildlife viewing

Finding the campground: Take US 14/16/20 west out of Cody for 45 miles. The campground is on the left side of the road.

About the campground: Bears visit more regularly now, and hard-sided RVs are required for camping. Pine and fir trees shade the picnic tables and most of the parking spots. Two loops offer fairly private places, with seven sites on the right and thirteen on the left upon entering. All of the units are within a very short distance of the river. Sitting in the shade stoking a campfire can be a most relaxing experience as well.

18 Three Mile

Location: 49 miles west of Cody
GPS: N44 29.79' / W109 56.85'
Facilities and amenities: Vault toilets, fire rings, picnic tables, food storage, trash receptacles, drinking water
Elevation: 6,656 feet
Road conditions: Gravel
Hookups: None
Sites: 21 basic sites (hard-sided campers only)
Maximum RV length: 60 feet long
Season: July–Sept
Fees: $$ per night, Golden Age and Access Passport holders half price
Maximum stay: 16 days
Management: Shoshone National Forest, Wapiti Ranger District, 203A Yellowstone Ave., Cody, WY 82414; (307) 527-6921 or (800) 517-0413
Reservations: National Recreation Reservation Service toll-free at (877) 444-6777 or online at recreation.gov
Pets: Pets must be on a leash.
Quiet hours: 10 p.m. to 6 a.m. (turn off generators)
ADA compliance: No
Activities: Fishing, hiking, wildlife viewing
Finding the campground: Take US 14/16/20 west out of Cody for 49 miles. The campground is on the left side of the road.
About the campground: The North Fork Shoshone River echoes off of the encroaching mountain sides as it slides by, with some traffic noise interrupting the serenade during the day. Tall fir trees offer shade, and when a breeze makes its way through the branches, another source of nature's music joins the chorus. The sun can get hot, but nights usually always cool off, so keep your jackets handy.

Buffalo Bill State Park

19 North Fork

Location: 16 miles west of Cody
GPS: N44 29.17' / W109 19.89'
Facilities and amenities: Host on-site, flush toilets, showers, fire rings, picnic tables, trash receptacles, drinking water
Elevation: 5,431 feet
Road conditions: Paved
Hookups: Electric (50 amp)
Sites: 6 tents-only, 60 basic sites
Maximum RV length: 60 feet long
Season: May–Sept
Fees: Day use: $ per day resident, $$ per day nonresident. Plus, camping fee: $$ per night resident, $$$ per night nonresident.
Maximum stay: 14 days
Management: Buffalo Bill State Park, 4192 North Fork Hwy., Cody, WY 82414; (307) 587-9227
Reservations: Online at wyomingstateparks.reserveamerica.com or by phone at (877) 996-7275
Pets: All pets must be in a vehicle or on a leash no longer than 10 feet and physically controlled at all times.
Quiet hours: 10 p.m. to 6 a.m. (turn off generators)
ADA compliance: Yes
Activities: Fishing, hiking
Finding the campground: Take US 14/16/20 west out of Cody for 15 miles. Turn left on CR 6KV and travel about 0.10 mile. Turn right onto the campground access road and travel about 0.75 mile.
About the campground: The lower loop of this campground puts anglers closer to the North Fork Shoshone River, though it will still take some footwork and shoreline evaluation. There is limited shade with enough space between units to allow for a semi-isolated experience. The upper section consists of three loops with the tent area on the end. The tent sites must be reserved, though any of the available RV sites can be utilized with tents and may prove more appealing dependent upon what shade and scenery preference is desired. Please note the more detailed regulations regarding Wyoming State Parks listed in the "Camping in Wyoming" section at the beginning of the book.

20 Lake Shore

Location: 10 miles west of Cody
GPS: N44 30.23' / W109 14.68'
Facilities and amenities: Host on-site, flush toilets, showers, fire rings, picnic tables, trash receptacles, boat ramp, drinking water
Elevation: 5,422 feet
Road conditions: Paved
Hookups: Electric (50 amp) and water
Sites: 5 tent sites, 32 basic sites
Maximum RV length: 60 feet long
Season: Year-round
Fees: Day use: $ per day resident, $$ per day nonresident. Plus, camping fee: $$ per night resident, $$$$ per night nonresident.
Maximum stay: 14 days
Management: Buffalo Bill State Park, 4192 North Fork Hwy., Cody, WY 82414; (307) 587-9227
Reservations: Online at wyomingstateparks.reserveamerica.com or by phone at (877) 996-7275
Pets: All pets must be in a vehicle or on a leash no longer than 10 feet and physically controlled at all times.
Quiet hours: 10 p.m. to 6 a.m. (turn off generators)
ADA compliance: Yes
Activities: Fishing, boating, swimming
Finding the campground: Take US 14/16/20 west out of Cody for 10 miles. The campground access is on the left.
About the campground: The three loops occupy three separate peninsulas of the Buffalo Bill Reservoir with limited shade and no lack of wind. The boat ramp is a short drive from the camping area, but it's convenient for those taking advantage of the water sports calling out on a hot day. Another popular function is to cruise into nearby Cody and take in any one or all of the five museums of the Buffalo Bill Center of the West. Should one decide to take it all in, there will be more than one day involved. Please note the more detailed regulations regarding Wyoming State Parks listed in the "Camping in Wyoming" section at the beginning of the book.

Green River Area

Brilliant-colored badlands and dynamic fishing abundantly adorn the countryside. Much of the terrain shows little, if any, change from when wagon trains lumbered across. Reaching forested mountains takes some travel time but rewards the seeker in a typically wonderful Wyoming way. So many of the hidden treasures defy the cynical belief that anywhere so beautiful could not exist in the midst of such stark contrast.

Fossils and agates abound all through this vast expanse, to the delight of rock hounds. In fact, some fossils and petrified wood have been agatized over the course of time, making them very collectible. Most can be found on the surface, with a semi-polish making them easy to identify.

High desert landscape of the Flaming Gorge area.

#		Group sites	Tents	RV sites	Total # of sites	Picnic area	Toilets	Showers	Drinking water	Dump station	Handicap	Recreation	Fee	Season	Can reserve	Stay limit
1	Meeks Cabin			24	24		V		X			FBoSHi	$$$	6/1-9/30		14
2	Firehole			40	40	X	Fl	X	X	X		FHiBoPi	$$$	5/1-9/30	X	16
3	Buckboard Crossing			66	66	X	Fl	X	X	X		FBSWsPi	$$-$$$	5/1-9/15	X	16
4	Hams Fork			13	13		V		X			FHiPi	$	5/1-9/30		14
5	Hobble Creek			18	18		V		X			FHiPi	$	6/1-9/30		14
6	Sacajawea			24	24		V		X			FHiPi	$	5/29-9/4		14
7	Slate Creek				Dis		V					FBoW	None	Year-round		14
8	Weeping Rock			10	Dis		V					FBOHiW	None	Year-round		14
9	Tailrace			3	Dis		V					FBoW	None	Year-round		14
10	Fontenelle Creek			55	55	X	FV		X		X	FBoSHiPiBr	$	Year-round		14

Bo = boating, Br = boat ramp, Dis = dispersed, F = fishing, Fl = flush toilet, Hi = hiking, Pi = picnicking, S = swimming, W = wildlife viewing, Ws = water sports

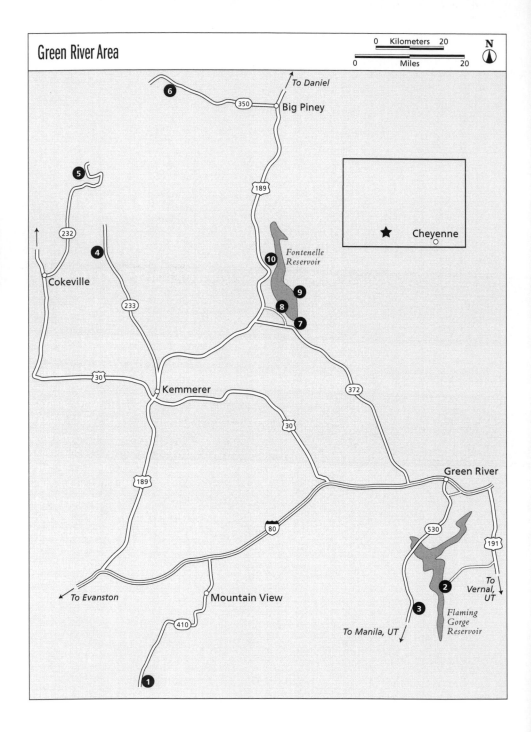

Green River Area

0 Kilometers 20

0 Miles 20

N

To Daniel

6

350 Big Piney

5

232

4

189

Cokeville

233

10 *Fontenelle Reservoir*

9

8

7

30 Kemmerer

372

30

189

Green River

80

530

191

To Evanston

Mountain View

2

3

To Vernal, UT

410

To Manila, UT

Flaming Gorge Reservoir

1

★ Cheyenne

1 Meeks Cabin

Location: 25 miles southwest of Mountain View
GPS: N40 59.91' / W110 35.51'
Facilities and amenities: Vault toilets, fire rings, trash receptacles, picnic tables, drinking water (Trailers, campers, and RVs should be filled before arriving at the campground. There is no place to fill up at the campground, and hooking up to the spigots is not allowed.)
Elevation: 8,708 feet
Road conditions: Gravel
Hookups: None
Sites: 24 basic sites
Maximum RV length: 40 feet long
Season: June–Sept, weather permitting
Fees: $$$ per night, $ per night per additional vehicle
Maximum stay: 14 days
Management: Evanston–Mountain View Ranger District, (307) 789-6555. Go Camp Utah / Utah Recreation Company, 564W 700S, Ste. 305, Box #5, Pleasant Grove, UT 84062; (385) 273-1100; gocamputah.com (concessionaire)
Reservations: First-come, first-served
Pets: Pets must be on a leash and under control at all times.
Quiet hours: 10 p.m. to 7 a.m.
ADA compliance: No
Activities: Fishing, boating, swimming, hiking
Finding the campground: Take WY 410 south and west out of Mountain View for 13 miles. Bear left on the gravel Meeks Cabin Access Road and travel 12 miles.
About the campground: Evergreen trees and sandstone surround this reservoir at almost 9,000 feet above sea level. A host occupies one of the units. Most are back-in sites of different lengths. Fishing is not always the best, but the water offers a cool way of dealing with the heat.

2 Firehole

Location: 29 miles south of Rock Springs
GPS: N41 20.98' / W109 26.77'
Facilities and amenities: Host on-site, flush toilets, showers, water spigots, picnic table and shelters, fire rings, boat ramp
Elevation: 6,123 feet
Road conditions: Paved
Hookups: None
Sites: 32 basic sites, 4 double sites
Maximum RV length: 40 feet long
Season: May–Sept, weather permitting
Fees: $$$ per night
Maximum stay: 16 days

Management: Ashley National Forest, 355 North Vernal Ave., Vernal, UT 84078; (435) 789-1181. American Land & Leisure, (801) 226-3564 or (800) 342-2267; info@americanll.com (concessionaire).

Reservations: National Recreation Reservation Service toll-free at (877) 444-6777 or online at recreation.gov

Pets: Pets must be on a leash and under control at all times.

Quiet hours: 10 p.m. to 6 a.m. (turn off generators)

ADA compliance: No

Activities: Fishing, hiking, boating

Finding the campground: Take I-80 west of Rock Springs toward Green River about 6 miles to the junction with US 191/Flaming Gorge Road. Take US 191 13 miles south. From US 191, go west on FR 106 about 10 miles to the campground.

About the campground: Sagebrush, cedar trees, and dramatic rock formations provide a scenic drive to the campground. The cedar trees tend to disappear at the camping area, but the rock formations make up for the absence. The paved road continues all the way through the camping area, including the parking aprons. Long trailers could fit, but they will need to be unhooked. The comfort station includes flush toilets, showers, sinks, and electrical outlets. Willow trees don't provide a lot of shade yet. The sturdy shelters built over the tables grant welcome relief for lunchtime picnickers.

3 Buckboard Crossing

Location: 25 miles southwest of Green River

GPS: N41 14.85' / W109 36.15'

Facilities and amenities: Flush toilets, showers, fire rings, picnic tables, shelters, drinking water

Elevation: 6,103 feet

Road conditions: Gravel

Hookups: Electric hookups

Sites: 66 basic sites

Maximum RV length: 50 feet long

Season: May–Sept, weather permitting

Fees: $$ per night, $$$ per night with electric hookup

Maximum stay: 16 days

Management: Ashley National Forest, 355 North Vernal Ave., Vernal, UT 84078; (435) 789-1181. American Land & Leisure, (801) 226-3564 or (800) 342-2267; info@americanll.com (concessionaire).

Reservations: National Recreation Reservation Service toll-free at (877) 444-6777 or online at recreation.gov

Pets: Pets must be on a leash and under control at all times.

Quiet hours: 10 p.m. to 6 a.m. (turn off generators)

ADA compliance: No

Activities: Fishing, boating, swimming, water sports

Finding the campground: Take WY 530 south out of Green River for 23 miles. Turn left at the sign onto the paved access road and travel 2 miles. The campground is on the right side of the access road.

About the campground: You might think of a desert oasis on first sight of this campground. Willow trees pop up out of the desert in stark contrast to their arid surroundings. These trees are watered from a man-made system—they don't drink from a lakeshore. Two loops hold thirty-four parking units apiece, with comfort stations centrally located. Willow trees offer welcome shade on a hot summer day and individual shelters cover the tables for those who want to enjoy being outdoors. At times the wind can be a real blessing. Only a few spaces were still available on our visit, testifying to the popularity of the area. The biggest attraction seemed to be the fairly easily accessible water recreation—boats, jet skis, and so forth.

4 Hams Fork

Location: 38 miles northwest of Kemmerer
GPS: N42 15.0.09' / W110 43.82'
Facilities and amenities: Vault toilets, fire rings, trash receptacles, picnic tables, drinking water
Elevation: 8,011 feet
Road conditions: Gravel
Hookups: None
Sites: 13 basic sites
Maximum RV length: 20 feet long
Season: May–Sept, weather permitting
Fees: $ per night
Maximum stay: 14 days
Management: Bridger National Forest, Kemmerer Ranger District, (307) 877-4415
Reservations: First-come, first-served
Pets: Pets must be on a leash and under control at all times.
Quiet hours: 10 p.m. to 6 a.m. (turn off generators)
ADA compliance: No
Activities: Fishing, hiking, picnicking
Finding the campground: Take US 189 north out of Kemmerer about 1 mile to WY 233. Turn left onto WY 233 and travel 19 miles. Continue on Hams Fork Road/CR 305 for 12 miles. Continue on Kelley-Hams Fork Road/FR 10062 for 6 miles. The campground is on the right.
About the campground: The road divides this campground, and the toilets and water are found in the main camping area on the east. Three units sit under the pine trees, with less distance to the Hams Fork River, which is more of a creek here. Tall willow brush shades the cool waters, inviting anglers and hot feet alike.

5 Hobble Creek

Location: 35 miles north of Cokeville
GPS: N42 23.88' / W110 47.04'
Facilities and amenities: Vault toilets, fire rings, trash receptacles, picnic tables, drinking water
Elevation: 7,349 feet

Road conditions: Gravel

Hookups: None

Sites: 18 basic sites

Maximum RV length: 20 feet long

Season: June–Sept, weather permitting

Fees: $ per night

Maximum stay: 14 days

Management: Bridger National Forest, Kemmerer Ranger District, (307) 877-4415

Reservations: First-come, first-served

Pets: Pets are welcome but must be kept under control at all times.

Quiet hours: 10 p.m. to 6 a.m. (turn off generators)

ADA compliance: No

Activities: Fishing, hiking, picnicking

Finding the campground: Take WY 232 north out of Cokeville for 13 miles to the end of the pavement. Bear right at the fork onto what will become FR 10062. It is a steady climb from here on a single-lane dirt road with small, narrow pullouts. Continue on FR 10062 for about 8 miles. Bear left onto FR 10066, following the signs to Lake Alice. The road signs get scarce, so continue following directions to Lake Alice for about 14 miles. The single-lane narrow portion with hairpin turns clinging to the mountainside is not a place you would want to meet a trailer. A river ford is also required near the last 1.5 miles of access. Water can be high in the early summer (July).

About the campground: This is not the place to arrive only to discover you forgot the matches, or anything else for that matter. The last 1.5 miles of the road must be reached by fording Hobble Creek. Water can be high well into July, making access difficult. If you like little company, this could be a welcome place to settle in for a while.

6 Sacajawea

Location: 24 miles from Big Piney

GPS: N42 37.11' / W110 31.86'

Facilities and amenities: Vault toilets, fire rings, trash receptacle, picnic tables, drinking water

Elevation: 8,341 feet

Road conditions: Gravel

Hookups: None

Sites: 24 basic sites

Maximum RV length: 30 feet long

Season: Memorial Day Weekend through Labor Day, weather permitting

Fees: $ per night

Maximum stay: 14 days

Management: Bridger-Teton National Forest, Big Piney Ranger District, (307) 276-5203

Reservations: First-come, first-served

Pets: Pets must be on a leash and under control at all times.

Quiet hours: 10 p.m. to 6 a.m. (turn off generators)

ADA compliance: No

Activities: Fishing, hiking, picnicking

Finding the campground: Take WY 350 west out of Big Piney for 10 miles. Continue dead ahead on the gravel road for 17 miles. The campground is on the left side of the road.

About the campground: Middle Piney Creek rushes past the pine forest housing these well-placed units. Nestled comfortably in the bottom of this forested canyon, you wouldn't know the campground existed if you weren't looking for it. Signs posted all over advise visitors that the water and other services are only for paying campers. Fishing could be challenging, with the thick willow brush choking the banks. Don't forget the bug spray, especially if your visit occurs during late June or early July.

7 Slate Creek

Location: 35 miles northeast of Kemmerer
GPS: N41 59.02' / W110 2.74'
Facilities and amenities: Vault toilets, fire rings, picnic tables
Elevation: 6,378 feet
Road conditions: Gravel to unimproved dirt
Hookups: None
Sites: Dispersed
Maximum RV length: 60 feet long
Season: Year-round
Fees: None
Maximum stay: 14 days
Management: Bureau of Land Management, Kemmerer Field Office, (307) 828-4500; kemmerer_wymail@blm.gov
Reservations: First-come, first-served
Pets: Pets are welcome but must be kept under control at all times.
Quiet hours: Campers courtesy
ADA compliance: No
Activities: Fishing, boating, wildlife viewing
Finding the campground: Take US 189 northeast out of Kemmerer for 25 miles. Turn right onto WY 372 and travel about 9 miles. Continue dead ahead at the Fontenelle store on the gravel road for 1 mile. The campground is on the left side of the road along the banks of the Green River.

About the campground: Parking outnumbers tables in this stretched-out camping area. About forty RVs could park in here with some forethought, but your neighbors would be closer than they are in most suburbs. The majority of the units follow the Green River below the Fontenelle Reservoir. When the large trout start moving into these waters to spawn, there will likely be very few vacant spots. If you must have a campfire for your needs, it would be best to pack some wood along. Shade can be found under the large cottonwoods still alive and standing, though the better spots fill first.

8 Weeping Rock

Location: 37 miles northeast of Kemmerer
GPS: N41 1.24' / W110 2.91'
Facilities and amenities: Vault toilet, fire rings, grills, picnic tables
Elevation: 6,398 feet
Road conditions: Gravel
Hookups: None
Sites: Dispersed camping with 10 designated sites
Maximum RV length: 50 feet long
Season: Year-round
Fees: None
Maximum stay: 14 days
Management: Bureau of Land Management, Kemmerer Field Office, (307) 828-4500; kemmerer_wymail@blm.gov
Reservations: First-come, first-served
Pets: Pets are welcome but must be kept under control at all times.
Quiet hours: Campers courtesy
ADA compliance: No
Activities: Fishing, boating, hiking, wildlife viewing
Finding the campground: From Kemmerer, take US 189 east 25 miles to WY 372. Go 8.4 miles and turn left onto County Line Road. Weeping Rock is right next to the dam.
About the campground: About twenty RVs would be the limit for this tight little river corner. Cottonwoods offer shade and, when they die, some firewood. This campground is somewhat concealed and therefore tends to have more activity.

9 Tailrace

Location: 36 miles northeast of Kemmerer
GPS: N42 1.48' / W110 3.67'
Facilities and amenities: Vault toilet, fire rings
Elevation: 6,412 feet
Road conditions: Gravel to improved dirt
Hookups: None
Sites: 3 basic sites
Maximum RV length: 40 feet long
Season: Year-round
Fees: None
Maximum stay: 14 days
Management: Bureau of Land Management, Kemmerer Field Office, (307) 828-4500; kemmerer_wymail@blm.gov
Reservations: First-come, first-served

Pets: Pets are welcome but must be kept under control at all times.

Quiet hours: Campers courtesy

ADA compliance: No

Activities: Fishing, boating, wildlife viewing

Finding the campground: To access the campground, travel east on WY 372 for 1 mile, cross the Green River Bridge, then immediately turn left (north) and travel 4 miles. Turn left (west) before the dam to access the river and travel 1 mile farther.

About the campground: Parking along the riverbank might hold ten RVs with some forethought, though a rainstorm would make life very miserable and possibly make an exit impossible. There is better ground up away from the bank, but one of the other campgrounds would offer closer access.

10 Fontenelle Creek

Location: 36 miles northeast of Kemmerer

GPS: N42 4.43' / W110 9.62'

Facilities and amenities: Flush and vault toilets, fire rings, barbecue grills, trash receptacles, covered picnic tables, drinking water, boat ramp, dump station

Elevation: 6,526 feet

Road conditions: Paved, including a paved access road to the reservoir

Hookups: None

Sites: 55 basic sites

Maximum RV length: 50 feet long

Season: Year-round (amenities available weather permitting)

Fees: $ per night, Golden Age and Access Passport holders half price

Maximum stay: 14 days

Management: Bureau of Land Management, Kemmerer Field Office, (307) 828-4500; kemmerer_wymail@blm.gov

Reservations: First-come, first-served

Pets: Pets allowed but must be leashed

Quiet hours: None enforced

ADA compliance: Yes

Activities: Fishing, boating, swimming, hiking, picnicking

Finding the campground: Take US 189 northeast out of Kemmerer for 36 miles. The campground is on the right side of the road.

About the campground: This campground has a sort of ghost-town appeal with its abandoned appearance. The history all around the area enhances that appeal when combining local information with your stay. The Names Hill Historic Site, about 4 miles away, is where pioneers on their way to Oregon in the mid-1800s carved their names in the soft limestone after crossing the Green River as a testament of their arrival and continued journey for those coming behind them. Native Americans left their pictographic messages before the pioneers, though most have eroded away. There is some documentation in the pioneers' journals for those who wish to explore this history in greater depth.

Camping here can be thought of as a glass half-full or half-empty situation, depending on the camper. In an effort to help those choosing the half-full approach, some thoughts about how to adjust to the infamous "Wyoming wind" seem appropriate. One of the first unwritten laws with regard to Wyoming wind is: Do not open the driver's side door and the passenger's side door at the same time. Most papers and other lightweight items will not be fully recovered if that is done. It's a scenario my wife and I are very much familiar with. The same wind has even "placed" lawn chairs and moderately heavy picnic items in an active fire pit. With that in mind as you tour the camping area, establish the dominant direction of the wind for the best possible positioning of your camp, with an understanding that "dominant" is not permanent. Think of it as a game where the "dust devils" are deliberately trying to irritate you. If they succeed, they win. On the other hand, if you recognize their devious plan, laugh it off and adjust accordingly, and you win!

Jackson Area

Mountain men frequented this scenic region even after the beaver were trapped out, and capable individuals can still revisit their steps in the backcountry—with the proper permission and equipment. The visitor center at Moose offers an excellent place to research your options.

Mountains jut out of the ground in stark beauty on both sides. Some less-visited campgrounds on the west must be accessed from Idaho, though they are in Wyoming. Grand Teton National Park is the major attraction here, though there are some wonderful and moderately secret hideaways nearby, like the Curtis Canyon Campground near the National Elk Refuge. Most travelers do not spend a lot of time exploring them, instead hurrying on their way to nearby Yellowstone National Park.

The thick underbrush and forest provide a sort of solitude.

#	Name	Group sites	Tents	RV sites	Total # of sites	Hookups	Picnic area	Toilets	Showers	Drinking water	Dump station	Phone	Handicap	Recreation	Fee	Season	Can reserve	Stay limit
1	Trail Creek			11	11		X	V		X				FHiWPi	$$	5/1–9/30	X	14
2	Teton Canyon			18	18			V		X				FHiW	$$	5/15–9/15	X	16
3	Cave Falls			23	23			V		X				FHiW	$	6/1–9/30		16
4	Curtis Canyon			12	12		X	V		X				HiWPh	$$	5/1–9/30		14
5	Gros Ventre	4	35	271	310	El	X	C		X	X	X	X	FHiWPh	$$$$$	5/1–10/10	X	14
6	Atherton Creek			20	20			V		X				FBoHiWsBr	$	5/1–9/30		14
7	Hatchet			9	33			V		X				HiM	$–$$	5/15–9/15		14
8	Turpin Meadow			18	18		X	V		X				FHiHrHuCoHtSt	$$	5/15–9/15		14
9	Jenny Lake		61	0	61		X	C	X	X		X	X	FHiBoMPhW	$$–$$$$$	5/15–9/15	X	7
10	Signal Mountain		4	81	85	El	X	C	X	X	X	X	X	FHiWPhPi	$$$$$	5/15–10/15	X	14
11	Colter Bay	10	10	324	354	El	X	C	X	X	X	X	X	FHiWPhPi	$$$$$	5/1–10/31	X	14
12	Colter Bay RV Park			112	112	ElWaSe			X	X	X	X	X	FHiPh	$$$$$	5/1–10/31	X	14
13	Colter Bay Tent Village				66			C						FHiPh	$$$$$	5/15–9/5	X	14
14	Lizard Creek		25	38	63			C		X				FHiW	$$$$$	6/15–9/15	X	14
15	Sheffield			12	12			V		X				FHi	$	5/15–9/15		16
16	Headwaters		34	97	131	EwaSe		Fl		X		X		FWHr	$$$$$	5/15–10/31	X	14

Bo = boating, Br = boat ramp, C = comfort station, Co = corrals, El = electric hookups, F = fishing, Hi = hiking, Hr = horseback riding, Ht = hitching posts, Hu = hunting, M = mountain biking, Ph = photography, Pi = picnicking, S = swimming, Se = sewer hookup, St = stock tanks, V = vault toilet, W = wildlife viewing, Wa = water hookup, Ws = water sports

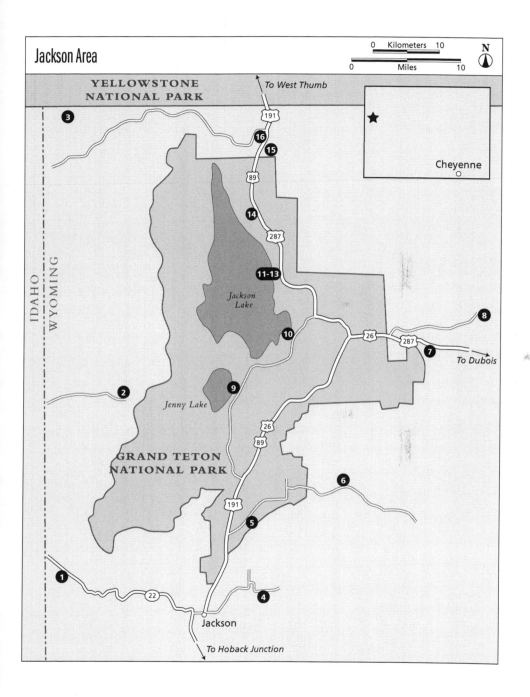

Jackson Area

Kilometers 10

Miles 10

N

YELLOWSTONE
NATIONAL PARK

To West Thumb

191

16

15

89

14

287

11-13

Jackson
Lake

10

26

287

8

7

To Dubois

2

9

Jenny Lake

26

89

GRAND TETON
NATIONAL PARK

6

191

5

1

22

4

Jackson

To Hoback Junction

IDAHO

WYOMING

Cheyenne

1 Trail Creek

Location: 18 miles west of Jackson
GPS: N43 32.48' / W111 2.48'
Facilities and amenities: Vault toilets, fire rings, barbecue grills, food-storage lockers, trash receptacles, picnic tables, drinking water
Elevation: 6,715 feet
Road conditions: Gravel
Hookups: None
Sites: 11 basic sites
Maximum RV length: 40 feet long
Season: May–Sept, weather permitting. *Note:* Dispersed camping allowed during the off-season.
Fees: $$ per night, $ per additional vehicle
Maximum stay: 14 days
Management: Caribou-Targhee National Forest, AuDi Campground Services Inc., HC 82 Box 1158, Duck Creek Village, UT 84762; (541) 351-1182; audi1@scinternet.net (concessionaire)
Reservations: National Recreation Reservation Service toll-free at (877) 444-6777 or online at recreation.gov
Pets: Pets must be kept on a leash and under control at all times.
Quiet hours: 10 p.m. to 6 a.m.
ADA compliance: No
Activities: Fishing, hiking, wildlife viewing, picnicking
Finding the campground: Take WY 22 west out of Jackson for 18 miles. *Note:* Teton Pass has 10 percent grades and sharp corners.
About the campground: Aspen trees greet campers at the entrance, while spruce trees take over the back portion. The semi-level parking spots are spread out between the highway and the raging Trail Creek. It will take a while for the sun to reach campers in this deep canyon. Traffic could be noisy during the day, though it is likely to get quiet after dark. A host is available at the campground.

2 Teton Canyon

Location: 9 miles east of Driggs, Idaho
GPS: N43 45.42' / W110 55.26'
Facilities and amenities: Vault toilets, fire rings, barbecue grills, trash receptacles, picnic tables, drinking water
Elevation: 6,955 feet
Road conditions: Gravel
Hookups: None
Sites: 18 basic sites
Maximum RV length: 20 feet long
Season: June–Sept, weather permitting

Fees: $$ single site per night, $6 per additional vehicle
Maximum stay: 16 days
Management: Caribou-Targhee National Forest, AuDi Campground Services Inc., HC 82 Box 1158, Duck Creek Village, UT 84762; (541) 351-1182; audi1@scinternet.net (concessionaire)
Reservations: National Recreation Reservation Service toll-free at (877) 444-6777 or online at recreation.gov
Pets: Pets must be kept on a leash and under control at all times.
Quiet hours: 10 p.m. to 6 a.m.
ADA compliance: No
Activities: Fishing, hiking, wildlife viewing
Finding the campground: In Driggs turn at the Targhee National Forest Recreation sign and travel 7 miles. Turn right onto the gravel FR 009 and travel 4 miles.
About the campground: Spruce trees shade the more popular units along a noisy creek. Other units fill the open area between the forest and trailhead parking. A few aspen trees pop out at various locations in this deep canyon. Photos of the western side of the Teton Mountains can be taken along the access road. After arriving at the campground, the steep, forested mountainsides hide the peaks, requiring a hike to view them.

3 Cave Falls

Location: 26 miles east of Marysville, Idaho
GPS: N44 7.92' / W111 0.93'
Facilities and amenities: Vault toilets, fire rings, food-storage lockers, trash receptacles, picnic tables, drinking water
Elevation: 6,148 feet
Road conditions: Gravel
Hookups: None
Sites: 23 basic sites
Maximum RV length: 60 feet long
Season: June–Sept, weather permitting
Fees: $ per night, $ per night per additional vehicle
Maximum stay: 16 days
Management: Caribou-Targhee National Forest, AuDi Campground Services Inc., HC 82 Box 1158, Duck Creek Village, UT 84762; (541) 351-1182; audi1@scinternet.net (concessionaire)
Reservations: First-come, first-served
Pets: Pets must be kept on a leash and under control at all times.
Quiet hours: 10 p.m. to 6 a.m.
ADA compliance: No
Activities: Fishing, hiking, wildlife viewing
Finding the campground: Take ID 47 east of Marysville for about 7 miles. Turn right at the sign onto the paved Grassy Lake Road and travel 19 miles. Thirteen miles of gravel divide two paved stretches across the national forest.

About the campground: This scenic little part of Wyoming is seldom visited, perhaps because it must be accessed from Idaho. The Grassy Lake Road does go through to Flag Ranch, in Grand Teton National Park, though four-wheel drives are advised. Cars were making the trip on our visit; however, a good rainstorm would stop their advance in one of the meadows. Water flows continuously from a pipe at the end of the campground, but not as fast as the Bechler River beside it. The first units are above the river out of sight of the noisy rapids. The farthest units are the closest to the river. Pine trees allow a few spruce into the long distances between camping spots. Regardless of whether you want to be close to the river or farther up, the rapids provide plenty of background music. The Cave Falls are a short distance past the campground. These wide and noisy falls are well worth the extra distance to get photographs. At the time of our visit, it appeared that the drinking water had been shut off in the picnic area and that trash service had been discontinued.

4 Curtis Canyon

Location: 8 miles east of Jackson
GPS: N43 30.83' / W110 39.67'
Facilities and amenities: Vault toilets, fire rings, grills, picnic tables, trash receptacles, drinking water
Elevation: 7,042 feet
Road conditions: Gravel, with a warning "No RVs over 30 feet in length due to narrow rough road"
Hookups: None
Sites: 12 basic sites
Maximum RV length: 20 feet long
Season: May–Sept, weather permitting
Fees: $$ per night, $ per extra vehicle
Maximum stay: 14 days
Management: Bridger-Teton National Forest, AuDi Campground Services Inc., HC 82 Box 1158, Duck Creek Village, UT 84762; (541) 351-1182; audi1@scinternet.net (concessionaire)
Reservations: First-come, first-served
Pets: Pets must be kept on a leash and under control at all times.
Quiet hours: 10 p.m. to 6 a.m.
ADA compliance: No
Activities: Hiking, wildlife viewing, photography
Finding the campground: From Jackson proceed through the National Elk Refuge on the northeast side. Take the gravel road past the Twin Creek Ranch to the national forest access sign. Turn right and travel up the switchbacks for 3 miles. The campground is on the right.
About the campground: This secret hideaway is neatly tucked into the evergreen forest out of sight from Jackson. A very short hike brings the Jackson Hole back into sight. Be sure to bring your camera and binoculars. The Elk Refuge lies below with a lot of area to study. A host is present at the campground. The rough road could prove very disheartening if the units are full. The reward for your perseverance would be isolated places to meditate on the panoramic mountains.

5 Gros Ventre

Location: 12 miles northeast of Jackson
GPS: N43 37.23' / W110 40.19'
Facilities and amenities: RV dump station, flush toilets, fire rings, picnic tables, trash receptacles, drinking water
Elevation: 6,573 feet
Road conditions: Loop roads are paved with compact gravel aprons.
Hookups: 39 electric (50 amp)
Sites: 271 basic sites, 35 tents-only, 4 group sites
Maximum RV length: 45 feet long
Season: May through Oct 10
Fees: $$$$$$ per night for basic sites, Golden Age and Access Passport holders half price, $$$$$$ per night for electric hookup, $$$ per night per person for group site
Maximum stay: 14 days
Management: Grand Teton National Park, PO Drawer 170, Moose, WY 83012-0170; (307) 739-3399; park website nps.gov/grte
Reservations: Make reservations 6 months in advance at recreation.gov.
Pets: Pets must be on a leash no longer than 6 feet at all times within 30 feet of roadways; not allowed on the multiuse pathway, park trails, or in the backcountry.
Quiet hours: 10 p.m. to 6 a.m.
ADA compliance: Yes
Activities: Fishing, hiking, wildlife viewing, photography
Finding the campground: Take US 26/89/191 north out of Jackson for 8 miles. Turn right onto Gros Ventre Road and travel 4 miles. The campground is on the right side of the road.
About the campground: The Tetons provide a spectacular backdrop for this campground. Mature cottonwood trees grant a lot of shade but little firewood. Drinking water is located at the comfort stations. RVs should fill drinking water tanks from the provided spigot at the dump station. The Gros Ventre River meanders past to the east, inviting anglers. This could work well for a base camp.

6 Atherton Creek

Location: 20 miles northeast of Jackson
GPS: N43 38.31' / W110 31.33'
Facilities and amenities: Vault toilets, fire rings, picnic tables, trash receptacles, drinking water, picnic area, boat ramp
Elevation: 6,961 feet
Road conditions: Gravel
Hookups: None
Sites: 20 basic sites
Maximum RV length: 25 feet long
Season: May–Sept, weather permitting
Fees: $ per day, Golden Age and Access Passport holders half price

Maximum stay: 14 days
Management: Bridger-Teton National Forest, AuDi Campground Services Inc., HC 82 Box 1158, Duck Creek Village, UT 84762; (541) 351-1182; audi1@scinternet.net (concessionaire)
Reservations: First-come, first-served
Pets: Pets must be kept on a leash and under control at all times.
Quiet hours: 10 p.m. to 6 a.m.
ADA compliance: No
Activities: Fishing, boating, hiking, water sports
Finding the campground: Take US 26/89/191 north out of Jackson for 8 miles. Turn right at Gros Ventre Junction and travel 6 miles, passing through Kelly. Turn right onto the paved Gros Ventre Road and travel 6 miles.
About the campground: The aspen and spruce trees share this sloping side hill along the banks of Lower Slide Lake. A landslide created this lake in 1923. The dam broke two years later, resulting in six deaths and a smaller lake. Three loops offer back-in sites with shorter aspen and spruce trees granting some shade. There are sites with excellent views, though they tend to fill quickly.

7 Hatchet

Location: 9 miles east of Moran Junction
GPS: N43 49.48' / W110 21.31'
Facilities and amenities: Vault toilet, fire rings, picnic tables, trash receptacles, food storage, drinking water
Elevation: 6,868 feet
Road conditions: Gravel
Hookups: None
Sites: 9 basic sites, 24 overflow parking
Maximum RV length: 18 feet long, 60 feet long in the overflow parking
Season: Mid-May through mid-Sept
Fees: $$ basic sites, $ overflow park, Golden Age and Access Passport holders half price
Maximum stay: 14 days
Management: Bridger-Teton National Forest, AuDi Campground Services Inc.; HC 82 Box 1158, Duck Creek Village, UT 84762; (541) 351-1182; audi1@scinternet.net (concessionaire)
Reservations: First-come, first-served
Pets: Pets must be on a leash and under physical control at all times.
Quiet hours: 10 p.m. to 6 a.m. (turn off generators)
ADA compliance: No
Activities: Hiking, mountain biking
Finding the campground: Take US 26/287 east of Moran Junction for 9 miles. The campground is on the right side of the road just before the Blackrock Ranger Station.
About the campground: The campground sits almost within a forest of lodgepole pine. The parking units appear to have been placed so as to avoid cutting trees. A 24-foot-long RV will fit in the pull-through, though that site is usually the first to be occupied so do not count on it. Both Yellowstone and Grand Teton National Parks campgrounds are reserved up to a year in advance. Reservations do get canceled, but timing can't. If your travels run late, this campground could

very well be the last place to camp. Firewood is for sale here. This is bear country. Be aware of the procedures.

8 Turpin Meadow

Location: 44 miles north of Jackson
GPS: N43 51.39' / W110 15.93'
Facilities and amenities: Vault toilets, fire rings, picnic tables, trash receptacles, corrals, hitching posts, stock tank
Elevation: 6,930 feet
Road conditions: Gravel
Hookups: None
Sites: 18 basic sites (including 4 pull-throughs)
Maximum RV length: 60 feet long
Season: Mid-May through mid-Sept
Fees: $$ per night, Golden Age and Access Passport holders half price
Maximum stay: 14 days
Management: Bridger-Teton National Forest, AuDi Campground Services Inc., HC 82 Box 1158, Duck Creek Village, UT 84762; (541) 351-1182; audi1@scinternet.net (concessionaire)
Reservations: First-come, first-served
Pets: Pets must be kept on a leash and under control at all times.
Quiet hours: 10 p.m. to 6 a.m.
ADA compliance: No
Activities: Fishing, hiking, horseback riding, hunting
Finding the campground: Take US 26/89/191 north out of Jackson for 30 miles. At Moran Junction continue on US 26/287 for 4 miles. Turn left onto the paved Buffalo Fork Road and travel 10 miles. Turn left onto the gravel access road just before crossing the Buffalo Fork River.
About the campground: Pine trees tower above grassy open spaces between units, where horses are allowed. The adjacent trailhead appeared more active than the campground upon our visit. This camping area is geared more toward horse riders, as evidenced by the extra-long parking units. Bear boxes located in the campground are not there for looks. Be aware of the proper procedures. Gathering firewood will require some hiking, so you may want to acquire some beforehand.

9 Jenny Lake

Location: 21 miles north of Jackson
GPS: N43 45.18' / W110 43.16'
Facilities and amenities: Coin-operated showers nearby, flush toilets, fire rings, picnic tables, leveled sites, bear-proof food-storage lockers, drinking water
Elevation: 6,802 feet
Road conditions: Paved

Hookups: NA
Sites: 51 tents-only, 10 hiker/biker sites
Maximum RV length: NA
Season: June–Sept
Fees: $$$$$$ base rate per night, $$ hiker/biker sites, Golden Age and Access Passport holders half price
Maximum stay: 7 days
Management: Contact information: (877) 444-6777; Grand Teton National Park, PO Drawer 170, Moose, WY 83012-0170; (307) 739-3399; park website nps.gov/grte
Reservations: National Recreation Reservation Service toll-free at (877) 444-6777 or online at recreation.gov
Pets: Pets must be kept on a leash and under control at all times.
Quiet hours: 10 p.m. to 6 a.m.
ADA compliance: Yes
Activities: Fishing, hiking, boating, mountain biking, photography, wildlife viewing
Finding the campground: Take US 26/89/191 north out of Jackson for 13 miles. Turn left at Moose Junction onto the paved Teton Park Road and travel 8 miles. Turn left at the South Jenny Lake access road and travel 0.25 mile.
About the campground: The boating activity listed above includes canoeing and kayaking, while hiking includes backpacking. Paved access winds through large boulders and tall spruce, pine, and fir trees. Sagebrush is scattered about with tall grass in places. The Tetons loom over the treetops, offering plenty of photographic views. This campground fills quickly every day. It has been reported that as one pulls out, two are waiting. It is a most beautiful spot, though it's somewhat maddening to obtain a unit.

10 Signal Mountain

Location: 33 miles north of Jackson
GPS: N43 50.53' / W110 36.65'
Facilities and amenities: RV dump station, pay showers and laundry nearby, flush toilets, fire rings, picnic tables, trash receptacles, drinking water
Elevation: 6,823 feet
Road conditions: Paved with compact gravel aprons
Hookups: 24 with electric hookups (30- and 50-amp)
Sites: 81 basic sites, 4 tents-only
Maximum RV length: 30 feet long
Season: Mid-May through mid-Oct
Fees: $$$$$$ per night for basic sites, $$$$$$ per night for site with electric hookups, Golden Age and Access Passport holders half price
Maximum stay: 14 days
Management: Grand Teton National Park: Signal Mountain Lodge, PO Box 50, Moran, WY 83013; (307) 543-2831; www.signalmountainlodge.com/signal-mountain-camping/signal-mountain-campground

Reservations: National Recreation Reservation Service toll-free at (877) 444-6777 or online at recreation.gov

Pets: All pets must be on a leash no longer than 6 feet and not left unattended. Runners and pens are not permitted.

Quiet hours: 10 p.m. to 7 a.m. (Generator hours are from 8 a.m. to 8 p.m.)

ADA compliance: Yes

Activities: Fishing, hiking, wildlife viewing, photography

Finding the campground: Take US 26/89/191 north out of Jackson for 13 miles. Turn left at Moose Junction onto the paved Teton Park Road and travel 20 miles.

About the campground: Stubby pine trees and tall sagebrush flow over the steep hillside overlooking Jackson Lake. Some of the units provide better mountain views than other spots. The units are well positioned, providing a sort of privacy. The Signal Mountain Trail, taking off from the camping area, is an excellent photographic tour. Moose, deer, and other wildlife are often spotted in the area as well.

11 Colter Bay

Location: 40 miles north of Jackson

GPS: N43 54.35' / W110 38.40'

Facilities and amenities: RV dump, pay showers and laundry nearby, flush toilets, fire rings, picnic tables, trash receptacles, drinking water

Elevation: 6,799 feet

Road conditions: Paved to gravel

Hookups: 13 with electricity (50-amp)

Sites: 324 basic sites, 10 hiker/biker sites, 10 group sites

Maximum RV length: 45 feet long

Season: May–Oct

Fees: $$$$$$ per night basic sites, $$$$$$ per night with electric, $$ per night per person group site, $$ per night hiker/biker site, Golden Age and Access Passport holders half price

Maximum stay: 14 days

Management: Grand Teton National Park: Colter Bay Campground, PO Box 250, Moran, WY 83013; (307) 543-2811; www.gtlc.com/camping/colter-bay-campground

Reservations: National Recreation Reservation Service toll-free at (877) 444-6777 or online at recreation.gov

Pets: Pets must be on a leash no longer than 6 feet at all times within 30 feet of roadways; not allowed on the multiuse pathway, park trails, or in the backcountry.

Quiet hours: 10 p.m. to 6 a.m.

ADA compliance: Yes

Activities: Fishing, hiking, wildlife viewing, photography

Finding the campground: Take US 26/89/191 north out of Jackson for 30 miles. At Moran Junction turn left onto US 89/191/287 and travel 10 miles. Turn left at the Colter Bay Village sign just past the convenience store and gas station. The campground entrance is a short distance from the highway on the right side.

About the campground: The Tetons peek through mature evergreen trees and in roadway clearings. Paved access is provided to the fifteen separate loops, with plenty of space between campers. Firewood tends to be rather scarce. Jackson Lake requires a short hike from the camping units, though some are a little closer than others. On an average summer day, this campground fills by noon. Some loops are set aside for tents only.

12 Colter Bay RV Park

Location: 40 miles north of Jackson
GPS: N43 54.36' / W110 38.44'
Facilities and amenities: Pay showers and laundry nearby, picnic tables. *Note:* There are no fire rings.
Elevation: 6,816 feet
Road conditions: Paved with gravel parking
Hookups: Electric (20-, 30-, 50-amp), water and sewer
Sites: 102 pull-through full-hookup sites, 10 back-in full-hookup sites
Maximum RV length: 45 feet long
Season: May–Oct
Fees: $$$$$$ per night for RVs up to 45 feet long at pull-through sites, $$$$$$ per night for RVs up to 30 feet long at back-in sites, Golden Age and Access Passport holders half price
Maximum stay: 14 days
Management: Grand Teton National Park: Colter Bay RV Park, PO Box 250, Moran, WY 83013; (307) 543-3100; www.gtlc.com/rv/colter-bay-rv-park
Reservations: National Recreation Reservation Service toll-free at (877) 444-6777 or online at recreation.gov
Pets: Pets must be on a leash no longer than 6 feet at all times within 30 feet of roadways; not allowed on the multiuse pathway, park trails, or in the backcountry.
Quiet hours: 10 p.m. to 6 a.m.
ADA compliance: Yes
Activities: Fishing, hiking, photography
Finding the campground: Take US 26/89/191 north out of Jackson for 30 miles. At Moran Junction turn left onto US 89/191/287 and travel 10 miles. Turn left at the Colter Bay Village sign just past the convenience store and gas station. The campground entrance is a short distance from the highway on the right side.
About the campground: Lodgepole pine provide plenty of shade with a need to pay attention while getting positioned just right. There are a lot of amenities in the area, but probably the biggest advantage is having the comforts of home at a base camp.

13 Colter Bay Tent Village

Location: 40 miles north of Jackson
GPS: N43 54.29' / W110 38.25'
Facilities and amenities: Potbellied woodstove, exterior fire ring, picnic table, lighting (no outlets), pull-down bunks
Elevation: 6,867 feet
Road conditions: Gravel
Hookups: None
Sites: 66 tent cabins
Maximum RV length: NA
Season: Mid-May through early Sept
Fees: $$$$$$ per night
Maximum stay: 14 days
Management: Grand Teton National Park: Colter Bay Tent Village, PO Box 250, Moran, WY 83013. Connect via the website email contact form. Colter Bay Tent Village, Grand Teton National Park (US National Park Service, nps.gov).
Reservations: National Recreation Reservation Service toll-free at (877) 444-6777 or online at recreation.gov
Pets: Pets must be on a leash no longer than 6 feet.
Quiet hours: 10 p.m. to 6 a.m.
ADA compliance: No
Activities: Fishing, hiking, photography
Finding the campground: Take US 26/89/191 north out of Jackson for 30 miles. At Moran Junction turn left onto US 89/191/287 and travel 10 miles. Turn left at the Colter Bay Village sign just past the convenience store and gas station and travel 0.7 mile. At the four-way intersection, turn left onto Douglas Fir Road and travel 0.1 mile. Turn left at the sign onto the Colter Bay Tent Village Road.
About the campground: These tent structures combine two log walls with two weatherproof canvas walls and a weatherproof roof to create a one-of-kind deluxe tent cabin. Camping gear is available for sale nearby but not provided. Even though reservations are required, there have been opportunities to fill a vacancy due to a cancellation. So if you are a tent camper and find that setting up a tent in the rain is not desirable, this could be a pleasant one-of-a-kind option.

14 Lizard Creek

Location: 15 miles north of Moran
GPS: N44 0.40' / W110 41.06'
Facilities and amenities: Comfort stations (flush toilets, running water), fire rings, picnic tables, trash receptacles, drinking water
Elevation: 6,813 feet
Road conditions: Paved with gravel aprons

Hookups: None
Sites: 38 basic sites, 25 tents-only
Maximum RV length: 25 feet long
Season: Mid-June through mid-Sept
Fees: $$$$$$ per night, Golden Age and Access Passport holders half price
Maximum stay: 14 days
Management: Grand Teton National Park: Signal Mountain Lodge, PO Box 50, Moran, WY 83013; (307) 543-2831; www.signalmountainlodge.com/signal-mountain-camping/lizard-creek-campground
Reservations: National Recreation Reservation Service toll-free at (877) 444-6777 or online at recreation.gov
Pets: All pets must be on a leash no longer than 6 feet and not left unattended. Runners and pens are not permitted.
Quiet hours: 10 p.m. to 7 a.m. (Generator hours are from 8 a.m. to 8 p.m.)
ADA compliance: No
Activities: Fishing, hiking, wildlife viewing
Finding the campground: Take US 26/89/191 north out of Jackson for 30 miles. At Moran Junction turn left onto US 89/191/287 and travel about 15 miles. The campground is on the left side of the road.
About the campground: Spruce and pine trees of various heights shelter these units, with a healthy helping of underbrush in places. Overall, there is a sort of "sanctuary" feeling here. Water levels of Jackson Lake will dictate whether or not fishing from shore can be done, among other things, but nothing that a short road trip doesn't take care of.

15 Sheffield

Location: 24 miles north of Moran
GPS: N44 5.59' / W110 39.82'
Facilities and amenities: Vault toilet, fire rings, picnic tables, trash receptacles, drinking water
Elevation: 6,900 feet
Road conditions: Gravel. *Note:* Access requires fording a local creek. Water levels can change quickly.
Hookups: None
Sites: 12 basic sites
Maximum RV length: 30 feet long
Season: Mid-May through mid-Sept, weather permitting
Fees: $ per night, Golden Age and Access Passport holders half price
Maximum stay: 16 days
Management: Bridger-Teton National Forest, AuDi Campground Services Inc., HC 82 Box 1158, Duck Creek Village, UT 84762; (541) 351-1182; audi1@scinternet.net (concessionaire)
Reservations: First-come, first-served
Pets: Pets must be on a leash and under physical control at all times.

Quiet hours: 10 p.m. to 6 a.m. (turn off generators)
ADA compliance: No
Activities: Fishing, hiking
Finding the campground: Take US 89 north for about 24 miles and be on the lookout for the Sheffield Campground sign—it tends to sneak up on you. Turn right onto the gravel-to-dirt road and travel 0.5 mile (including fording Sheffield Creek). Bear to the right to enter the campground.
About the campground: There are some older pine trees here, but most are not. The open spaces are filled with an assortment of grasses and brush common to mountain country. The camping units are spaced well enough, but there are not enough trees to hide, although this does allow for some scenic landscapes for a backdrop. The creek ford has concrete "bars" to help, and it shouldn't be much of a problem, but stay alert all the same.

16 Headwaters

Location: 22 miles north of Moran
GPS: N44 6.32' / W110 40.08'
Facilities and amenities: Host on-site, phone (cell phone service nonexistent)
Elevation: 6,900 feet
Road conditions: Gravel
Hookups: Electric (20-, 30-, and 50-amp), water and sewer
Sites: 97 RV sites, 34 tents-only
Maximum RV length: 45 feet long
Season: Mid-May through Oct
Fees: $$$$$$ per night for RV site, $$$$$$ for tent site, Golden Age and Access Passport holders half price
Maximum stay: 14 days
Management: Grand Teton National Park: Headwaters Campground, PO Box, Moran, WY 83013; (307) 543-2861; www.gtlc.com/camping/headwaters-campground-at-flagg-ranch
Reservations: National Recreation Reservation Service toll-free at (877) 444-6777 or online at recreation.gov
Pets: Pets must be kept on a leash and under control at all times.
Quiet hours: 10 p.m. to 6 a.m.
ADA compliance: No
Activities: Fishing, wildlife viewing, horseback riding
Finding the campground: Heading north from Jackson on US 26/89/191, turn left (west) at Moran Junction. Continue north on US 89/191/287 for 22 miles to Flagg Ranch. Turn left (west) and follow the signs.
About the campground: The pine forest offers shade, and a hike presents postcard-quality photo opportunities of the mountains to take home for show. It can be an excellent base camp, depending on where you prefer to explore.

Lander Area

Mountains meet desert in random locations without offering an explanation. Some of the resulting formations include the historical sites known as Devil's Gate and Independence Rock. The unique geology also contains an abundance of agates and the famous Wyoming jade.

The Oregon Trail traversed this region, leaving a massive amount of outstanding evidence. Wagon ruts are still obvious to this day in select areas. The historical markers along the route are well worth the time to examine.

In a majority of places, you can turn completely around and not see any fences, power lines, or houses. Cattle have replaced the buffalo, and here and there two parallel ruts indicate current travel routes. Otherwise, the scene remains much the same as when the mountain men and western emigrants passed through.

Mountain majesty in view.

#	Name	Group sites	Tents	RV sites	Total # of sites	Hookups	Picnic area	Toilets	Showers	Drinking water	Dump station	Phone	Handicap	Recreation	Fee	Season	Can reserve	Stay limit
1	Horse Creek			9	9			V						FHiW	$$	5/15-9/6		16
2	Double Cabin			14	14			V						FHiW	$$	5/15-9/6		16
3	Pinnacles			21	21			V						FHiW	$$	6/15-9/6		16
4	Brooks Lake			13	13			V		X				FBoHiWBr	$	6/15-9/6		16
5	Falls			54	54	El		V		X			X	FHiW	$$	6/1-9/15		16
6	Sinks Canyon			14	14			V		X			X	FHiW	$$	5/15-9/15		16
7	Worthen Meadows			28	28		X	V						FBoHiWBrPi	$$	6/1-9/15		16
8	Fiddlers Lake			16	20		X	V		X			X	FHiBoPi	$$	6/15-9/15		16
9	Little Popo Agie			4	4			V		X				FHiW	None	7/1-9/15		16
10	Louis Lake			9	9			V		X				FBoWBr	$	6/1-9/15		16
11	Cottonwood			18	18			V		X				HiMPhW	$	6/1-10/31		14
12	Big Atlantic Gulch			8	8			V		X				FHiMPhW	$	6/1-10/31		14
13	Atlantic City			18	18			V		X				HiMPhW	$	6/1-10/31		14

Boysen State Park

#	Name	Group sites	Tents	RV sites	Total # of sites	Hookups	Picnic area	Toilets	Showers	Drinking water	Dump station	Phone	Handicap	Recreation	Fee	Season	Can reserve	Stay limit
14	Lower Wind River			39	39		X	V		X			X	FPgPi	$$-$$$	5/1-9/30	X	14
15	Upper Wind River		2	37	39			V		X			X	FPg	$$-$$$	5/1-9/30	X	14
16	Brannon			10	10		X	V		X				FBoPgBrPi	$$-$$$	5/1-9/30	X	14
17	Tamarask			25	25		X	V		X			X	FBoPgBrPi	$$-$$$	5/1-9/30	X	14
18	Tough Creek	6		76	82			V		X			X	FBoSBr	$$-$$$	5/1-9/30	X	14
19	Lakeside			8	8		X	V						FBoS	$$-$$$	5/1-9/30	X	14
20	Fremont Bay	1		5	Dis		X	V		X			X	FBoPg	$$-$$$	5/1-9/30	X	14

Sinks Canyon State Park

#	Name	Group sites	Tents	RV sites	Total # of sites	Hookups	Picnic area	Toilets	Showers	Drinking water	Dump station	Phone	Handicap	Recreation	Fee	Season	Can reserve	Stay limit
21	Popo Agi		4	20	24			V		X				FHiW	$$-$$$	5/1-9/30	X	14
22	Sawmill			5	5			V		X			X	FHiW	$$-$$$	5/1-9/30	X	14

Bo = boating
Br = boat ramp
Dis = dispersed
El = electric hookups
F = fishing
Hi = hiking
M = mountain biking
Pg = playground
Ph = photography
Pi = picnicking
S = swimming
V = vault toilet
W = wildlife viewing

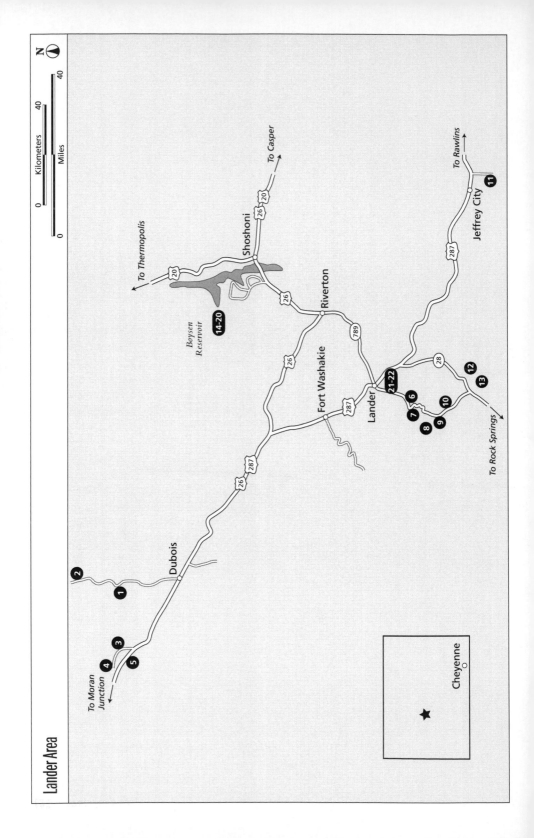

Lander Area

1 Horse Creek

Location: 11 miles north of Dubois
GPS: N43 39.93' / W109 38.17'
Facilities and amenities: Vault toilet, fire rings, bear boxes, trash receptacles, picnic tables
Elevation: 7,659 feet
Road conditions: Gravel
Hookups: None
Sites: 9 basic sites
Maximum RV length: 32 feet long
Season: Mid-May through Sept 6
Fees: $$ per night, Golden Age and Access Passport holders half price
Maximum stay: 16 days
Management: Shoshone National Forest, Wind River Ranger District, (307) 455-2466
Reservations: First-come, first-served
Pets: Pets must be leashed and under control at all times.
Quiet hours: 10 p.m. to 6 a.m. (no generators)
ADA compliance: No
Activities: Fishing, hiking, wildlife viewing
Finding the campground: Take the Wiggins Fork Road/FR 285 north out of Dubois for 11 miles. The first 3 miles are paved.
About the campground: The level parking areas sit along the banks of Horse Creek. Some shade comes from the spruce and pine trees scattered about. Willow brush and grass spread out between trees and parking spots. The road gets rough in spots, making a longer stay more desirable. The units to the right tend to get a bit of dust from passing traffic. A host occupies one of the sites. Firewood will take some effort, though deadfall appears at various places.

2 Double Cabin

Location: 27 miles north of Dubois
GPS: N43 48.40' / W109 33.65'
Facilities and amenities: Vault toilet, fire rings, trash receptacles, picnic tables
Elevation: 8,009 feet
Road conditions: Gravel with good to very rough rocky road at various places
Hookups: None
Sites: 14 basic sites
Maximum RV length: 32 feet long
Season: Mid-May through Sept 6
Fees: $$ per night, Golden Age and Access Passport holders half price
Maximum stay: 16 days
Management: Shoshone National Forest, Wind River Ranger District, (307) 455-2466
Reservations: First-come, first-served
Pets: Pets must be leashed and under control at all times.

Quiet hours: 10 p.m. to 6 a.m. (no generators)
ADA compliance: No
Activities: Fishing, hiking, wildlife viewing
Finding the campground: Take the Wiggins Fork Road/FR 285 north out of Dubois for 27 miles. The first 3 miles are paved. There are numerous roads shooting off of this one, but a directional sign was present at each intersection as of our visit.
About the campground: The pine forest closes in on these camping units. Some sites offer pull-throughs while the rest are back-in. Just outside the camping area, a sagebrush meadow slopes away into the Wiggins Fork. Huge mountains loom far into the sky on all sides. A nearby trailhead grants access to wilderness. For rock hounds the riverbed offers fresh specimens of agate and petrified wood every year, as high waters from spring thaw flush new rocks to the surface. Firewood will take some effort, though a short stop along the way in could make it easier. There were vacant spots with more than enough campers just outside the area to fill them at the time of our visit. A host is available at the campground. Keep in mind that this is grizzly bear country.

3 Pinnacles

Location: 28 miles northwest of Dubois
GPS: N43 45.06' / W109 59.80'
Facilities and amenities: Vault toilet, fire rings, bear boxes, trash receptacles, drinking water
Elevation: 9,121 feet
Road conditions: Gravel
Hookups: None
Sites: 21 basic sites
Maximum RV length: 32 feet long
Season: Mid-June through early Sept
Fees: $$ per night, Golden Age and Access Passport holders half price
Maximum stay: 16 days
Management: Shoshone National Forest, Wind River Ranger District, (307) 455-2466
Reservations: First-come, first-served
Pets: Pets must be leashed and under control at all times.
Quiet hours: 10 p.m. to 6 a.m. (no generators)
ADA compliance: No
Activities: Fishing, hiking, wildlife viewing
Finding the campground: Take US 26/287 west out of Dubois for 23 miles. Turn right onto the gravel FR 515 and travel 5 miles. Follow the directions as posted for the last mile.
About the campground: A lot of rolling knolls spotted with spruce and pine trees lie between the parking units here. Individual sites offer privacy and mountain scenery. Some pull-throughs are available. Brooks Lake settles into the shadows just west of the campground with some spots within view. Deadfall appeared plentiful at the time of our visit, but at some point in the future, campers will need to go beyond the camping area for their firewood. The washboard access road tests nerves and endurance, but it's an acceptable sacrifice for such a beautiful haven. A host is available at the campground.

4 Brooks Lake

Location: 28 miles northwest of Dubois
GPS: N43 44.94' / W110 0.29'
Facilities and amenities: Vault toilet, fire rings, trash receptacles, picnic tables, drinking water, boat ramp
Elevation: 9,121 feet
Road conditions: Gravel
Hookups: None
Sites: 13 basic sites
Maximum RV length: 32 feet long
Season: Mid-June through early Sept
Fees: $ per night, Golden Age and Access Passport holders half price
Maximum stay: 16 days
Management: Shoshone National Forest, Wind River District, (307) 455-2466
Reservations: First-come, first-served
Pets: Pets must be leashed and under control at all times.
Quiet hours: 10 p.m. to 6 a.m. (no generators)
ADA compliance: No
Activities: Fishing, boating, hiking, wildlife viewing
Finding the campground: Take US 26/287 west out of Dubois for 23 miles. Turn right onto the gravel FR 515 and travel 5 miles.
About the campground: Brooks Lake snuggles up to a few of the parking units here. More isolated and private spots climb into the forest. Spruce trees inhabit the campground almost to the shoreline. Larger units will have to search some to find usable sites, but they do exist. Brooks Lake would be a good place for a canoe. Huge mountains overlook both the lake and campground, offering plenty of postcard-quality pictures. If you want scenic views including a mountain lake, this is the campground.

5 Falls

Location: 24 miles northwest of Dubois
GPS: N43 42.52' / W109 58.34'
Facilities and amenities: Vault toilet, fire rings, bear boxes, trash receptacles, drinking water
Elevation: 8,350 feet
Road conditions: Gravel
Hookups: Electric
Sites: 54 basic sites
Maximum RV length: 32 feet long
Season: June through mid-Sept
Fees: $$ per night, Golden Age and Access Passport holders half price
Maximum stay: 16 days

Management: Shoshone National Forest, Wind River District, (307) 455-2466
Reservations: First-come, first-served
Pets: Pets must be leashed and under control at all times.
Quiet hours: 10 p.m. to 6 a.m. (no generators)
ADA compliance: Yes
Activities: Fishing, hiking, wildlife viewing
Finding the campground: Take US 26/287 west out of Dubois for 24 miles. The campground is on the left side of the road.
About the campground: Engelmann spruce and lodgepole pine shade both loops in equal percentages, with an open grassy meadow between. Brooks Lake Creek provides a smashing encore for an already serene setting. A waterfall crashes over a cliff edge so abruptly, one would not expect it. Obviously, this pleasant addition resulted in the campground's name. Many travelers pass by never realizing the beauty they're missing. A parking area near the falls allows vehicles access with little effort. Firewood gathering doesn't require a lot of work yet, as this quiet spot seems to be passed by more frequently than other campgrounds. This would be an excellent place to relax either before or after a whirlwind tour of Yellowstone National Park. A host is available in the campground.

6 Sinks Canyon

Location: 7 miles southwest of Lander
GPS: N42 4.25' / W108 50.20'
Facilities and amenities: Vault toilet, fire rings, trash receptacles, picnic tables, drinking water
Elevation: 6,886 feet
Road conditions: Paved with numerous pothole repairs
Hookups: None
Sites: 14 basic sites
Maximum RV length: No trailers over 20 feet long
Season: Mid-May through mid-Sept
Fees: $$ per night, Golden Age and Access Passport holders half price
Maximum stay: 16 days
Management: Shoshone National Forest, Washakie Ranger District, (307) 332-5460 (concessionaire)
Reservations: First-come, first-served
Pets: Pets must be on a leash and under control at all times.
Quiet hours: 10 p.m. to 6 a.m. (turn off generators)
ADA compliance: Yes
Activities: Fishing, hiking, wildlife viewing
Finding the campground: In Lander go south on 5th Street to the end of the road. Turn right (west) onto the paved Sinks Canyon Road/SR 131 and travel 7 miles. The Sinks Canyon Road will turn south as you leave Lander. The campground is on the left side of the road.

About the campground: This campground is not the most user-friendly for large RVs and those with trailers, but that does not diminish its popularity. The crashing water of the Popo Agie stream offers a welcome complaint to the ears of those that choose to exercise their skills at backing up. The assortment of boulders and pine trees come in all different sizes, with thick underbrush squeezed in between the units along the riverbank. There is a good-sized parking area with more open grassy sites. The units here are not as close to the creek, but as the sun sets and traffic dies down, the crashing water music has no trouble reaching these units as well.

7 Worthen Meadows

Location: 18 miles southwest of Lander
GPS: N42 4.86' / W108 55.76'
Facilities and amenities: Vault toilets, fire rings, trash receptacles, picnic tables, drinking water, boat ramp
Elevation: 8,848 feet
Road conditions: Gravel
Hookups: None
Sites: 28 basic sites
Maximum RV length: No trailers over 24 feet long
Season: June through mid-Sept
Fees: $$ per night, Golden Age and Access Passport holders half price
Maximum stay: 16 days
Management: Shoshone National Forest, Washakie Ranger District, (307) 332-5460 (concessionaire)
Reservations: First-come, first-served
Pets: Pets must be on a leash and under control at all times
Quiet hours: 10 p.m. to 6 a.m. (turn off generators)
ADA compliance: No
Activities: Fishing, boating, hiking, wildlife viewing
Finding the campground: In Lander go south on 5th Street to the end of the road. Turn right (west) onto the paved Sinks Canyon Road/SR 131 and travel 18 miles. The Sinks Canyon Road will turn south as you leave Lander and will become gravel in about 9 miles. Steep gravel switchbacks begin just after the pavement ends as well.
About the campground: This campground is separated into two locations with parking units well spaced in mature pine trees, taking advantage of available shoreline boundaries of peninsulas along a mountain lake. The boat ramp and picnic area divide the Hilltop and Lakeside camping areas. The eight units located in Hilltop are on a knoll with a little more of a hike to the lakeshore. Tents or RVs up to 20 feet long find Hilltop suitable. Longer RVs and trailers will fit much easier in the Lakeside area. Lodgepole pine are thicker in the Lakeside sites, with plenty of deadfall for firewood. The forest does not quite classify as dog-hair, but it is close. Trout and grayling jump for lunch, leaving plenty of surface rings on the water for proof.

8 Fiddlers Lake

Location: 24 miles southwest of Lander
GPS: N42 38.12' / W108 52.51'
Facilities and amenities: Vault toilets, fire pits, barbecue grills, bear-proof storage, trash receptacles, drinking water
Elevation: 9,425 feet
Road conditions: Gravel
Hookups: None
Sites: 16 basic sites, 4 tents-only
Maximum RV length: No trailers over 40 feet long
Season: Mid-June through mid-Sept
Fees: $$ per day, Golden Age and Access Passport holders half price
Maximum stay: 16 days
Management: Shoshone National Forest, Washakie Ranger District, (307) 332-5460 (concessionaire)
Reservations: First-come, first-served
Pets: Pets must be leashed at all times.
Quiet hours: 10 p.m. to 6 a.m. (turn off generators)
ADA compliance: Yes
Activities: Fishing, boating, hiking
Finding the campground: From Lander go south on WY 131 to FR 300, then continue south for 12 miles. The campground is on the right.
About the campground: A tents-only camping area is located a short distance away from the main access road. These are walk-in sites with a bit of a hike from the parking area that helps promote an isolation of sorts. The mature pine trees and underbrush blend well within the multicolored igneous rocks for a one-of-a-kind sort of setting. A small brook tumbles down over an assortment of small to large rocks, creating a chorus of its own.

Combined camping units are found farther away, closer to the shoreline of Fiddler Lake. There are water fountains, though as of our visit we could not find one that delivered any water. The spaces are well spaced from other units with enough open area for some pleasant views. There is a boat ramp for access to the lake, though there is plenty of shoreline to settle into a lawn chair and wait for a fish to bite if that is more to your liking. The mountainous forest offers plenty of choices for an adventurous hiker or children with active imaginations. As with other campgrounds in the area, the drive getting to it creates a desire to take advantage of the 16-day maximum stay.

9 Little Popo Agie

Location: 23 miles southwest of Lander
GPS: N42 36.50' / W108 51.30'
Facilities and amenities: Vault toilet, fire rings, picnic tables
Elevation: 8,778 feet

Road conditions: Gravel (rough)

Hookups: None

Sites: 4 basic sites

Maximum RV length: 16 feet long

Season: July through mid-Sept

Fees: None

Maximum stay: 16 days

Management: Shoshone National Forest, Washakie Ranger District, (307) 332-5460

Reservations: First-come, first-served

Pets: Pets must be on a leash and never unattended.

Quiet hours: 10 p.m. to 6 a.m. (turn off generators)

ADA compliance: No

Activities: Fishing, hiking, wildlife viewing

Finding the campground: From Lander, go south on WY 131, then FR 300 for about 23 miles.

About the campground: The toilet and a few other amenities settle into this very old campground in stark contrast with the ground-level fire "chimneys" in various stages of decay and repair. It is kind of like visiting an old ghost town. The clear mountain water of the Little Popo Agie stream has witnessed many campers in its travel on its way down. Trailers will be difficult to level and turn around for those with "backing" issues. A high-profile unit, as in both truck and trailer, is definitely advised. Upon our arrival at the campground access, the sign was missing the word "Little." Not that it made any difference, as we had been here before, but it is the place. With the camping area so close to the main access road, dust and noise will be something to deal with, at least until the latter part of the day. The "bubbling" of Little Popo Agie stream will no doubt be a welcome sort of lullaby, especially after the dust storms created by the passing traffic dies off in the evening. When that happens, all is forgiven with an unforgettable reward.

10 Louis Lake

Location: 41 miles southwest of Lander via WY 28

GPS: N42 35.15' / W108 51.20'

Facilities and amenities: Vault toilets, fire pits, picnic tables, drinking water, boat ramp

Elevation: 8,582 feet

Road conditions: The gravel access road is less rough than some of the main road from WY 28, but it is not there for speed anyway.

Hookups: None

Sites: 9 basic sites

Maximum RV length: 24 feet long

Season: June through mid-Sept

Fees: $ per day, Golden Age and Access Passport holders half price

Maximum stay: 16 days

Management: Shoshone National Forest, Washakie Ranger District, (307) 332-5460

Reservations: First-come, first-served

Pets: Pets must be on a leash and never unattended.

Quiet hours: 10 p.m. to 6 a.m.

ADA compliance: No

Activities: Fishing, boating, wildlife viewing

Finding the campground: Take US 287/WY 789 south out of Lander for 8.5 miles. Stay to the right (actually straight ahead) onto WY 28 and travel 22.5 miles. Turn right at FR 300 and proceed to the gravel road, then travel 9 miles to the campground sign. Turn right and travel 1 mile to the campground.

About the campground: The units settle into the pine trees in this rather compact but inviting campground. Louis Lake is not in sight, though it is more due to forest interference than distance. Trailers will fit in the parking units though they all require backing in. Our first thought about bringing a trailer here, or to any one of the campgrounds on FR 300 (otherwise known as the Loop Road), was the narrowness, combined with multiple corners and rough road conditions. This would not be a choice for a short one-night stay and an early wakeup to move down the road to wherever. The 16-day maximum stay would be a definite consideration. The campground can be reached from the Lander side, but the WY 28 access is by far the most time efficient and the least amount of narrow road.

11 Cottonwood

Location: 73 miles southeast of Lander

GPS: N42 21.74' / W107 41.74'

Facilities and amenities: Vault toilets, fire rings, picnic tables, trash receptacles, drinking water

Elevation: 7,721 feet

Road conditions: Gravel (with numerous rough areas)

Hookups: None

Sites: 18 basic sites

Maximum RV length: 20 feet long

Season: June–Oct, weather permitting

Fees: $ per day, Golden Age and Access Passport holders half price

Maximum stay: 14 days

Management: Bureau of Land Management, Lander Field Office, (307) 332-8400; lander_wymail@blm.gov

Reservations: First-come, first-served

Pets: Pets allowed

Quiet hours: Campers courtesy

ADA compliance: No

Activities: Hiking, mountain biking, photography, wildlife viewing

Finding the campground: Take US 287 southeast out of Lander for 62 miles (passing through Jeffrey City). Turn right onto the gravel Green Mountain Road/BLM 2411 and travel 11 miles.

About the campground: Tall lodgepole pine share this mountain campground with an ever-increasing number of fast-growing aspen trees. These trees are well watered, with the bubbly creek flowing past camping units as it happily makes its way to the Sweetwater River miles downstream. Fishing and horseback riding are listed on the BLM website, though it seems those activities will require some additional travel. Rockhounding would be a consideration for this area as jade and agates are found in the nearby desert—again a little travel is required to get there.

The drive to this paradise can test the limits of patience and would not be a good choice for those who want to catch some rest and then make an early morning departure. This is more of "set and stay for a while" type of place.

12 Big Atlantic Gulch

Location: 28 miles south of Lander
GPS: N42 31.16' / W108 42.87'
Facilities and amenities: Vault toilets, fire pits, trash receptacles, picnic tables, hand-pumped drinking water
Elevation: 8,042 feet
Road conditions: About 0.5 mile before the campground, the paved road changes to gravel.
Hookups: None
Sites: 8 basic sites
Maximum RV length: 40 feet long
Season: June 1 through Oct 31
Fees: $ per day, Golden Age and Access Passport holders half price
Maximum stay: 14 days
Management: Bureau of Land Management, Lander Field Office, (307) 332-8400; lander_wymail@blm.gov
Reservations: First-come, first-served
Pets: Pets must be on a leash and must not be left unattended.
Quiet hours: 10 p.m. to 7 a.m.
ADA compliance: No
Activities: Fishing, hiking, mountain biking, photography, wildlife viewing
Finding the campground: Take US 287/WY 789 south out of Lander 8.5 miles. Stay to the right (actually straight ahead) onto WY 28 and travel 19.5 miles. At the brown Atlantic City–South Pass sign, turn left onto the WY 28 bypass road. Travel down this road about 2 miles. A brown sign stating "BLM CG 2 - 1 mile" directs seekers to turn left onto the paved Atlantic City Road. Turn left—the road turns to gravel in 1 mile. A short distance past the pavement, turn left at the sign, then drive 0.5 mile to the campground entrance on the left.
About the campground: Aspen trees seem more dominant, with lodgepole pine mingled between. The camping units are separated with just enough space to maintain a sort of isolation while close enough to make sharing a campfire and fellowship with neighbors possible if desired. The Atlantic City Road is far enough away to keep dust from drifting into the campground, however, the campground road will provide plenty if the speed limit is not followed. Toward nightfall the traffic generally comes to a nonexistent status, providing some very quiet nights. Physical labor is involved for obtaining the drinking water from a hand pump. Most of the units are back-in with a few pull-through. Leveling will take some forethought and evaluation. As of our visit the coyotes offered up a nighttime concert and an occasional cow bellowed no doubt in search of a wayward calf. All in all, as the darkness settled in, quiet came with it.

13 Atlantic City

Location: 28 miles south of Lander
GPS: N42 30.96' / W108 43.34'
Facilities and amenities: Vault toilets, fire pits, trash receptacles, picnic tables, drinking water
Elevation: 8,094 feet
Road conditions: About 0.5 mile before the campground, the paved road changes to gravel.
Hookups: None
Sites: 18 basic sites
Maximum RV length: 30 feet long
Season: June 1 through Oct 31
Fees: $ per day, Golden Age and Access Passport holders half price
Maximum stay: 14 days
Management: Bureau of Land Management, Lander Field Office, (307) 332-8400; lander_wymail@blm.gov
Reservations: First-come, first-served
Pets: Pets must be on a leash and not left unattended.
Quiet hours: 10 p.m. to 7 a.m.
ADA compliance: No
Activities: Hiking, mountain biking, photography, wildlife viewing
Finding the campground: From Lander take US 287/WY 789 south 8.5 miles. Stay to the right (actually straight ahead) onto WY 28 and travel 19.5 miles. At the brown Atlantic City–South Pass sign, turn left onto the WY 28 bypass road. Just before the turn there will be another brown sign pointing left with "BLM Campgrounds (2)" on it. Travel down this road about 2 miles. Turn left onto the paved Atlantic City Road and travel about 1 mile. About 0.2 mile from the campground, the road will turn to gravel. The campground is on the right.
About the campground: The lodgepole pine mix with aspen and provide shade along with an occasional wind serenade from the needles combined with the shimmering leaves of the aspen. This is a very quiet campground and a very popular spot. The unit does not have to be vacated until 2 p.m. so it is possible to arrive later in the day just in time to take possession, though that is by no means any guarantee. The Atlantic City Road does have a fair amount of travel during the week with an increase on weekends, but the camping units are far enough off the road that the dust is not noticed. As the sun sets, the traffic seems to go with it, leaving a very noticeable silence, with the exception of when the wind is passing through the needles. Drinking water is provided by a well through a number of well-placed spigots. With a little scouting, one can park in a unit where the freshwater tank can be filled by combining a number of hoses, thus avoiding the "bucket brigade" routine if needed. There are a lot of interesting places to visit here including the Miners Delight Ghost Town, Fort Stambaugh, South Pass Historic Area, and Atlantic City. Not to mention the not-too-distant fishing and hiking adventures awaiting in Shoshone National Forest. For those who have the time, taking advantage of the 14-day maximum stay would be a very inviting option.

Boysen State Park

Overview

Management: Wyoming State Parks, Historic Sites & Trails, (307) 777-6323

Reservations: Online at wyomingstateparks.reserveamerica.com or by phone at (877) 996-7275

Pets:

- All pets must be in a vehicle or on a leash no longer than 10 feet and physically controlled at all times.
- Pets shall not be left unattended for any time greater than 1 hour.
- Persons with pets on lawns and picnic and camping areas will be responsible for proper removal of their animals' waste.
- Parcels of parkland may be closed permanently or for a specified period of time to domestic pets in order to protect wildlife or adjacent landowners' rights.

Quiet hours: 10 p.m. to 6 a.m. Turn off generators. All generators and electronic devices or any actions that may disturb the peace are prohibited during these hours.

Conduct:

- Glass beverage containers are prohibited outside vehicles and all camping units on parkland except on established commercial premises and designated historic sites.
- Draining or dumping refuse or waste, including gray water, from any source, except in places or receptacles provided for such use, is prohibited.

14 Lower Wind River

Location: 16 miles north of Shoshoni
GPS: N43 26.45' / W108 10.28'
Facilities and amenities: Vault toilets, fire rings, picnic tables, trash dumpsters, drinking water
Elevation: 4,630 feet
Road conditions: Paved
Hookups: None
Sites: 39 basic sites
Maximum RV length: 60 feet long
Season: May–Sept
Fees: $$ per resident per vehicle, $$$ per nonresident per vehicle, not including reservation or daily pass fee
Maximum stay: 14 days

Management: Wyoming State Parks, Historic Sites & Trails, (307) 777-6323. Boysen State Park Superintendent, (307) 876-2796.

Reservations: Online at wyomingstateparks.reserveamerica.com or by phone at (877) 996-7275

Pets: All pets must be kept on a leash at all times.

Quiet hours: 10 p.m. to 6 a.m.

ADA compliance: Yes

Activities: Fishing, playground

Finding the campground: Take US 26 east out of Riverton for 25 miles. At Shoshoni turn left onto US 20 and travel 15 miles. Turn left at the sign.

About the campground: The entrance divides this campground into two loops. Large cottonwood trees provide more shade on the northern loop. The southern portion hosts a group area and playground along with the parking spots. Parking spots are gravel with a paved access road. As with the previous campground, traffic noise can get intense. When things quiet down, the Wind River can be heard working its way through the canyon. Three nearby tunnels add an orchestra of echoing car horns from time to time. Keep in mind that fishing downstream from Boysen State Park will put you onto the Wind River Indian Reservation. A special permit is required. There are pull-throughs on the south side that accommodate longer RVs. However, the majority of the sites are in the range of 30 to 40 feet long.

15 Upper Wind River

Location: 15 miles north of Shoshoni

GPS: N43 26.07' / W108 10.61'

Facilities and amenities: Vault toilets, fire rings, picnic tables, trash receptacles, drinking water

Elevation: 4,629 feet

Road conditions: Gravel

Hookups: None

Sites: 37 basic sites, 2 tents-only

Maximum RV length: 50 feet long

Season: May–Sept

Fees: $$ per resident per vehicle, $$$ per nonresident per vehicle, not including reservation or daily pass fee

Maximum stay: 14 days

Management: Wyoming State Parks, Historic Sites & Trails, (307) 777-6323. Boysen State Park Superintendent, (307) 876-2796.

Reservations: Online at wyomingstateparks.reserveamerica.com or by phone at (877) 996-7275

Pets: Pets must be kept on a leash at all times.

Quiet hours: 10 p.m. to 6 a.m. (no generators, no exceptions)

ADA compliance: Yes

Activities: Fishing, playground

Finding the campground: Take US 26 east out of Riverton for 24 miles. At Shoshoni turn left onto US 20 and travel 14 miles. Turn left at the sign.

About the campground: Large cottonwood trees shade both sides of the paved access and parking units, but the sun can still get pretty intense by around noon. During our visit a host occupied a site toward the back of the campground. Firewood will need to be acquired before reaching this place. The green-colored Wind River rushes by to the west. Traffic noise gets a little heavy with the main highway directly beside and above the camping area.

16 Brannon

Location: 13 miles north of Shoshoni
GPS: N43 24.11' / W108 10.13'
Facilities and amenities: Vault toilet, fire rings, picnic tables, trash receptacles, boat ramp, drinking water
Elevation: 4,730 feet
Road conditions: Gravel
Hookups: None
Sites: 10 basic sites
Maximum RV length: 60 feet long
Season: May–Sept
Fees: $$ per resident per vehicle, $$$ per nonresident per vehicle, not including reservation or daily pass fee
Maximum stay: 14 days
Management: Wyoming State Parks, Historic Sites & Trails, (307) 777-6323. Boysen State Park Superintendent, (307) 876-2796.
Reservations: Online at wyomingstateparks.reserveamerica.com or by phone at (877) 996-7275
Pets: Pets must be kept on a leash at all times.
Quiet hours: 10 p.m. to 6 a.m. (no generators, no exceptions)
ADA compliance: No
Activities: Fishing, boating, playground
Finding the campground: Take US 20 north out of Shoshoni for 13 miles to the main access on the left.
About the campground: It was difficult to tell where the picnic area started and the camping stopped. Watered and mowed grass marked what appeared to be the picnic area. Other roads took off toward the lake to the right of this area. Trailers were parked within sight of a sign giving directions to a swimming area.

17 Tamarask

Location: 14 miles north of Shoshoni
GPS: N43 23.58' / W108 9.61'
Facilities and amenities: Vault toilet, fire rings, picnic tables, trash receptacles, boat ramp, drinking water

Elevation: 7,746 feet
Road conditions: Gravel
Hookups: None
Sites: 25 basic sites
Maximum RV length: 50 feet long
Season: May–Sept
Fees: $$ per resident per vehicle, $$$ per nonresident per vehicle, not including reservation or daily pass fee
Maximum stay: 14 days
Management: Wyoming State Parks, Historic Sites & Trails, (307) 777-6323. Boysen State Park Superintendent, (307) 876-2796.
Reservations: Online at wyomingstateparks.reserveamerica.com or by phone at (877) 996-7275
Pets: Pets must be kept on a leash at all times.
Quiet hours: 10 p.m. to 6 a.m. (no generators, no exceptions)
ADA compliance: Yes
Activities: Fishing, boating, playground
Finding the campground: Take US 20 north out of Shoshoni for 13 miles to the main access on the left. Go left to the fee booth and past the marina access a total of about 1 mile. The campground is on the right.
About the campground: Tables and shade trees, of sorts, line separate peninsulas on a dead-end road. Drinking water appears to be relatively easy to obtain from one of the spigots. Driftwood makes a good fire when it can be found.

18 Tough Creek

Location: 32 miles northeast of Riverton
GPS: N43 19.29' / W108 7.48'
Facilities and amenities: Vault toilet, fire rings, picnic tables, shelter, trash receptacles, boat ramp, drinking water
Elevation: 4,732 feet
Road conditions: Paved access gravel parking
Hookups: None
Sites: 76 basic sites, 6 group sites
Maximum RV length: 80 feet long
Season: May–Sept
Fees: $$ per resident per vehicle, $$$ per nonresident per vehicle, not including reservation or daily pass fee
Maximum stay: 14 days
Management: Wyoming State Parks, Historic Sites & Trails, (307) 777-6323. Boysen State Park Superintendent, (307) 876-2796.
Reservations: Online at wyomingstateparks.reserveamerica.com or by phone at (877) 996-7275
Pets: Pets must be kept on a leash at all times.
Quiet hours: 10 p.m. to 6 a.m. (no generators, no exceptions)

ADA compliance: Yes
Activities: Fishing, boating, swimming
Finding the campground: Take US 20 north out of Shoshoni for 6 miles. Turn left at the Tough Creek Campground sign onto the paved road and travel 1 mile. There is a very active railroad crossing just before reaching the campground. Be alert!
About the campground: Given a choice, this would be the campground to stay in while visiting the state park. Most of the units find shade under one or more cottonwood trees. Fire rings, grills, and tables almost outnumber the trees. Firewood could be a problem so be sure to bring what you need, though driftwood makes a good fire when it's available. The wind can be brutal and at times will arrive without any warning. Any unsecured light items, such as lawn chairs, could take flight. Before taking off for whatever adventure, whether it's for minutes or hours, take time to "windproof" your site, including awnings.

19 Lakeside

Location: 3 miles west of Shoshoni
GPS: N43 13.17' / W108 10.77'
Facilities and amenities: Vault toilet, fire rings, picnic tables
Elevation: 4,727 feet
Road conditions: Paved to gravel
Hookups: None
Sites: Undetermined (8 plus or minus)
Maximum RV length: 40 feet long
Season: May–Sept
Fees: $$ per resident per vehicle, $$$ per nonresident per vehicle, not including reservation or daily pass fee
Maximum stay: 14 days
Management: Wyoming State Parks, Historic Sites & Trails, (307) 777-6323. Boysen State Park Superintendent, (307) 876-2796.
Reservations: Online at wyomingstateparks.reserveamerica.com or by phone at (877) 996-7275
Pets: Pets must be kept on a leash at all times.
Quiet hours: 10 p.m. to 6 a.m. (no generators, no exceptions)
ADA compliance: No
Activities: Fishing, boating, swimming
Finding the campground: Take US 26 west out of Shoshoni for 5 miles. The campground is on the right.
About the campground: As of our visit this campground appeared to be a relatively new one. It could still be under construction, however, the fee station was functional, implying it is available to camp in. There are trees along the shoreline, though none close enough to the camping units for shade. As with other spots in this country, wind can be a serious force to deal with.

20 Fremont Bay

Location: 9 miles northwest of Shoshoni
GPS: N43 15.75' / W108 11.58'
Facilities and amenities: Vault toilet, fire rings, picnic tables, boat ramp, drinking water
Elevation: 4,733 feet
Road conditions: Gravel
Hookups: None
Sites: 4 basic and dispersed
Maximum RV length: 25 feet long
Season: May–Sept
Fees: $$ per resident per vehicle, $$$ per nonresident per vehicle
Maximum stay: 14 days
Management: Wyoming State Parks, Historic Sites & Trails, (307) 777-6323. Boysen State Park Superintendent, (307) 876-2796.
Reservations: First-come, first-served, group site reservable at wyo-park.com or by calling Reserve America at (877) 996-7275
Pets: Pets must be kept on a leash at all times.
Quiet hours: 10 p.m. to 6 a.m.
ADA compliance: Yes (group site only)
Activities: Fishing, boating, playground
Finding the campground: Take US 26 west out of Shoshoni for 5 miles. Turn right at the Boysen West Shore Road sign and travel about 1 mile. Turn right onto the West Shore Loop 1 road and travel about 4 miles to the access road on the right.
About the campground: Water recreation attracts campers to this desert reservoir. For the most part evenings are spent resting up for the next day's water sports. The group area here can be reserved and offers the best shelter from an intense sun—if it's not spoken for, individuals can use it. Other than the group area, there are only three fire rings with tables. A volleyball court settles into the sandy soil along with other playground equipment.

Sinks Canyon State Park

Overview

Management: Wyoming State Parks, Historic Sites & Trails, (307) 777-6323

Reservations: Online at wyomingstateparks.reserveamerica.com or by phone at (877) 996-7275

Pets:

- All pets must be in a vehicle or on a leash no longer than 10 feet and physically controlled at all times.
- Pets shall not be left unattended for any time greater than 1 hour.
- Persons with pets on lawns and picnic and camping areas will be responsible for proper removal of the animals' waste.
- Parcels of parkland may be closed permanently or for a specified period of time to domestic pets in order to protect wildlife or adjacent landowners' rights.

Quiet hours: 10 p.m. to 6 a.m. Turn off generators. All generators and electronic devices or any actions that may disturb the peace are prohibited during these hours.

Conduct:

- Glass beverage containers are prohibited outside vehicles and all camping units on parkland except on established commercial premises and designated historic sites.
- Draining or dumping refuse or waste, including gray water, from any source, except in places or receptacles provided for such use, is prohibited.

21 Popo Agi

Location: 7 miles southwest of Lander

GPS: N43 44.56' / W108 49.21'

Facilities and amenities: Vault toilets, fire rings, trash receptacles, picnic tables, drinking water

Elevation: 6,640 feet

Road conditions: Paved

Hookups: None

Sites: 20 basic sites, 4 walk-in tent sites

Maximum RV length: 40 feet long

Season: May 1 through Sept 30

Fees: $ for Wyoming residents, $$ for nonresidents

Maximum stay: 14 days in any 30-day period

Management: Sinks Canyon State Park

Reservations: All sites must be reserved by logging on to wyo-park.com or calling Reserve America at (877) 996-7275.

Pets: All pets must be leashed. Pet waste must be cleaned up and properly disposed of.

Quiet hours: 10 p.m. to 6 a.m. Turn off generators. Excessive noise is prohibited.

ADA compliance: No

Activities: Fishing, hiking, wildlife viewing

Finding the campground: In Lander go south on 5th Street to the end of the road. Turn right (west) onto the paved Sinks Canyon Road/SR 131 and travel 7 miles. The Sinks Canyon Road will turn south as you leave Lander. The campground is on the left side of the road.

About the campground: Every available inch seems to be accounted for to accommodate larger RVs. The pine trees here are engulfed in an assortment of aspen and underbrush thick enough that travel is maintained along the paved roads and cement walking areas. Even though the units seem very close, the foliage presents a type of isolation and noise curtain. Firewood is listed on the website as available (donations suggested). No firewood can be gathered or transported into the camping area.

22 Sawmill

Location: 6 miles southwest of Lander

GPS: N43 45.44' / W108 47.98'

Facilities and amenities: Vault toilets, fire rings, trash receptacles, picnic tables, drinking water

Elevation: 6,161 feet

Road conditions: Paved

Hookups: None

Sites: 5 basic sites

Maximum RV length: 40 feet long

Season: May 1 through Sept 30

Fees: $ for Wyoming residents, $$ for nonresidents

Maximum stay: 14 days in any 30-day period

Management: Sinks Canyon State Park

Reservations: All sites must be reserved by logging on to wyo-park.com or calling Reserve America at (877) 996-7275.

Pets: All pets must be leashed. Pet waste must be cleaned up and properly disposed of.

Quiet hours: 10 p.m. to 6 a.m. Turn off generators. Excessive noise is prohibited.

ADA compliance: Yes

Activities: Fishing, hiking, wildlife viewing

Finding the campground: In Lander go south on 5th Street to the end of the road. Turn right (west) onto the paved Sinks Canyon Road/SR 131 and travel 6 miles. The Sinks Canyon Road will turn south as you leave Lander. The campground is on the left side of the road.

About the campground: This is mainly a day-use area, but there are five units for tents or RVs that tend to be held for late arrivals even though the reservation process still must be utilized. We found that particular feature a "good idea" with no way to really exercise it at the campground with no cell service, but the thought was good. The drinking water still comes from a hand pump and the large day-use picnic area can provide some extra noise common to social gatherings. In the end, that quiets down as the sun sets.

Laramie Area

Campers have a choice between windy, flat prairie reservoirs and high-elevation cold in the Laramie area. The more popular campgrounds reside at elevations that generate cool days and cold nights all summer. Weather plays an important role in opening and closing dates for most of the campgrounds, with some not available until late July.

The Vedauwoo Rocks between Laramie and Cheyenne offer rock climbers and adventure seekers an unforgettable experience. The unusual formations and placement of these ancient granite rocks go beyond the imagination. Golden aspen leaves make for an even greater enhancement for fall visitors.

Cheyenne Frontier Days may officially be the last week of July, but camping areas fill up and prices go up long before the events begin and extend well past the "bucking bronco" dust cloud settles to the ground. Should this be of no interest to you, plan ahead to move toward Laramie or Casper.

Picture-postcard mountain view.

#	Name	Group sites	Tents	RV sites	Total # of sites	Picnic area	Toilets	Hookups	Showers	Drinking water	Dump station	Handicap	Recreation	Fee	Season	Can reserve	Stay limit
1	Vedauwoo		14	12	26	X	V			X		X	HiRcPi	$	6/1-10/31		14
2	Tie City			18	18		V						FHiM	$	6/1-10/31	X	14
3	Yellow Pine			19	19		V						FHi	$	6/1-8/31		14
4	Pine			6	6		V						FHi	$	6/1-9/30		14
5	Bow River			13	13		V			X			FHi	$	6/15-9/15		14
6	Deep Creek			11	11		V			X			FHi	$	7/1-9/30		14
7	Willow			16	16		V			X			FHi	$	6/1-9/30		14
8	North Fork			60	60		V						FHiW	$	6/1-9/30		14
9	Nash Fork			27	27		V						FHiPi	$	6/1-9/30		14
10	Brooklyn Lake			19	19		V			X			FHiW	$	6/1-9/30		14
11	Sugar Loaf			16	16		V			X			FHiWPh	$	7/15-9/15		14
12	Silver Lake			17	17		V			X			FHiWPh	$	7/15-9/30		14
13	Lake Owen			35	35		V						FHiWPh	$	6/1-10/31		14
14	Pelton Creek			16	16		V			X			FHRm	$	6/15-10/15		14
15	Rob Roy			65	65	X	V			X			FBoPiRm	$	6/15-10/15		14
16	Hawk Springs State Park		24				V			X			FBoSBrBdBe	$-$$	Year-round	X	14

A = archery, Bd = boat dock, Be = beach, Bo = boating, Br = boat ramp, El = electric hookups, F = fishing, Hi = hiking, Hr = horseback riding, M = mountain biking, Pg = playground, Ph = photography, Pi = picnicking, Rc = rock climbing, Rm = rocks and minerals, S = swimming, V = vault toilet, W = wildlife viewing, Wa = water hookups

Curt Gowdy State Park

#	Name	Group sites	Tents	RV sites	Total # of sites	Picnic area	Toilets	Hookups	Showers	Drinking water	Dump station	Handicap	Recreation	Fee	Season	Can reserve	Stay limit
17	Tumble Weeds			17	17		V	ElWa		X		X	FBoPi	$-$$	5/1–9/30	X	14
18	Hecla Point	1		7	7		V						FHi	$-$$	5/1–9/30	X	14
19	Federal Bay	1		3	4	X	V					X	FBoPi	$-$$	5/1–9/30	X	14
20	Jerre's Haven		4	13	17	X	V	El		X			FPi	$-$$	5/1–9/30	X	14
21	Silver Crown			9	9	X	V			X			FBoPiBrPg	$-$$	5/1–9/30	X	14
22	Camp Russell	1		9	10	X	V	El		X		X	FPiPg	$-$$	5/1–9/30	X	14
23	Happy Jack	4		3	7	X	V	El		X		X	F	$-$$	5/1–9/30	X	14
24	North Causeway		3	5	8		V						HiMHrA	$-$$	5/1–9/30	X	14
25	Aspen Grove			13	13		V						FPi	$-$$	5/1–9/30	X	14
26	South Causeway		3	16	19		V					X	F	$-$$	5/1–9/30	X	14
27	Pole Mountain		4		4		V						Hi	$-$$	5/1–9/30	X	14
28	Twin Bays		7		7		V						FHi	$-$$	5/1–9/30	X	14
29	Sherman Hills	1		9	10	X	V			X		X	FBoBrPgPi	$-$$	5/1–9/30	X	14
30	Granite Point	1		9	11	X	V			X			FBoBrPiPg	$-$$	5/1–9/30	X	14
31	Crystal Lake West			13	13	X	V			X		X	FPi	$-$$	5/1–9/30	X	14
32	Twin Lakes Creek			4	4	X	V			X			FPi	$-$$	5/1–9/30	X	14
33	Crystal Lake East			21	21	X	V			X			FBoBrPiPg	$-$$	5/1–9/30	X	14

A = archery, Bd = boat dock, Be = beach, Bo = boating, Br = boat ramp, El = electric hookups, F = fishing, Hi = hiking, Hr = horseback riding, M = mountain biking, Pg = playground, Ph = photography, Pi = picnicking, Rc = rock climbing, Rm = rocks and minerals, S = swimming, V = vault toilet, W = wildlife viewing, Wa = water hookups

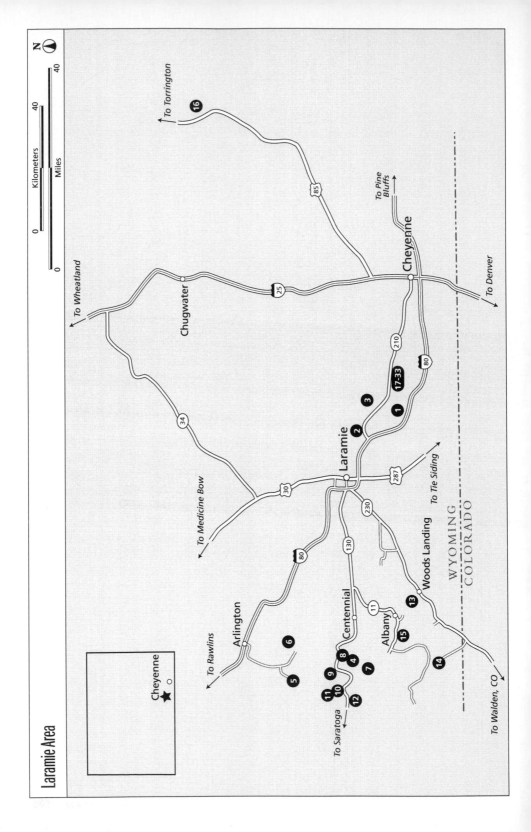

Laramie Area

1 Vedauwoo

Location: 17 miles east of Laramie
GPS: N41 9.28' / W105 22.91'
Facilities and amenities: Vault toilets, fire rings, trash receptacles, picnic tables, drinking water
Elevation: 8,280 feet
Road conditions: Paved
Hookups: None
Sites: 12 basic sites, 14 tents-only
Maximum RV length: 32 feet long
Season: June–Oct, weather permitting
Fees: $ per night, Golden Age and Access Passport holders half price
Maximum stay: 14 days
Management: Medicine Bow National Forest, Laramie Ranger District, 2468 Jackson St., Laramie, WY 82070; (307) 745-2300
Reservations: First-come, first-served
Pets: Pets must be on a leash.
Quiet hours: 10 p.m. to 6 a.m. (turn off generators)
ADA compliance: Yes
Activities: Hiking, rock climbing, picnicking
Finding the campground: Take I-80 east of Laramie for 15.8 miles to the Vedauwoo Road/exit 329. Turn left and travel 1.2 miles. Turn left at the Vedauwoo Recreation Area sign and travel 0.3 mile.
About the campground: Native Americans gave these dynamic rock formations their name, which means "earth born." Reportedly, they believed spirits piled these rocks up during a playful period. Paved roads and parking areas along with easy access to the interstate add up to a lot of use. There are both easy and technical climbing opportunities here, along with all of the related dangers, including death. Gnarly pine trees struggle for survival while stunted aspen seem to be less tormented in this environment. Level paved parking units make exploring more inviting. Our visit during the week found a few empty places. Even if you do not prefer to climb rocks, a camera is a must. Dynamic pictures can still be had without the dangers. A host occupies one of the sites. Firewood gathering requires some work.

2 Tie City

Location: 12 miles east of Laramie
GPS: N41 15.18' / W105 26.25'
Facilities and amenities: Vault toilet, fire rings, trash receptacle, picnic tables
Elevation: 8,618 feet
Road conditions: Gravel, narrow and rough in places
Hookups: None
Sites: 18 basic sites

Maximum RV length: 32 feet long

Season: June–Oct, weather permitting

Fees: $ per night, Golden Age and Access Passport holders half price

Maximum stay: 14 days

Management: Medicine Bow National Forest, Laramie Ranger District, 2468 Jackson St., Laramie, WY 82070; (307) 745-2300

Reservations: National Recreation Reservation Service toll-free at (877) 444-6777 or online at recreation.gov

Pets: Pets must be on a leash.

Quiet hours: 10 p.m. to 6 a.m. (turn off generators)

ADA compliance: No

Activities: Fishing, hiking, mountain biking

Finding the campground: Take I-80 east of Laramie for 9.5 miles to WY 210/exit 323; take exit 323 at the Summit Rest Area. Turn left onto Happy Jack Road/WY 210 and travel 1 mile. Turn right at the campground sign and travel 0.25 mile.

About the campground: Old aspens hedge in the single-lane dirt road at the entrance to the campground. Spruce trees and tall grass take over gradually and have established complete control at the end of the campground. The pull-throughs look like the easiest to level in this rolling terrain. A host occupies one of the units. Firewood appears to be easily gathered from nearby deadfall. Getting into the campground may seem like a roller coaster, but the layout makes each site unique.

3 Yellow Pine

Location: 13 miles east of Laramie

GPS: N41 15.14' / W105 24.68'

Facilities and amenities: Vault toilet, fire rings, picnic tables

Elevation: 8,348 feet

Road conditions: Improved dirt

Hookups: None

Sites: 19 basic sites

Maximum RV length: 32 feet long

Season: June–Aug, weather permitting

Fees: $ per night, Golden Age and Access Passport holders half price

Maximum stay: 14 days

Management: Medicine Bow National Forest, Laramie Ranger District, 2468 Jackson St., Laramie, WY 82070; (307) 745-2300

Reservations: First-come, first-served

Pets: Pets must be on a leash.

Quiet hours: 10 p.m. to 6 a.m. (turn off generators)

ADA compliance: No

Activities: Fishing, hiking

Finding the campground: Take I-80 east of Laramie for 9.5 miles to WY 210/exit 323; take exit 323 at the Summit Rest Area. Turn left onto Happy Jack Road/WY 210 and travel 2 miles. Turn right at the Happy Jack Recreation Area sign and travel 1 mile, bearing left.

The sign on FR 719 showed the Pole Creek Campground being 1 mile away as well, though we found the access with a locked gate and an unmaintained sort of roadway. In our search we found it listed as a group camping site that will require a phone call to the ranger district to access.

About the campground: Aspen and pine trees in the camping area are just tall enough to provide shade and promote a sense of privacy, with more mature trees defining the campground boundary. The units are far enough apart to allow a time of solitude or open up to making new friends with a wave and an invitation to share a campfire. As of our visit, there was no designated host, but that could change. This would be an excellent place to set up a base camp and go exploring. There is no major evidence of a lot of usage here, which could be very pleasing for those who like to feel alone, though there is no guarantee. Be sure to bring plenty of drinking water, as there is none at the campground. Brook trout are available in the south fork of Lodgepole Creek but will take a little legwork to get to.

4 Pine

Location: 31 miles west of Laramie
GPS: N41 19.22' / W106 9.95'
Facilities and amenities: Vault toilet, fire rings, picnic tables
Elevation: 8,620 feet
Road conditions: Paved with gravel spurs
Hookups: None
Sites: 6 basic sites
Maximum RV length: 16 feet long
Season: June–Sept, weather permitting
Fees: $ per night, Golden Age and Access Passport holders half price
Maximum stay: 14 days
Management: Medicine Bow National Forest, Laramie Ranger District, 2468 Jackson St., Laramie, WY 82070; (307) 745-2300
Reservations: First-come, first-served
Pets: Pets must be leashed at all times and kept within your designated campsite.
Quiet hours: 10 p.m. to 6 a.m. (turn off generators)
ADA compliance: No
Activities: Fishing, hiking
Finding the campground: Take WY 130 west out of Laramie for 30 miles, passing through Centennial. Turn left onto the paved Barber Lake Road and travel 1 mile. The campground is on the right side of the road.
About the campground: Shade is lacking, with plenty of stumps to prove it was here at one time. When clouds are absent, the tradeoff is a much better night sky view for stargazers with an added benefit of much easier trailer positioning (no tree branch racing stripes). The heat is not that overbearing in this high-elevation campground, and the nearby Libby Creek delivers plenty of rock-bashing background music. The units are all back-in with a one-way entrance and exit. If you

miss the main gate, don't try sneaking in the back way. If another trailer is on the way out, a real nightmare comes to life. Be sure to bring plenty of drinking water. The pump was padlocked as of our visit and the official website states that available water is dependent upon well and/or pump maintenance and water-testing requirements.

5 Bow River

Location: 15 miles south of Elk Mountain
GPS: N41 30.92' / W106 22.20'
Facilities and amenities: Pit toilets, fire rings, picnic tables, drinking water
Elevation: 8,588 feet
Road conditions: Gravel to improved dirt
Hookups: None
Sites: 13 basic sites
Maximum RV length: 32 feet long
Season: Mid-June through mid-Sept, weather permitting
Fees: $ per night, $ per day for additional vehicle, Golden Age and Access Passport holders half price
Maximum stay: 14 days
Management: Medicine Bow National Forest, Brush Creek Ranger District, (307) 326-5258
Reservations: First-come, first-served
Pets: Pets must be on a leash no longer than 6 feet and under control at all times.
Quiet hours: 10 p.m. to 6 a.m. (turn off generators)
ADA compliance: No
Activities: Fishing, hiking
Finding the campground: Coming from the west on I-80, take the Elk Mountain/WY 72 exit 255, travel about 3.5 miles, and turn left, crossing the bridge just past the museum. Follow this road for about 0.5 mile. Continue straight ahead (south) on CR 101, which turns into FR 101 at the national forest boundary, for 15 miles. Turn right onto FR 100 and travel about 0.2 mile. The campground is on the left, a short distance after crossing the bridge.

From the east on I-80, take CR 402/exit 260, travel about 2 miles, and turn left onto CR 101.
About the campground: The forest housing this isolated camping area contains spruce, fir, and aspen, with construction in progress to remove hazardous dead ones. Most of the camping sites were closed as of our visit but are anticipated to be completed by the time this book is published. The back-in spaces are adequately placed to create a sense of privacy but will require some effort to get level. Medicine Bow River is close by for the anglers in your group, though it appeared to be challenging to fish in. Do not forget bug spray. Mosquitoes have no mercy and invite all living relatives to the funeral of the one you crush. This is a perfect place to spend some quality quiet time for those who prefer a more "primitive" type of setting.

6 Deep Creek

Location: 55 miles west of Laramie
GPS: N41 27.45' / W106 16.43'
Facilities and amenities: Vault toilets, fire rings, picnic tables, drinking water (not guaranteed)
Elevation: 10,084 feet
Road conditions: Gravel
Hookups: None
Sites: 11 basic sites
Maximum RV length: 20 feet long
Season: July–Sept, weather permitting
Fees: $ per night, Golden Age and Access Passport holders half price
Maximum stay: 14 days
Management: Medicine Bow National Forest, Brush Creek/Hayden Ranger District, 2171 Highway 130, Saratoga, WY 82331; (307) 326-5258
Reservations: First-come, first-served
Pets: Pets must be leashed or under physical restrictive control.
Quiet hours: 10 p.m. to 6 a.m. (turn off generators)
ADA compliance: No
Activities: Fishing, hiking
Finding the campground: Coming from the west on I-80, take the Elk Mountain/WY 72 exit 255, travel about 3.5 miles, and turn left, crossing the bridge just past the museum. Follow this road for about 0.5 mile. Continue straight ahead (south) on CR 101, which turns into FR 101 at the national forest boundary, for 25 miles. The campground is on the left.

From the east on I-80, take CR 402/exit 260, travel about 2 miles, and turn left onto CR 101.
About the campground: Old fir trees stand guard over this time-worn area, with plenty of stories to tell about past visitors. Drinking water is not guaranteed, so be sure to bring plenty. A sign at the entrance explains that due to budget cuts, this will no longer be a full-service campground. If donations are ample enough, the water will continue to be tested. There is no trash service or host. Deadfall makes firewood gathering rather easy. If you are looking for an isolated place to hide out, this could be it.

7 Willow

Location: 32 miles west of Laramie
GPS: N41 19.31' / W106 10.32'
Facilities and amenities: Vault toilet, fire rings, trash receptacles, picnic tables, limited to non-available drinking water
Elevation: 8,638 feet
Road conditions: Gravel
Hookups: None

Sites: 16 basic sites
Maximum RV length: 22 feet long
Season: June–Sept, weather permitting
Fees: $ per night, Golden Age and Access Passport holders half price
Maximum stay: 14 days
Management: Medicine Bow National Forest, Laramie Ranger District, 2468 Jackson St., Laramie, WY 82070; (307) 745-2300
Reservations: First-come, first-served
Pets: Pets must be leashed at all times and kept within your designated campsite.
Quiet hours: 10 p.m. to 6 a.m. (turn off generators)
ADA compliance: No
Activities: Fishing, hiking
Finding the campground: Take WY 130 west out of Laramie for 30 miles, passing through Centennial. Turn left onto the paved Barber Lake Road and travel 1.5 miles. Turn right at the campground sign and travel 0.5 mile.
About the campground: Libby Creek makes a bend here that divides this campground into two areas. The willow brush hiding the ice-cold water of the creek grows high overhead, with pine trees adding to the shadows in various places. A 22-foot trailer can fit but will take some maneuvering and backing skills for a spot along the Libby Creek bank near the entrance. There is easier parking at the end of the campground, but it is a single-lane road so there will be times that it takes a combined effort of more than one party to arrive. As with the previous campground, be sure to bring plenty of drinking water as it is not guaranteed to be available.

8 North Fork

Location: 35 miles west of Laramie
GPS: N41 21.60' / W106 10.22'
Facilities and amenities: Vault toilets, fire rings, trash receptacles, picnic tables
Elevation: 9,186 feet
Road conditions: Gravel
Hookups: None
Sites: 60 basic sites
Maximum RV length: 30 feet long
Season: June–Sept, weather permitting
Fees: $ per night, Golden Age and Access Passport holders half price
Maximum stay: 14 days
Management: Medicine Bow National Forest, Laramie Ranger District, 2468 Jackson St., Laramie, WY 82070; (307) 745-2300
Reservations: First-come, first-served
Pets: Pets must be leashed at all times and kept within your designated campsite.
Quiet hours: 10 p.m. to 6 a.m. (turn off generators)
ADA compliance: No

Activities: Fishing, hiking, wildlife viewing

Finding the campground: Take WY 130 west out of Laramie for 34 miles, passing through Centennial. Turn right onto the gravel Sand Lake Road/FR 101 and travel 1 mile. The campground is on the left.

About the campground: The lower the elevation, the higher the spruce, fir, and pine trees. Rainbow and brook trout dwell in the nearby North Fork Little Laramie River. Weather may not allow camping in this popular area until well into July. The units have plenty of space in between and appear to be well positioned so your neighbors don't come into view too much. Fishing will take some footwork unless you're one of the lucky ones to find a campsite along the bank of the North Fork Little Laramie River. A variety of trout await your attempt to invite them for a meal.

⑨ Nash Fork

Location: 33 miles west of Laramie
GPS: N41 21.52' / W106 14.00'
Facilities and amenities: Vault toilets, fire rings, grills, trash receptacles, picnic tables
Elevation: 10,209 feet
Road conditions: Gravel
Hookups: None
Sites: 27 basic sites
Maximum RV length: 22 feet long
Season: June–Sept, weather permitting
Fees: $ per night, Golden Age and Access Passport holders half price
Maximum stay: 14 days
Management: Medicine Bow National Forest, Laramie Ranger District, (307) 745-2300
Reservations: First-come, first-served
Pets: Pets must be on a leash no longer than 6 feet and under control at all times.
Quiet hours: 10 p.m. to 6 a.m. (turn off generators)
ADA compliance: No
Activities: Fishing, hiking, picnicking
Finding the campground: Take WY 130 west out of Laramie for 33 miles. Turn right at the sign and travel 0.5 mile.
About the campground: Spruce and scattered lodgepole pine fill the gaps between large boulders at this spot, which is at 10,000 feet. On our visit here in the middle of July, the snowdrifts still stood 4 feet high or more. The brushy alpine meadows hosted an icy breeze and wildflowers. The sun might feel warm from time to time, but there is a whole lot more cold than heat in the area. A host is present at the campground.

1O Brooklyn Lake

Location: 34 miles west of Laramie
GPS: N41 22.44' / W106 14.83'
Facilities and amenities: Vault toilets, fire rings, grills, trash receptacles, picnic tables, drinking water
Elevation: 10,584 feet
Road conditions: Gravel
Hookups: None
Sites: 19 basic sites
Maximum RV length: 22 feet long
Season: Mid-July through mid-Sept
Fees: $ per night, Golden Age and Access Passport holders half price
Maximum stay: 14 days
Management: Medicine Bow National Forest, Laramie Ranger District, (307) 745-2300
Reservations: First-come, first-served
Pets: Pets must be on a leash no longer than 6 feet and under control at all times.
Quiet hours: 10 p.m. to 6 a.m. (turn off generators)
ADA compliance: No
Activities: Fishing, hiking, wildlife viewing
Finding the campground: Take WY 130 west out of Laramie for 33 miles. Turn right at the sign onto Brooklyn Lake Road and travel 2 miles.
About the campground: This campground does not open until late summer, and exactly when it does is a function of weather. On our visit in the middle of July, the opening date appeared to be some time further into the future. Brooklyn Lake is nestled in alpine meadows close to the campground. Spruce trees living here show signs of a difficult life. The elevation probably makes things a bit different—since it is more than 10,000 feet above sea level. Breathing gets hard for some individuals at this height.

11 Sugar Loaf

Location: 37 miles west of Laramie
GPS: N41 21.29' / W106 17.66'
Facilities and amenities: Vault toilets, fire rings, trash receptacles, picnic tables, drinking water
Elevation: 10,810 feet
Road conditions: Narrow gravel road with small campsites
Hookups: None
Sites: 16 basic sites
Maximum RV length: 22 feet long
Season: Mid-July through Sept, dependent upon snowmelt
Fees: $ per night, Golden Age and Access Passport holders half price
Maximum stay: 14 days

Management: Medicine Bow National Forest, Laramie Ranger District, (307) 745-2300

Reservations: First-come, first-served

Pets: Pets must be on a leash no longer than 6 feet and under control at all times.

Quiet hours: 10 p.m. to 6 a.m. (turn off generators)

ADA compliance: No

Activities: Fishing, hiking, wildlife viewing, photography

Finding the campground: Directions from Laramie: 40 miles west on WY 130, then 1 mile north into the recreation area.

About the campground: Mountain scenery is abundant here—do not forget your camera and some winter clothes. At 11,000 feet when the sun goes down, so does the temperature. Douglas fir reside here with other alpine vegetation, with a fair distance between units. Keep in mind that generators are not allowed to run during the quiet hours so alternative heating may be required if the RV you have gets chilled.

12 Silver Lake

Location: 56 miles west of Laramie

GPS: N41 18.89' / W106 21.55'

Facilities and amenities: Vault toilets, fire rings, trash receptacles, picnic tables, drinking water

Elevation: 10,474 feet

Road conditions: Gravel

Hookups: None

Sites: 17 basic sites

Maximum RV length: 32 feet long

Season: July–Sept, weather permitting

Fees: $ per night, Golden Age and Access Passport holders half price

Maximum stay: 14 days

Management: Medicine Bow National Forest, Brush Creek/Hayden Ranger District, (307) 326-5258

Reservations: First-come, first-served

Pets: Pets must be leashed or under physical restrictive control.

Quiet hours: 10 p.m. to 6 a.m. Turn off generators. Keep voices and music down.

ADA compliance: No

Activities: Fishing, hiking, wildlife viewing, photography

Finding the campground: From Saratoga travel south on WY 130 for 8 miles to the 130/230 intersection. Turn left and travel 24 miles up WY 130 to Silver Lake Campground. From Centennial stay on WY 130 for 18 miles to reach Silver Lake Campground.

About the campground: The spruce trees have been thinned out in the campground with a well-defined boundary away from the camping units. The snow can still be present well into July among these units so don't forget warmer clothes. This campground is advertised to open on July 1, but don't count on it. The elevation is more than 10,000 feet. Between the height and lack of sun in the thick forest, opening day might well be at the end of July. A foot trail leads to Silver Lake and fishing opportunities.

13 Lake Owen

Location: 36 miles west of Laramie
GPS: N41 8.66' / W106 6.27'
Facilities and amenities: Vault toilets, fire rings, trash receptacles, picnic tables
Elevation: 8,966 feet
Road conditions: Gravel
Hookups: None
Sites: 35 basic sites
Maximum RV length: 22 feet long
Season: June–Oct
Fees: $ per night, $ per additional vehicle, Golden Age and Access Passport holders half price
Maximum stay: 14 days
Management: Medicine Bow National Forest, Laramie Ranger District, 2468 Jackson St., Laramie, WY; (307) 745-2300
Reservations: First-come, first-served
Pets: Pets must be leashed.
Quiet hours: 10 p.m. to 6 a.m. (turn off generators)
ADA compliance: No
Activities: Fishing, hiking, wildlife viewing, photography
Finding the campground: From Laramie take WY 130 west for 21.7 miles to WY 11. Turn left onto WY 11 and continue through Albany 10.9 miles. The pavement ends at Albany. Continue on the gravel road past the forest boundary for 2.2 miles to FR 513 on the left. The FR 513 sign is not visible until you make the turn. It is basically the first left turn after entering the national forest. Turn left onto FR 513 and travel for 2.5 miles to FR 517. Turn left onto FR 517 and continue for 1.5 miles to FR 540—this road sign is also not visible until you make the turn. Turn right and travel 2.8 miles to campground.
About the campground: An aspen thicket engulfs one side of the campground, and the remaining area finds shade under pine trees. Firewood is not too far away, though you might consider picking up some deadfall along the way. A host may occupy one of the sites depending upon personnel availability. On a sunny morning the snowcapped mountains to the north stand above the green forest in stark contrast. It could prove difficult to keep your eye on a bobber if you are fishing. A caboose is still in place at the trailhead parking area just before embarking on the main campground access road. A forest fire has altered the appearance, though it is still easy to identify. This is part of Medicine Bow Rail line of days long gone by. There are also some skeletons of camping units ravaged by the fire that may or may not be resurrected in the future, but it is a stark reminder of how devastating and unforgiving a fire can be.

14 Pelton Creek

Location: 52 miles southwest of Laramie
GPS: N41 4.35' / W106 18.19'
Facilities and amenities: Vault toilets, fire rings, picnic tables, drinking water
Elevation: 8,259 feet
Road conditions: Gravel
Hookups: None
Sites: 16 basic sites
Maximum RV length: 16 feet long
Season: Mid-June through mid-Oct
Fees: $ per night, Golden Age and Access Passport holders half price
Maximum stay: 14 days
Management: Medicine Bow National Forest, Laramie Ranger District, 2468 Jackson St., Laramie, WY 82070; (307) 745-2300
Reservations: First-come, first-served
Pets: Pets must be leashed at all times and kept within your designated campsite.
Quiet hours: 10 p.m. to 6 a.m. (turn off generators)
ADA compliance: No
Activity: Fishing, hiking, gold panning
Finding the campground: From Laramie take WY 230 west for 40.6 miles to the National Forest Recreation Area sign on FR 898. Turn right onto FR 898 and go 8.7 miles to the campground.
About the campground: As of our visit in 2022, there were "Campground Closed" signs posted on the access road just off of WY 230. Apparently, the Mullen Fire is the reported cause for the closure, with ongoing efforts to bring the campground back into use. It is expected to be back in service by the time this book is on the market, though it is difficult to say how much it will change the individual camping sites. A call to the Laramie Ranger District is recommended before making the trip into this area.

15 Rob Roy

Location: 46 miles west of Laramie
GPS: N41 13.22' / W106 15.01'
Facilities and amenities: Vault toilets, fire rings, trash receptacles, picnic tables, drinking water, boat ramp
Elevation: 9,546 feet
Road conditions: Gravel
Hookups: None
Sites: 65 basic sites
Maximum RV length: 35 feet long
Season: Mid-June through mid-Oct, dependent upon snow conditions
Fees: $ per night, $ for day use (picnicking), Golden Age and Access Passport holders half price

Maximum stay: 14 days
Management: Medicine Bow National Forest, Laramie Ranger District, (307) 745-2300
Reservations: First-come, first-served
Pets: Pets must be on a leash.
Quiet hours: 10 p.m. to 6 a.m. (turn off generators)
ADA compliance: No
Activities: Fishing, boating, picnicking, rockhounding
Finding the campground: Take WY 130 west out of Laramie for 24 miles. Turn left onto the paved WY 11 and travel 11 miles. Continue through Albany on the gravel FR 500 for 11 miles. Turn left at the campground sign.
About the campground: Rock hounds may find gold panning in Douglas Creek rewarding. Douglas Creek flows into and out of Rob Roy Reservoir. The back-in units are not that difficult to negotiate, but finding an empty one on a weekend might be. The lure of cold water and big fish draws plenty of visitors. The picnic area is closest to the lake. Camping units are uniformly located along several loops that get progressively farther from the reservoir. The ones closest to the lake are the closest to the entrance and also the first to be occupied.

16 Hawk Springs State Park

Location: 55 miles northeast of Cheyenne
GPS: N41 42.76' / W104 11.82'
Facilities and amenities: Vault toilets, fire rings, trash receptacles, drinking water, boat ramp, boat dock, beach, playground
Elevation: 4,486 feet
Road conditions: Very rough gravel
Hookups: None
Sites: 24 primitive sites, walk-in only
Maximum RV length: None
Season: May 1 through Sept 30, drinking water available; Oct 1 through Apr 30 no water
Fees: Wyoming resident fees: Daily use $, camping $. Nonresident fees: Daily use $$, camping $$
Maximum stay: 14 days in a 30-day period
Management: Hawk Springs State Recreation Area, (307) 836-2334
Reservations: All sites must be reserved online at wyomingstateparks.reserveamerica.com or by phone at (877) 996-7275.
Pets: Pets must be on a leash.
Quiet hours: 10 p.m. to 6 a.m.
ADA compliance: No
Activities: Fishing, boating, swimming
Finding the campground: Take I-25 north out of Cheyenne to exit 17. Take US 85 north for 51 miles. At the Hawk Springs sign, turn right onto the gravel CR 225/K4 and travel 3 miles.
About the campground: Huge cottonwood trees shade the compact parking spaces. Water recreation draws the largest group of visitors. Reports of blue heron could motivate bird-watchers to pack their binoculars. This popular spot is often full on weekends and holidays. *Note:* Glass containers must be used in vehicles and camping structures.

Curt Gowdy State Park

Overview

Season: May–Sept
Fees: Reservation fee: $4 residents, $8 nonresidents
Maximum stay: 14 days
Management: Wyoming State Parks, Historic Sites & Trails, (307) 777-6323. Curt Gowdy State Park, (307) 632-7946.
Reservations: Online at wyomingstateparks.reserveamerica.com or by phone at (877) 996-7275
Pets:

- All pets must be in a vehicle or on a leash no longer than 10 feet and physically controlled at all times.
- Pets shall not be left unattended for any time greater than 1 hour.
- Persons with pets on lawns and picnic and camping areas will be responsible for proper removal of the animals' waste.
- Parcels of parkland may be closed permanently or for a specified period of time to domestic pets in order to protect wildlife or adjacent landowners' rights.

Quiet hours: 10 p.m. to 6 a.m. Turn off generators. All generators and electronic devices or any actions that may disturb the peace are prohibited during these hours.
Conduct:

- Glass beverage containers are prohibited outside vehicles and all camping units on parkland except on established commercial premises and designated historic sites.
- Draining or dumping refuse or waste, including gray water, from any source, except in places or receptacles provided for such use, is prohibited.

17 Tumble Weeds

Location: 25 miles west of Cheyenne
GPS: N41 10.75' / W105 14.21'
Facilities and amenities: Vault toilets, fire rings, picnic tables, playground, drinking water
Elevation: 7,259 feet
Road conditions: Gravel
Hookups: Water and 50-amp electricity
Sites: 17 basic sites
Maximum RV length: 50 feet long
Season: May–Sept
Fees: Wyoming resident fees: Daily use $, camping $. Nonresident fees: Daily use $$, camping $$.
Maximum stay: 14 days
Management: Curt Gowdy State Park, 1264 Granite Springs Rd., Cheyenne, WY; (307) 632-7946 (superintendent)
Reservations: All sites must be reserved online at wyomingstateparks.reserveamerica.com or by phone at (877) 996-7275.
Pets: All pets must be in a vehicle or on a leash no longer than 10 feet and physically controlled at all times.
Quiet hours: 10 p.m. to 6 a.m. (turn off generators)
ADA compliance: Yes
Activities: Fishing, boating, picnicking
Finding the campground: Take I-80 east of Laramie for 9.5 miles to WY 210/exit 323; take exit 323 at the Summit Rest Area. Turn left onto Happy Jack Road/WY 210 and travel 14 miles. Or at Cheyenne take exit 10B/Happy Jack Road and follow it west out of Cheyenne for 24 miles. Either of these will arrive at the main north access road. There is a south gate, however, as of our visit, we found the gravel road access to be very rough. Take the main access road/Granite Springs Road south for 0.9 mile. Turn left, travel a short distance, turn left onto the gravel access road, and travel 0.1 mile.
About the campground: No swimming is allowed here so if that is an important activity for you, this is not the place to be. Shade is absent, but the electricity keeps the air-conditioning going when it is needed. There is a lot of open space here, so wind can visit with a vengeance, but the views are worth it.

18 Hecla Point

Location: 25.3 miles west of Cheyenne
GPS: N41 10.80' / W105 14.04'
Facilities and amenities: Vault toilet, fire rings, picnic tables
Elevation: 7,246 feet
Road conditions: Gravel
Hookups: None

Sites: 7 basic sites
Maximum RV length: 40 feet long
Season: May–Sept
Fees: Wyoming resident fees: Daily use $, camping $. Nonresident fees: Daily use $$, camping $$.
Maximum stay: 14 days
Management: Curt Gowdy State Park, 1264 Granite Springs Rd., Cheyenne, WY; (307) 632-7946 (superintendent)
Reservations: First-come, first-served
Pets: All pets must be in a vehicle or on a leash no longer than 10 feet and physically controlled at all times.
Quiet hours: 10 p.m. to 6 a.m. (turn off generators)
ADA compliance: No
Activities: Fishing, hiking
Finding the campground: Take I-80 east of Laramie for 9.5 miles to WY 210/exit 323; take exit 323 at the Summit Rest Area. Turn left onto Happy Jack Road/WY 210 and travel 14 miles. Or at Cheyenne take exit 10B/Happy Jack Road and follow it west out of Cheyenne for 24 miles. Either of these will arrive at the main north access road. There is a south gate, however, as of our visit, we found the gravel road access to be very rough. Take the main access road/Granite Springs Road south for 0.9 mile. Turn left, travel a short distance, turn left onto the gravel access road, and travel 0.3 mile.
About the campground: There is good shoreline access here and a sort of isolation with a good amount of space between the units. There is some foliage that helps, but it is not overabundant or available at each spot. The more desirable spots are occupied quickly.

19 Federal Bay

Location: 25.4 miles west of Cheyenne
GPS: N41 10.82' / W105 13.87'
Facilities and amenities: Vault toilet, fire rings, picnic tables, shelters, boat ramp, picnic shelter
Elevation: 7,523 feet
Road conditions: Gravel
Hookups: None
Sites: 3 basic sites, 1 group
Maximum RV length: 30 feet long
Season: May–Sept
Fees: Wyoming resident fees: Daily use $, camping $. Nonresident fees: Daily use $$, camping $$.
Maximum stay: 14 days
Management: Curt Gowdy State Park, 1264 Granite Springs Rd., Cheyenne, WY; (307) 632-7946 (superintendent)
Reservations: All sites must be reserved online at wyomingstateparks.reserveamerica.com or by phone at (877) 996-7275.
Pets: All pets must be in a vehicle or on a leash no longer than 10 feet and physically controlled at all times.

Quiet hours: 10 p.m. to 6 a.m. (turn off generators)

ADA compliance: Yes

Activities: Fishing, boating, picnicking

Finding the campground: Take I-80 east of Laramie for 9.5 miles to WY 210/exit 323; take exit 323 at the Summit Rest Area. Turn left onto Happy Jack Road/WY 210 and travel 14 miles. Or at Cheyenne take exit 10B/Happy Jack Road and follow it west out of Cheyenne for 24 miles. Either of these will arrive at the main north access road. There is a south gate, however, as of our visit, we found the gravel road access to be very rough. Take the main access road/Granite Springs Road south for 0.9 mile. Turn left, travel a short distance, turn left onto the gravel access road, and travel 0.4 mile.

About the campground: The sites might be a long way apart, but there isn't much between them to block the view. It might take a little work to get the windows pointing in a direction toward a view you would like. Of course, that is all relative to what your interests are.

20 Jerre's Haven

Location: 26 miles west of Cheyenne

GPS: N41 10.82' / W105 14.47'

Facilities and amenities: Vault toilet, fire rings, picnic tables, playground, shelters, drinking water

Elevation: 7,295 feet

Road conditions: Gravel

Hookups: Electricity (50-amp)

Sites: 13 pull-through sites, 4 tents-only

Maximum RV length: 100 feet long

Season: May–Sept

Fees: Wyoming resident fees: Daily use $, camping $. Nonresident fees: Daily use $$, camping $$.

Maximum stay: 14 days

Management: Curt Gowdy State Park, 1264 Granite Springs Rd., Cheyenne, WY; (307) 632-7946 (superintendent)

Reservations: All sites must be reserved online at wyomingstateparks.reserveamerica.com or by phone at (877) 996-7275.

Pets: All pets must be in a vehicle or on a leash no longer than 10 feet and physically controlled at all times.

Quiet hours: 10 p.m. to 6 a.m. (turn off generators)

ADA compliance: No

Activities: Fishing, picnicking

Finding the campground: Take I-80 east of Laramie for 9.5 miles to WY 210/exit 323; take exit 323 at the Summit Rest Area. Turn left onto Happy Jack Road/WY 210 and travel 14 miles. Or at Cheyenne take exit 10B/Happy Jack Road and follow it west out of Cheyenne for 24 miles. Either of these will arrive at the main north access road. There is a south gate, however, as of our visit, we found the gravel road access to be very rough. Take the main access road/Granite Springs Road south for 1 mile. The campground is on the right.

About the campground: The views are good but leveling is not. The activities help to make camping worthwhile, but if you are one for setting at a campfire most of the day, one of the other campgrounds might be better.

21 Silver Crown

Location: 26 miles west of Cheyenne
GPS: N41 10.80' / W105 14.40'
Facilities and amenities: Vault toilets, fire rings, picnic tables, group picnic shelter, playground, boat ramp, drinking water
Elevation: 7,266 feet
Road conditions: Gravel
Hookups: None
Sites: 9 basic sites
Maximum RV length: 30 feet long
Season: May–Sept
Fees: Wyoming resident fees: Daily use $, camping $. Nonresident fees: Daily use $$, camping $$.
Maximum stay: 14 days
Management: Curt Gowdy State Park, 1264 Granite Springs Rd., Cheyenne, WY; (307) 632-7946 (superintendent)
Reservations: All sites must be reserved online at wyomingstateparks.reserveamerica.com or by phone at (877) 996-7275.
Pets: All pets must be in a vehicle or on a leash no longer than 10 feet and physically controlled at all times.
Quiet hours: 10 p.m. to 6 a.m. (turn off generators)
ADA compliance: No
Activities: Fishing, boating, picnicking
Finding the campground: Take I-80 east of Laramie for 9.5 miles to WY 210/exit 323; take exit 323 at the Summit Rest Area. Turn left onto Happy Jack Road/WY 210 and travel 14 miles. Or at Cheyenne take exit 10B/Happy Jack Road and follow it west out of Cheyenne for 24 miles. Either of these will arrive at the main north access road. There is a south gate, however, as of our visit, we found the gravel road access to be very rough. Take the main access road/Granite Springs Road south for 1 mile. The campground access is on the left.
About the campground: The primary attraction here is the relatively close access to the boat ramp. There are still views and other activities to engage in when the waves are too tall.

22 Camp Russell

Location: 26 miles west of Cheyenne
GPS: N41 10.80' / W105 14.42'
Facilities and amenities: Vault toilet, fire rings, picnic tables, shelters, playground, drinking water
Elevation: 7,271 feet
Road conditions: Gravel
Hookups: Electric (50-amp)
Sites: 9 basic sites, 1 group
Maximum RV length: 55 feet long

Season: May–Sept

Fees: Wyoming resident fees: Daily use $, camping $. Nonresident fees: Daily use $$, camping $$.

Maximum stay: 14 days

Management: Curt Gowdy State Park, 1264 Granite Springs Rd., Cheyenne, WY; (307) 632-7946 (superintendent)

Reservations: All sites must be reserved online at wyomingstateparks.reserveamerica.com or by phone at (877) 996-7275.

Pets: All pets must be in a vehicle or on a leash no longer than 10 feet and physically controlled at all times.

Quiet hours: 10 p.m. to 6 a.m. (turn off generators)

ADA compliance: Yes

Activities: Fishing, picnicking

Finding the campground: Take I-80 east of Laramie for 9.5 miles to WY 210/exit 323; take exit 323 at the Summit Rest Area. Turn left onto Happy Jack Road/WY 210 and travel 14 miles. Or at Cheyenne take exit 10B/Happy Jack Road and follow it west out of Cheyenne for 24 miles. Either of these will arrive at the main north access road. There is a south gate, however, as of our visit, we found the gravel road access to be very rough. Take the main access road/Granite Springs Road south for 1 mile. The campground is on the left just past the Silver Crown access.

About the campground: Rolling grassy hills dominate this spacious area. The parking places snuggle up pretty close to the lake's edge, with a lot of distance between other campers. The terrain provides little wind protection, though it could be worse.

23 Happy Jack

Location: 26 miles west of Cheyenne

GPS: N41 10.79' / W105 14.50'

Facilities and amenities: Restroom, fire rings, picnic tables, shelters, drinking water

Elevation: 7,274 feet

Road conditions: Gravel

Hookups: Electric (50-amp)

Sites: 3 basic sites, 4 group sites

Maximum RV length: 40 feet long

Season: May–Sept

Fees: Wyoming resident fees: Daily use $, camping $. Nonresident fees: Daily use $$, camping $$.

Maximum stay: 14 days

Management: Curt Gowdy State Park, 1264 Granite Springs Rd., Cheyenne, WY; (307) 632-7946 (superintendent)

Reservations: All sites must be reserved online at wyomingstateparks.reserveamerica.com or by phone at (877) 996-7275.

Pets: All pets must be in a vehicle or on a leash no longer than 10 feet and physically controlled at all times.

Quiet hours: 10 p.m. to 6 a.m. (turn off generators)

ADA compliance: Yes, group site
Activities: Fishing, picnicking
Finding the campground: Take I-80 east of Laramie for 9.5 miles to WY 210/exit 323; take exit 323 at the Summit Rest Area. Turn left onto Happy Jack Road/WY 210 and travel 14 miles. Or at Cheyenne take exit 10B/Happy Jack Road and follow it west out of Cheyenne for 24 miles. Either of these will arrive at the main north access road. There is a south gate, however, as of our visit, we found the gravel road access to be very rough. Take the main access road/Granite Springs Road south for 1 mile. The campground access road is on the left.
About the campground: There are additional units scattered along the lakeshore, though they appear to be more for angler access than camping. Shade is scarce with the exception of the group shelter.

24 North Causeway

Location: 27.1 miles west of Cheyenne
GPS: N41 10.78' / W105 14.60'
Facilities and amenities: Vault toilet, fire rings, picnic tables
Elevation: 7,263 feet
Road conditions: Gravel
Hookups: None
Sites: 5 basic sites, 3 tents-only
Maximum RV length: 50 feet long
Season: May–Sept
Fees: Wyoming resident fees: Daily use $, camping $. Nonresident fees: Daily use $$, camping $$.
Maximum stay: 14 days
Management: Curt Gowdy State Park, 1264 Granite Springs Rd., Cheyenne, WY; (307) 632-7946 (superintendent)
Reservations: All sites must be reserved online at wyomingstateparks.reserveamerica.com or by phone at (877) 996-7275.
Pets: All pets must be in a vehicle or on a leash no longer than 10 feet and physically controlled at all times.
Quiet hours: 10 p.m. to 6 a.m. (turn off generators)
ADA compliance: No
Activities: Fishing
Finding the campground: Take I-80 east of Laramie for 9.5 miles to WY 210/exit 323; take exit 323 at the Summit Rest Area. Turn left onto Happy Jack Road/WY 210 and travel 14 miles. Or at Cheyenne take exit 10B/Happy Jack Road and follow it west out of Cheyenne for 24 miles. Either of these will arrive at the main north access road. There is a south gate, however, as of our visit, we found the gravel road access to be very rough. Take the main access road/Granite Springs Road south for 2.1 miles. The campground access road is on the left.
About the campground: This place might be more for those who like to get away from the crowds. Water access is still present but not as easy as other areas.

25 Aspen Grove

Location: 27.4 miles west of Cheyenne
GPS: N41 10.75' / W105 14.76'
Facilities and amenities: Vault toilet, fire rings, picnic tables, shelters
Elevation: 7,245 feet
Road conditions: Gravel
Hookups: None
Sites: 13 basic sites
Maximum RV length: 60 feet long
Season: May–Sept
Fees: Wyoming resident fees: Daily use $, camping $. Nonresident fees: Daily use $$, camping $$.
Maximum stay: 14 days
Management: Curt Gowdy State Park, 1264 Granite Springs Rd., Cheyenne, WY; (307) 632-7946 (superintendent)
Reservations: All sites must be reserved online at wyomingstateparks.reserveamerica.com or by phone at (877) 996-7275.
Pets: All pets must be in a vehicle or on a leash no longer than 10 feet and physically controlled at all times.
Quiet hours: 10 p.m. to 6 a.m. (turn off generators)
ADA compliance: No
Activities: Hiking, mountain biking, horseback riding, archery
Finding the campground: Take I-80 east of Laramie for 9.5 miles to WY 210/exit 323; take exit 323 at the Summit Rest Area. Turn left onto Happy Jack Road/WY 210 and travel 14 miles. Or at Cheyenne take exit 10B/Happy Jack Road and follow it west out of Cheyenne for 24 miles. Either of these will arrive at the main north access road. There is a south gate, however, as of our visit, we found the gravel road access to be very rough. Take the main access road/Granite Springs Road south for 2.1 miles. Turn to the right onto the gravel access road and travel 0.3 mile.
About the campground: This campground has more appeal for those who want to explore the country outside the fishing and boating activities.

26 South Causeway

Location: 28 miles west of Cheyenne
GPS: N41 10.55' / W105 14.24'
Facilities and amenities: Vault toilet, fire rings, picnic tables
Elevation: 7,232 feet
Road conditions: Gravel
Hookups: None
Sites: 16 basic sites, 3 tents-only
Maximum RV length: 55 feet long

Season: May–Sept
Fees: Wyoming resident fees: Daily use $, camping $. Nonresident fees: Daily use $$, camping $$.
Maximum stay: 14 days
Management: Curt Gowdy State Park, 1264 Granite Springs Rd., Cheyenne, WY; (307) 632-7946
Reservations: All sites must be reserved online at wyomingstateparks.reserveamerica.com or by phone at (877) 996-7275.
Pets: All pets must be in a vehicle or on a leash no longer than 10 feet and physically controlled at all times.
Quiet hours: 10 p.m. to 6 a.m. (turn off generators)
ADA compliance: Yes
Activities: Fishing, hiking
Finding the campground: Take I-80 east of Laramie for 9.5 miles to WY 210/exit 323; take exit 323 at the Summit Rest Area. Turn left onto Happy Jack Road/WY 210 and travel 14 miles. Or at Cheyenne take exit 10B/Happy Jack Road and follow it west out of Cheyenne for 24 miles. Either of these will arrive at the main north access road. There is a south gate, however, as of our visit, we found the gravel road access to be very rough. Take the main access road/Granite Springs Road south for 2.2 miles. The asphalt turns to gravel past here.
About the campground: There is some wind protection here, and this area is accessible to those with disabilities. It is also settled into an area that from all appearances should have less wind impact than some of the camping areas in the ridgetops.

27 Pole Mountain

Location: 28.2 miles north of Cheyenne
GPS: N41 10.43' / W105 14.24'
Facilities and amenities: Vault toilet, fire rings, grills, picnic tables
Elevation: 7,315 feet
Road conditions: Gravel
Hookups: None
Sites: 4 tents-only
Maximum RV length: RVs are not allowed here.
Season: May–Sept
Fees: Wyoming resident fees: Daily use $, camping $. Nonresident fees: Daily use $$, camping $$.
Maximum stay: 14 days
Management: Curt Gowdy State Park, 1264 Granite Springs Rd., Cheyenne, WY; (307) 632-7946 (superintendent)
Reservations: All sites must be reserved online at wyomingstateparks.reserveamerica.com or by phone at (877) 996-7275.
Pets: All pets must be in a vehicle or on a leash no longer than 10 feet and physically controlled at all times.
Quiet hours: 10 p.m. to 6 a.m. (turn off generators)
ADA compliance: No

Activities: Hiking

Finding the campground: Take I-80 east of Laramie for 9.5 miles to WY 210/exit 323; take exit 323 at the Summit Rest Area. Turn left onto Happy Jack Road/WY 210 and travel 14 miles. Or at Cheyenne take exit 10B/Happy Jack Road and follow it west out of Cheyenne for 24 miles. Either of these will arrive at the main north access road. There is a south gate, however, as of our visit, we found the gravel road access to be very rough. Take the main access road/Granite Springs Road south for 2.4 miles.

About the campground: This campground seems to be more focused on hiking than any water activities at the reservoir. There are trees and rock formations tempting the adventurous.

28 Twin Bays

Location: 28.1 miles west of Cheyenne
GPS: N41 10.39' / W105 14.36'
Facilities and amenities: Vault toilet, fire rings, picnic tables
Elevation: 7,309 feet
Road conditions: Gravel
Hookups: None
Sites: 7 tents-only
Maximum RV length: NA
Season: May–Sept
Fees: Wyoming resident fees: Daily use $, camping $. Nonresident fees: Daily use $$, camping $$.
Maximum stay: 14 days
Management: Curt Gowdy State Park, 1264 Granite Springs Rd., Cheyenne, WY; (307) 632-7946
Reservations: All sites must be reserved online at wyomingstateparks.reserveamerica.com or by phone at (877) 996-7275.
Pets: All pets must be in a vehicle or on a leash no longer than 10 feet and physically controlled at all times.
Quiet hours: 10 p.m. to 6 a.m. (turn off generators)
ADA compliance: No
Activities: Fishing, hiking
Finding the campground: Take I-80 east of Laramie for 9.5 miles to WY 210/exit 323; take exit 323 at the Summit Rest Area. Turn left onto Happy Jack Road/WY 210 and travel 14 miles. Or at Cheyenne take exit 10B/Happy Jack Road and follow it west out of Cheyenne for 24 miles. Either of these will arrive at the main north access road. There is a south gate, however, as of our visit, we found the gravel road access to be very rough. Take the main access road/Granite Springs Road south for 2.5 miles. The campground is on the left. The Granite Springs Road will turn to gravel.

About the campground: These rolling sandy hills sit in the most forested part of the park. Maneuvering could be tricky, but it's well worth the effort. Sites here are positioned to create a sense of privacy even with close neighbors. This place appears to be the first choice for most locals.

29 Sherman Hills

Location: 28.5 miles west of Cheyenne
GPS: N41 10.3' / W105 14.24'
Facilities and amenities: Vault toilet, fire rings, picnic tables, shelters, boat ramp, playground, drinking water
Elevation: 7,268 feet
Road conditions: Gravel
Hookups: None
Sites: 9 basic sites, 1 group site
Maximum RV length: 40 feet long
Season: May–Sept
Fees: Wyoming resident fees: Daily use $, camping $. Nonresident fees: Daily use $$, camping $$.
Maximum stay: 14 days
Management: Curt Gowdy State Park, 1264 Granite Springs Rd., Cheyenne, WY; (307) 632-7946 (superintendent)
Reservations: All sites must be reserved online at wyomingstateparks.reserveamerica.com or by phone at (877) 996-7275.
Pets: All pets must be in a vehicle or on a leash no longer than 10 feet and physically controlled at all times.
Quiet hours: 10 p.m. to 6 a.m. (turn off generators)
ADA compliance: Yes
Activities: Fishing, boating, picnicking
Finding the campground: Take I-80 east of Laramie for 9.5 miles to WY 210/exit 323; take exit 323 at the Summit Rest Area. Turn left onto Happy Jack Road/WY 210 and travel 14 miles. Or at Cheyenne take exit 10B/Happy Jack Road and follow it west out of Cheyenne for 24 miles. Either of these will arrive at the main north access road. There is a south gate, however, as of our visit, we found the gravel road access to be very rough. Take the main access road/Granite Springs Road south for 2.9 miles. The campground is on the left. The Granite Springs Road will turn to gravel.
About the campground: Pine trees hide this hollow from the road and the lake. A small bay pokes into one of the three sites. This compact place offers the best protection from both wind and sun. In exchange for the shelter, a hike is required to access the lake, unless you happen to be next in line for the unit beside the bay.

30 Granite Point

Location: 28.7 miles west of Cheyenne
GPS: N41 10.39' / W105 14.24'
Facilities and amenities: Vault toilet, fire rings, picnic tables, shelters, boat ramp, playground, drinking water
Elevation: 7,240 feet
Road conditions: Gravel

Hookups: None
Sites: 9 basic sites, 1 tents-only, 1 group
Maximum RV length: 40 feet long
Season: May–Sept
Fees: Wyoming resident fees: Daily use $, camping $. Nonresident fees: Daily use $$, camping $$.
Maximum stay: 14 days
Management: Curt Gowdy State Park, 1264 Granite Springs Rd., Cheyenne, WY; (307) 632-7946 (superintendent)
Reservations: All sites must be reserved online at wyomingstateparks.reserveamerica.com or by phone at (877) 996-7275.
Pets: All pets must be in a vehicle or on a leash no longer than 10 feet and physically controlled at all times.
Quiet hours: 10 p.m. to 6 a.m. (turn off generators)
ADA compliance: No
Activities: Fishing, boating, picnicking
Finding the campground: Take I-80 east of Laramie for 9.5 miles to WY 210/exit 323; take exit 323 at the Summit Rest Area. Turn left onto Happy Jack Road/WY 210 and travel 14 miles. Or at Cheyenne take exit 10B/Happy Jack Road and follow it west out of Cheyenne for 24 miles. Either of these will arrive at the main north access road. There is a south gate, however, as of our visit, we found the gravel road access to be very rough. Take the main access road/Granite Springs Road south for 3.1 miles. The campground is on the left. The Granite Springs Road will turn to gravel.
About the campground: The views are pleasant to the eye. Noise from the road could be problematic if it is a holiday or a weekend.

31 Crystal Lake West

Location: 30.3 miles west of Cheyenne
GPS: N41 10.61' / W105 14.43'
Facilities and amenities: Vault toilets, fire rings, picnic tables, shelters, drinking water
Elevation: 6,989 feet
Road conditions: Gravel
Hookups: None
Sites: 13 basic sites
Maximum RV length: 30 feet long
Season: May–Sept
Fees: Wyoming resident fees: Daily use $, camping $. Nonresident fees: Daily use $$, camping $$.
Maximum stay: 14 days
Management: Curt Gowdy State Park, 1264 Granite Springs Rd., Cheyenne, WY; (307) 632-7946 (superintendent)
Reservations: All sites must be reserved online at wyomingstateparks.reserveamerica.com or by phone at (877) 996-7275.

Pets: All pets must be in a vehicle or on a leash no longer than 10 feet and physically controlled at all times.

Quiet hours: 10 p.m. to 6 a.m. (turn off generators)

ADA compliance: Yes

Activities: Fishing, picnicking

Finding the campground: Take I-80 east of Laramie for 9.5 miles to WY 210/exit 323; take exit 323 at the Summit Rest Area. Turn left onto Happy Jack Road/WY 210 and travel 14 miles. Or at Cheyenne take exit 10B/Happy Jack Road and follow it west out of Cheyenne for 24 miles. Either of these will arrive at the main north access road. There is a south gate, however, as of our visit we found the gravel road access to be very rough. Take the main access road/Granite Springs Road south for 4.7 miles. The campground is on the left. The Granite Springs Road will turn to gravel.

About the campground: Fishing and pleasant views are calling from this area.

32 Twin Lakes Creek

Location: 30.5 miles west of Cheyenne

GPS: N41 9.45' / W105 12.53'

Facilities and amenities: Vault toilet, fire rings, picnic tables, drinking water

Elevation: 6,993 feet

Road conditions: Gravel

Hookups: None

Sites: 4 basic sites

Maximum RV length: 25 feet long

Season: May–Sept

Fees: Wyoming resident fees: Daily use $, camping $. Nonresident fees: Daily use $$, camping $$.

Maximum stay: 14 days

Management: Curt Gowdy State Park, 1264 Granite Springs Rd., Cheyenne, WY; (307) 632-7946 (superintendent)

Reservations: All sites must be reserved online at wyomingstateparks.reserveamerica.com or by phone at (877) 996-7275.

Pets: All pets must be in a vehicle or on a leash no longer than 10 feet and physically controlled at all times.

Quiet hours: 10 p.m. to 6 a.m. (turn off generators)

ADA compliance: No

Activities: Fishing, picnicking

Finding the campground: Take I-80 east of Laramie for 9.5 miles to WY 210/exit 323; take exit 323 at the Summit Rest Area. Turn left onto Happy Jack Road/WY 210 and travel 14 miles. Or at Cheyenne take exit 10B/Happy Jack Road and follow it west out of Cheyenne for 24 miles. Either of these will arrive at the main north access road. There is a south gate, however, as of our visit, we found the gravel road access to be very rough. Take the main access road/Granite Springs Road south for 4.9 miles. The campground is on the left. The Granite Springs Road will turn to gravel.

About the campground: Lakeshore appeal tops the list, with the boating and fishing opportunities as an added benefit.

33 Crystal Lake East

Location: 30.8 miles west of Cheyenne
GPS: N41 9.24' / W105 12.15'
Facilities and amenities: Vault toilets, fire rings, picnic tables, playground, drinking water, boat ramp
Elevation: 6,989 feet
Road conditions: Gravel
Hookups: None
Sites: 21 basic sites
Maximum RV length: 25 feet long
Season: May–Sept
Fees: Wyoming resident fees: Daily use $, camping $. Nonresident fees: Daily use $$, camping $$.
Maximum stay: 14 days
Management: Curt Gowdy State Park, 1264 Granite Springs Rd., Cheyenne, WY; (307) 632-7946 (superintendent)
Reservations: All sites must be reserved online at wyomingstateparks.reserveamerica.com or by phone at (877) 996-7275.
Pets: All pets must be in a vehicle or on a leash no longer than 10 feet and physically controlled at all times.
Quiet hours: 10 p.m. to 6 a.m. (turn off generators)
ADA compliance: No
Activities: Fishing, boating, picnicking
Finding the campground: Take I-80 east of Laramie for 9.5 miles to WY 210/exit 323; take exit 323 at the Summit Rest Area. Turn left onto Happy Jack Road/WY 210 and travel 14 miles. Or at Cheyenne take exit 10B/Happy Jack Road and follow it west out of Cheyenne for 24 miles. Either of these will arrive at the main north access road. There is a south gate, however, as of our visit, we found the gravel road access to be very rough. Take the main access road/Granite Springs Road south for 5.2 miles. The campground is on the left. The Granite Springs Road will turn to gravel.
About the campground: Almost all of the camping units are along Crystal Lake's shoreline here. It is only a short distance from those that are not.

Pinedale Area

Jim Bridger of mountain-man fame camped in this area many times. The Museum of the Mountain Man located in Pinedale is a must-see attraction, with its excellent displays of artifacts from the fur trade. Ice-cold mountain lakes snuggle into the canyons and other hideaways along the Bridger Wilderness boundary.

Most of the camping areas snuggle up against the Bridger Wilderness. Mountains climb upwards to more than 12,000 feet above sea level. Clear, cold natural lakes frequently reflect snowcapped splendor, with occasional disturbances of rising trout.

The surrounding desert offers plenty of specimens for the diligent rock hound. The petrified wood of the Farson area is well worth investigating.

Fremont Lake.

#	Name	Group sites	Tents	RV sites	Total # of sites	Picnic area	Toilets	Showers	Drinking water	Dump station	Phone	Handicap	Recreation	Fee	Season	Can reserve	Stay limit
1	Whiskey Grove			9	9		V		X				FHiHuWPi	$$	6/1-9/30		14
2	Green River Lakes	3		36	39	X	V		X				FBoHiHuWHrPhPi	$$-$$$$	6/15-9/15		14
3	New Fork Lake			15	15		V						FBoHiWPi	$	6/1-9/30		14
4	Narrows			19	19		V						FBoSHi	$$	5/1-9/30	X	14
5	Boulder Lake			15	15		V						FHiW	$	6/1-9/30		14
6	Fremont Lake	1		52	53	X	V		X				FBoBdBrHiWPi	$$-$$$$$$	5/1-9/30	X	14
7	Half Moon Lake			17	17		V						FBoHiW	$	6/1-9/30		14
8	Willow Lake				Dis		V						FBoBrS	None	6/1-9/30		14
9	Trails End			8	8		V						HiBaHr	$$	6/1-9/30		14
10	North Boulder Lake			4	Dis		V						FBoSHi	None	Year-round		14
11	South Boulder Lake			Dis	Dis		V						FBoSHi	None	Year-round		14
12	New Fork River			2	Dis		V						FBrHiPhWHr	None	Year-round		14
13	Scab Creek			9	9		V		X				FHiRcWPh	None	5/1-9/30		14
14	Warren Bridge			16	16		V		X	X			FHiW	$	5/1-10/31		14
15	Soda Lake				Dis		V						FBoHiM	None	5/1-11/30		14

Ba = backpacking, Bd = boat dock, Bo = boating, Br = boat ramp, Dis = dispersed, F = fishing, Hi = hiking, Hr = horseback riding, Hu = hunting, M = mountain biking, Ph = photography, Pi = picnicking, Rc = rock climbing, S = swimming, V = vault toilet, W = wildlife viewing

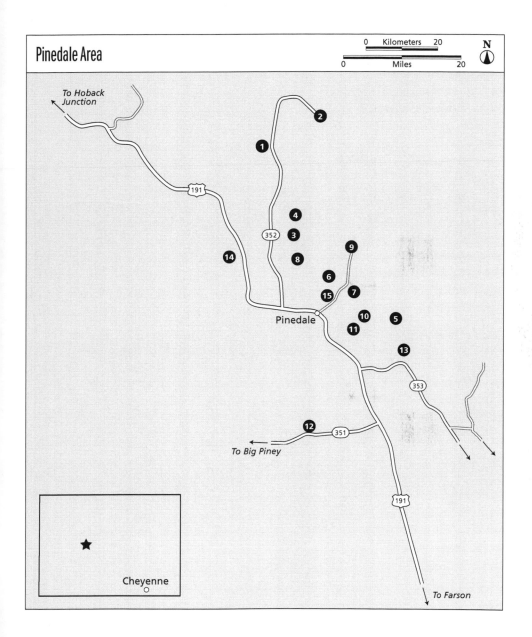

Pinedale Area

0　Kilometers　20

0　Miles　20

N

To Hoback
Junction

191

352

Pinedale

353

351

To Big Piney

191

Cheyenne

To Farson

1 Whiskey Grove

Location: 39.5 miles northwest of Pinedale
GPS: N43 15.23' / W110 1.12'
Facilities and amenities: Vault toilet, fire rings, picnic tables, trash receptacles, drinking water (hand pump)
Elevation: 7,685 feet
Road conditions: Improved dirt
Hookups: None
Sites: 9 basic sites
Maximum RV length: 30 feet long
Season: June–Sept, weather permitting
Fees: $$ per day, Golden Age and Access Passport holders half price
Maximum stay: 14 days
Management: Bridger-Teton National Forest, Pinedale Ranger District, 29 East Fremont Lake Rd. (PO Box 220), Pinedale, WY 82941; (307) 367-4326
Reservations: First-come, first-served
Pets: Pets must be on a leash at all times.
Quiet hours: 10 p.m. to 6 a.m. (turn off generators)
ADA compliance: No
Activities: Fishing, hiking, hunting, wildlife viewing, picnicking
Finding the campground: Take US 191 west out of Pinedale for 6 miles. Turn right (north) onto the paved WY 352 and travel 33 miles. Turn left (south) onto the improved dirt access road and travel 0.5 mile.
About the campground: The Green River runs past campers at this hidden spot, and the pine and spruce trees shading each unit are not visible from the sagebrush flats above. It is almost like someone took a great big bucketful out of the side hill. The camping loop circles around the extent of this "dugout," and just looking from the road going past it, you'd never know it was there.

2 Green River Lakes

Location: 56 miles northwest of Pinedale
GPS: N43 18.94' / W109 51.79'
Facilities and amenities: Vault toilet, fire rings, picnic tables, trash receptacles, drinking water
Elevation: 8,063 feet
Road conditions: Many miles of very rough rocky access road
Hookups: None
Sites: 36 basic sites, 3 group sites
Maximum RV length: 40 feet long
Season: Mid-June through mid-Sept, weather permitting
Fees: $$ per day per single site, Golden Age and Access Passport holders half price, $$$$ per day per group of up to 35 individuals

Maximum stay: 14 days
Management: Bridger-Teton National Forest, Pinedale Ranger District, 29 East Fremont Lake Rd. (PO Box 220), Pinedale, WY 82941; (307) 367-4326
Reservations: First-come, first-served
Pets: Pets must be on a leash at all times.
Quiet hours: 10 p.m. to 6 a.m. (turn off generators)
ADA compliance: No
Activities: Fishing, boating, hiking, hunting, wildlife viewing, horseback riding, photography, picnicking
Finding the campground: Take US 191 west out of Pinedale for 6 miles. Turn right onto the paved WY 352 and travel 50 miles. The road will turn to gravel in about 33 miles.
About the campground: The rough rocky road will test everyone and everything making the journey. Be prepared for a frustrating exercise in endurance and bolt-tightening redecoration of unsecured items. This campground has gone from light use to being packed. Additional traffic was created with the explosion of wilderness hikers and explorers racing to obtain parking at the trailhead. The benefits can be worth the grief, but a call to the Ranger District is recommended to make sure the campground is not full. The group areas can be reserved. Groups A and B accommodate thirty-five individuals each. Group C holds seventy, with all three areas requiring foot access.

3 New Fork Lake

Location: 23 miles northwest of Pinedale
GPS: N43 6.29' / W109 56.57'
Facilities and amenities: Vault toilet, fire rings, picnic tables
Elevation: 7,887 feet
Road conditions: Gravel to improved dirt
Hookups: None
Sites: 15 basic sites
Maximum RV length: 20 feet long
Season: June–Sept, weather permitting
Fees: $ per day, Golden Age and Access Passport holders half price
Maximum stay: 14 days
Management: Bridger-Teton National Forest, Pinedale Ranger District, 29 East Fremont Lake Rd. (PO Box 220), Pinedale, WY 82941; (307) 367-4326
Reservations: First-come, first-served
Pets: Pets must be on a leash at all times.
Quiet hours: 10 p.m. to 6 a.m. (turn off generators)
ADA compliance: No
Activities: Fishing, boating, hiking, wildlife viewing, picnicking
Finding the campground: Take US 191 west out of Pinedale for 6 miles. Turn right (north) onto the paved WY 352 and travel 15 miles. Turn right (east) onto the gravel New Fork Lake Road and travel 2 miles. The campground is to the right with a little dogleg sort of turn to access.

About the campground: Aspen trees roll up and down, blanketing the hills with no uniformity, concealing campers and creating a sort of exploration of discovery wondering what one will find. Level spots must be sought, but they can be found. However, if one doesn't mind spending extra time "engineering," a level trailer could create some very delightful memories that go beyond the normal routines. Don't get in a hurry here. The road disappears into cavernous holes and blind corners. The lake is not that far away, with its own secrets, so to speak.

4 Narrows

Location: 26 miles northwest of Pinedale
GPS: N43 6.24' / W109 56.35'
Facilities and amenities: Vault toilet, fire rings, picnic tables
Elevation: 7,832 feet
Road conditions: Gravel to improved dirt
Hookups: None
Sites: 19 basic sites
Maximum RV length: 35 feet long
Season: May–Sept, weather permitting
Fees: $$ per day, Golden Age and Access Passport holders half price
Maximum stay: 14 days
Management: Bridger-Teton National Forest, Pinedale Ranger District, 29 East Fremont Lake Rd. (PO Box 220), Pinedale, WY 82941; (307) 367-4326
Reservations: National Recreation Reservation Service toll-free at (877) 444-6777 or online at recreation.gov
Pets: Pets must be on a leash at all times.
Quiet hours: 10 p.m. to 6 a.m. (turn off generators)
ADA compliance: No
Activities: Fishing, boating, swimming, hiking
Finding the campground: Take US 191 west out of Pinedale for 6 miles. Turn right (north) onto the paved WY 352 and travel 15 miles. Turn right (east) onto the gravel New Fork Lake Road and travel 5 miles.
About the campground: There are so many aspen trees here it could almost qualify as a forest of its own. The lower loop bearing to the right at the entrance has some ups and downs with level parking. Tight turns make it a little compact. The upper loop bearing to the left at the entrance stretches out along somewhat flat ground above the lakeshore. Foot-worn paths work their way through wild roses, grass, and other shrubbery to the lake. The upper portion of New Fork Lake laps against the rocky shore below a fairly steep bank. To some extent, the Narrows Campground divides this lake into two separate bodies of water. A host may not be present, dependent on the availability of personnel. This is bear country, so be aware of the necessary precautions. Trash service and drinking water are not provided here. There are reviews stating that reserved sites have not been honored, and with no host on-site and no cell phone service, things can get very unpleasant. A phone call to the ranger district is advised to verify the presence of a host before making the trek.

5 Boulder Lake

Location: 25 miles southeast of Pinedale
GPS: N42 51.33' / W109 37.13'
Facilities and amenities: Vault toilet, fire rings, picnic tables
Elevation: 7,298 feet
Road conditions: Gravel
Hookups: None
Sites: 15 basic sites
Maximum RV length: 6 back-in from 12 to 49 feet long, 6 pull-through from 75 to 126 feet long
Season: June–Sept, weather permitting
Fees: $ per day, Golden Age and Access Passport holders half price
Maximum stay: 14 days
Management: Bridger-Teton National Forest, Pinedale Ranger District, 29 East Fremont Lake Rd. (PO Box 220), Pinedale, WY 82941; (307) 367-4326
Reservations: First-come, first-served
Pets: Pets must be on a leash at all times.
Quiet hours: 10 p.m. to 6 a.m. (turn off generators)
ADA compliance: No
Activities: Fishing, hiking, wildlife viewing
Finding the campground: Take US 191 south out of Pinedale for about 12 miles. Turn left (east) onto the paved WY 353 and travel 3 miles to Boulder Lake Road. Turn left (north) onto the CR 125, which will turn into FR 370780, and travel about 15 miles. Bear left at the lodge to cross Boulder Creek and access the campground.
About the campground: Camping units hide quite well in this mixed forest of pine and aspen trees. After crossing the bridge, a long continuous loop provides access to nice level parking spots. The very rough road getting here may deter many would-be campers. That or the easier access of other campgrounds not too far away.

6 Fremont Lake

Location: 7 miles northeast of Pinedale
GPS: N42 56.38' / W109 47.82'
Facilities and amenities: Host on-site, vault toilets, fire rings, grills, food-storage lockers, picnic tables, trash receptacles, drinking water, boat ramp and dock
Elevation: 7,516 feet
Road conditions: Paved to gravel at the end units
Hookups: None
Sites: 52 basic sites, 1 group site
Maximum RV length: 60 feet long
Season: May–Sept, weather permitting
Fees: $$ per day, $$$$$$ per day for group, Golden Age and Access Passport holders half price

Maximum stay: 14 days

Management: Bridger-Teton National Forest, Pinedale Ranger District, 29 East Fremont Lake Rd. (PO Box 220), Pinedale, WY 82941; (307) 367-4326

Reservations: National Recreation Reservation Service toll-free at (877) 444-6777 or online at recreation.gov

Pets: Pets must be on a leash at all times.

Quiet hours: 10 p.m. to 6 a.m. (turn off generators)

ADA compliance: No

Activities: Fishing, boating, hiking, wildlife viewing, picnicking

Finding the campground: Take the Fremont Lake Road northeast out of Pinedale, via South Pine Drive, and travel about 6 miles. Turn left (north) at the Fremont Lake sign and follow the signs to the campground. There are no signs designating the campground until arriving at the actual access.

About the campground: The steep ridge on the eastern edge of the campground does not allow sunshine until later hours of the morning, which can be appealing for sleeping in late in the early morning mountain chill. In addition, the longer daylight in the evening makes campfire fellowship a pleasant pastime. Large igneous rocks, ranging from marble size to huge car size, are scattered about in a disarray of piles, with mature Douglas fir staking claim to any available ground and cedar trees competing for anything that's left. The lower loop is the closest to the lakeshore, but the upper loop seems to offer a greater distance between units for those who want a little more isolation. There are some first-come, first-served sites, but they fill fast on holidays and warm weekends. For those who want to be assured of a camping spot, reservations would be best. Some of the parking aprons are difficult to level longer trailers. Trailers are not recommended in the farthest camping sites.

7 Half Moon Lake

Location: 10 miles north of Pinedale

GPS: N42 56.19' / W109 45.56'

Facilities and amenities: Vault toilet, fire pits, picnic tables

Elevation: 7,615 feet

Road conditions: Improved dirt

Hookups: None

Sites: 17 basic sites

Maximum RV length: A 30-foot trailer will fit but will require unhooking and some backing skills dependent on your site selection.

Season: June–Sept, weather permitting

Fees: $ per day, Golden Age and Access Passport holders half price. As of our visit, a notice of a proposed increase in the fee was posted at the main entrance information sign.

Maximum stay: 14 days

Management: Bridger-Teton National Forest, Pinedale Ranger District, 29 East Fremont Lake Rd. (PO Box 220), Pinedale, WY 82941; (307) 367-4326

Reservations: First-come, first-served

Pets: Pets must be on a leash at all times.

Quiet hours: 10 p.m. to 6 a.m. (turn off generators)
ADA compliance: No
Activities: Fishing, boating, hiking, wildlife viewing
Finding the campground: At the eastern end of Pinedale, turn at the Fremont Lake sign and travel 9 miles. Turn right at the Half Moon Lodge sign onto the gravel road and travel 1 mile.
About the campground: Aspen trees and a thick underbrush fill up the space between Douglas firs sheltering the camping sites here. It almost has a maze sort of structure, leaving one with a question of which fork in the road is the main road. Leveling will take some thought before making a final unhook, but it is not impossible. The boat ramp is farther down the road and well used.

There is no water or trash service provided so special thought and provisions are required to accommodate your needs based upon the length of stay.

8 Willow Lake

Location: 14 miles north of Pinedale
GPS: N42 59.47' / W109 54.02'
Facilities and amenities: Vault toilet, limited fire rings and picnic tables, boat ramp
Elevation: 7,710 feet
Road conditions: The main access is gravel, the campground improved dirt to sand
Hookups: None
Sites: Dispersed
Maximum RV length: 40 feet long
Season: June–Sept, weather permitting
Fees: None
Maximum stay: 14 days
Management: Bridger-Teton National Forest, Pinedale Ranger District, 29 East Fremont Lake Rd. (PO Box 220), Pinedale, WY 82941; (307) 367-4326
Reservations: First-come, first-served
Pets: Pets must be on a leash at all times.
Quiet hours: 10 p.m. to 6 a.m. (turn off generators)
ADA compliance: No
Activities: Fishing, boating, swimming
Finding the campground: On the western end of Pinedale, turn north at the Soda Lake Wildlife Management Area sign. Follow directions to and past Soda Lake on the gravel CR 119. Bear left at Soda Lake and travel a total of 7 miles from Pinedale. At the national forest boundary, bear left just after the cattle guard and travel 4 miles. The improved dirt road gets rough and very narrow toward the end.
About the campground: Pine trees carpet the northeast mountainsides in the distance, but not the campground. Sandy beaches move up well beyond the lakeshore into the parking areas along the south shore. The fire rings and picnic tables are scattered around with no uniformity in the midst of some very loose sand. They seem to be positioned for shade more than site designation. The high ridges surrounding this super-clear mountain lake seem to cut off the infamous Wyoming wind, although it might be more like just slowing it down a little. This pleasant lake produces a lot of photo opportunities with the Wind River Mountains in the background.

9 Trails End

Location: 16 miles north of Pinedale
GPS: N43 0.36' / W109 45.12'
Facilities and amenities: Vault toilets, fire rings, picnic tables
Elevation: 9,360 feet
Road conditions: Paved
Hookups: None
Sites: 8 basic sites
Maximum RV length: 60 feet long
Season: June–Sept, weather permitting
Fees: $$ per day, Golden Age and Access Passport holders half price
Maximum stay: 14 days
Management: Bridger-Teton National Forest, Pinedale Ranger District, 29 East Fremont Lake Rd. (PO Box 220), Pinedale, WY 82941; (307) 367-4326
Reservations: First-come, first-served
Pets: Pets must be on a leash at all times.
Quiet hours: 10 p.m. to 6 a.m. (turn off generators)
ADA compliance: No
Activities: Hiking, backpacking, horseback riding
Finding the campground: At the eastern end of Pinedale, turn north at the Fremont Lake sign and follow the directions to Elkhart Park, 16 miles away.
About the campground: Trailhead parking shares a portion of the lower part of the campground. The upper loop sneaks farther back into the pine forest, with parking spots better suited for pickup campers or tents. Trees seem larger but farther apart in the lower loop. With the possible exception of heavy traffic for the wilderness access, this spot proved lonely—a feature that you might find attractive. Corrals are available for those with horses.

10 North Boulder Lake

Location: 18 miles southeast of Pinedale
GPS: N42 50.49' / W109 42.22'
Facilities and amenities: Vault toilet, fire rings, picnic tables
Elevation: 7,303 feet
Road conditions: Gravel to improved dirt
Hookups: None
Sites: 4 basic sites plus dispersed sites
Maximum RV length: 60 feet long
Season: Year-round, weather permitting
Fees: None
Maximum stay: 14 days
Management: Bureau of Land Management, Pinedale Field Office, 1625 West Pine St., Pinedale, WY 82491; (307) 367-5300; pinedale_wymail@blm.gov

Reservations: First-come, first-served
Pets: Pets must be on a leash.
Quiet hours: Campers courtesy
ADA compliance: No
Activities: Fishing, boating, swimming, hiking
Finding the campground: Take US 191 south out of Pinedale for 11 miles. Turn left (east) onto the gravel Burnt Lake Road and travel 7 miles.
About the campground: Mature aspen trees provide shade here when the leaves are soaking up the available sunshine. It is not a forest by any means, but all the same it offers some very pleasant reprieve from direct wind blasts and intense sun rays on a summer day. Boating is listed as one of the activities on the various sources of information, but it will take some travel to the south side of the lake to get to the boat ramp. Be sure to take along plenty of drinking water as none is provided, and be prepared to deal with processing the trash as this is a pack-it-in, pack-it-out campground.

11 South Boulder Lake

Location: 23 miles southeast of Pinedale
GPS: N42 50.14' / W109 42.26'
Facilities and amenities: Vault toilet, fire rings, picnic tables
Elevation: 7,320 feet
Road conditions: Gravel to improved dirt
Hookups: None
Sites: Dispersed sites
Maximum RV length: 40 feet long
Season: Year-round, weather permitting
Fees: None
Maximum stay: 14 days
Management: Pinedale Field Office, 1625 West Pine St., Pinedale, WY 82491; (307) 367-5300; pinedale_wymail@blm.gov
Reservations: First-come, first-served
Pets: Pets must be on a leash.
Quiet hours: Campers courtesy
ADA compliance: No
Activities: Fishing, boating, swimming, hiking
Finding the campground: Take US 191 south out of Pinedale for 12 miles. Turn left (east) onto the paved WY 353 and travel 3 miles. Turn left (north) at the Boulder Lake Road sign/CR 23125 and travel 7 miles. Turn left (west) at the sign and travel 1 mile.
About the campground: There are no shade trees in this area. Boulders, sagebrush, and wide-open prairie scenes dominate the available parking spots. Evergreen trees, both dead and alive, populate the Boulder River stream banks below the dam, inviting explorers to tackle the challenging terrain for some stream fishing or other discoveries.

12 New Fork River

Location: 35 miles southwest of Pinedale
GPS: N42 36.34' / W109 51.41'
Facilities and amenities: Vault toilet, picnic tables, boat launch
Elevation: 6,844 feet
Road conditions: Gravel to improved dirt
Hookups: None
Sites: 2 plus undesignated dispersed sites
Maximum RV length: NA
Season: Year-round, weather permitting
Fees: None
Maximum stay: 14 days
Management: Pinedale Field Office, 1625 West Pine St., Pinedale, WY 82491; (307) 367-5300; pinedale_wymail@blm.gov
Reservations: First-come, first-served
Pets: Pets must be on a leash.
Quiet hours: Campers courtesy
ADA compliance: No
Activities: Fishing, hiking, photography, wildlife viewing, horseback riding
Finding the campground: Take US 191 south out of Pinedale for 23 miles. Turn right (west) onto WY 351 and travel 5 miles. The campground is across the bridge on the right (north) side of the road.
About the campground: Water failed the test for drinking here. New Fork River flows past with plenty, though it is unlikely that you will want to make your coffee with it. Anglers probably find this spot more appealing. A contractor takes care of the upkeep, though the weeds may get a bit high from time to time, and there is no host or firewood. If you are running late in the day, this might be a great stopover for an early morning departure.

13 Scab Creek

Location: 26 miles southeast of Pinedale
GPS: N42 49.06' / W109 33.80'
Facilities and amenities: Vault toilets, fire rings, picnic tables, drinking water
Elevation: 8,173 feet
Road conditions: Gravel to improved dirt
Hookups: None
Sites: 9 basic sites
Maximum RV length: 20 feet long
Season: May–Sept, weather permitting
Fees: None
Maximum stay: 14 days

Management: Pinedale Field Office, 1625 West Pine St., Pinedale, WY 82491; (307) 367-5300; pinedale_wymail@blm.gov
Reservations: First-come, first-served
Pets: Pets must be on a leash.
Quiet hours: Campers courtesy
ADA compliance: No
Activities: Fishing, hiking, climbing, wildlife viewing, photography
Finding the campground: From Pinedale, drive south on US 191 for 12 miles, turn left (east) at the gas station in the town of Boulder onto WY 353, and travel for 7 miles. Take another left (north) onto Scab Creek Road/CR-122, follow this road for 1.5 miles, and take a slight left onto Scab Creek Access Road/BLM 5423. Follow that until you reach Scab Creek Recreation Area, roughly 5.5 miles.
About the campground: Wilderness access produces a lot of vehicles in the parking area near the campground. Camping units divide the pine forest into nonuniform but semiprivate locations. Aspen trees of different sizes grow near the entrance, helping hide the camping units even more. This is a quiet camping area, with most visitors moving farther into the wilderness.

There are two camping areas with the nine basic units primarily for smaller units. The second area is for those with horse trailers and larger RVs with intentions of camping in the wilderness area via horseback.

14 Warren Bridge

Location: 20 miles northwest of Pinedale on US 191
GPS: N43 1.08' / W110 7.11'
Facilities and amenities: RV dump station, vault toilets, picnic tables, trash cans, fire rings, grills, drinking water
Elevation: 7,473 feet
Road conditions: Campground units and access roads are gravel
Hookups: None
Sites: 16 pull-through, 6 picnic sites
Maximum RV length: Any
Season: May–Oct, weather permitting
Fees: $ per day, Golden Age and Access Passport holders half of standard price
Maximum stay: 14 days
Management: Pinedale Field Office, 1625 West Pine St., Pinedale, WY 82491; (307) 367-5300; pinedale_wymail@blm.gov
Reservations: First-come, first-served
Pets: Pets must be on a leash.
Quiet hours: Campers courtesy
ADA compliance: No
Activities: Fishing, hiking, wildlife viewing
Finding the campground: Take US 191 northwest out of Pinedale for 20 miles. At the Warren Bridge sign, turn left (south) into the campground. (The turn is very close to the sign so slow down beforehand.)

About the campground: The Green River passes by this sagebrush-dominated flat portion of the otherwise rolling desert hills surrounding it. The units are all relatively level with water spigots well placed for use. The dump station is also a real benefit given the limited number of them and with the long-distance driving typically required in the wide-open spaces in Wyoming. Traffic can be heavy at times but does have a noticeable decrease at dark that adds a certain charm to the nighttime quiet. The wind can be difficult to ignore, but the other benefits outweigh the irritation in the long run. Should you find the wind noticeable upon arrival, don't open the driver's side and passenger doors at the same time. Every loose item in the cab will promptly take flight. Overall, this is an excellent area to set up a base camp to set out and explore the local attractions and points of interest.

15 Soda Lake

Location: 5 miles northwest of Pinedale
GPS: N42 57.59' / W109 50.35'
Facilities and amenities: Vault toilets, fire rings, picnic tables
Elevation: 7,589 feet
Road conditions: Gravel to improved dirt
Hookups: None
Sites: Dispersed
Maximum RV length: Any
Season: May–Nov
Fees: None
Maximum stay: 14 days
Management: Wyoming Game and Fish, Pinedale Office, (307) 777-4600
Reservations: First-come, first-served
Pets: Pets allowed
Quiet hours: Campers courtesy
ADA compliance: No
Activities: Fishing, boating, hiking, mountain biking
Finding the campground: On the western end of Pinedale, turn at the Soda Lake Wildlife Management Area sign. Travel 5 miles down the gravel CR 119. There are two access roads into Soda Lake. The second access road is shorter than the first.
About the campground: Wind is a constant companion here with no trees for shade or a wind break. For those that can adapt to enduring its relentless presence, the outdoor activities can be enjoyed without the multitudes found in other more popular spots. Parking is a matter of choice all around this lake. Most campers make use of the fishing activity. The wildlife and Wind River Mountains in the background just add that much more to the experience. Sagebrush and some grass leave plenty of open air to gaze at the mountains by day or stars on a clear night. You will need to bring your own firewood.

Saratoga Area

All-terrain vehicles (ATVs), or in some circles "side-by-sides," are a common sight in any one of the multiple backcountry roads here. Most of the roads, if not all, are remnants of the huge mining operations of Old West origin. Many go by old mine buildings and other historic areas that are not easily reached without an appropriate vehicle. The exact spot cannot be confirmed, but Thomas Edison reportedly discovered the material for the light filament as a result of a fishing trip at Battle Lake in the Saratoga area. As the report goes, a bamboo rod combined with a campfire triggered the event that ultimately gave us the light bulb. Fishing is still popular, though access is undoubtedly improved.

In the southwest portion of this area, moss beards frequently adorn a countless number of older trees, indicating that this is relatively untouched land. Plentiful oak trees make for a most panoramic view when pooled with aspen and mixed evergreens, especially in the fall.

Plenty of room for slide-outs in this spot.

#		Group sites	Tents	RV sites	Total # of sites	Picnic area	Toilets	Hookups	Drinking water	Dump station	Handicap	Recreation	Fee	Season	Can reserve	Stay limit
1	Lincoln Park			12	12		V		X		X	HuFOhv	$	6/15–9/30		14
2	South Brush Creek			20	20		V		X			FHOhvW	$	5/15–9/15		14
3	Ryan Park	1		49	50		V		X			FHi	$	6/1–9/30	X	14
4	French Creek			11	11		V		X			FHiHuOhv	$	6/1–9/30		14
5	Bennett Peak			11	11	X	V		X		X	FHiMWPiHu	$	6/1–11/15		14
6	Corral Creek			6	6	X	V					FHiMWPiHu	$	6/1–11/15		14
7	Six Mile Gap		5	4	9		V		X			FHi	$	6/15–9/15		14
8	Encampment River			8	8	X	V					FSHiMWPh	$	6/1–11/15		14
9	Bottle Creek			12	12	X	V		X			HiPi	$	6/1–9/31		14
10	Hog Park			50	50	X	V		X			FBoHiWPi	$	6/15–9/30	X	14
11	Lost Creek			13	13	X	V		X			HiOhvM	$	6/15–10/31		14
12	Jack Creek			16	16	X	V		X			FHiOhvPi	$	6/15–10/31		14
13	Teton Reservoir			5	5		V					FHiWsWPh	None	6/1–11/30		14
14	Dugway			5	5		V					FPi	None	6/1–10/31		14
	Seminoe State Park															
15	Sunshine Beach			38	38	X	V		X	X	X	FBoSPiOhv	$$–$$$$	Year-round	X	14
16	South Red Hills			19	19	X	V		X	X	X	FBoSPiOhv	$$–$$$$	Year-round	X	14
17	Red Hills North			30	30	X	V	El	X	X	X	FBoSPiOhvBeBdFpPg	$$–$$$	5/1–9/30	X	14

Bd = boat dock, Be = beach, Bo = boating, El = electric hookups, F = fishing, Fp = fishing pier, Hi = hiking, Hu = hunting, M = mountain biking, Ohv = off highway vehicle, Pg = playground, Ph = photography, Pi = picnicking, S = swimming, V = vault toilet, W = wildlife viewing, Ws = water sports

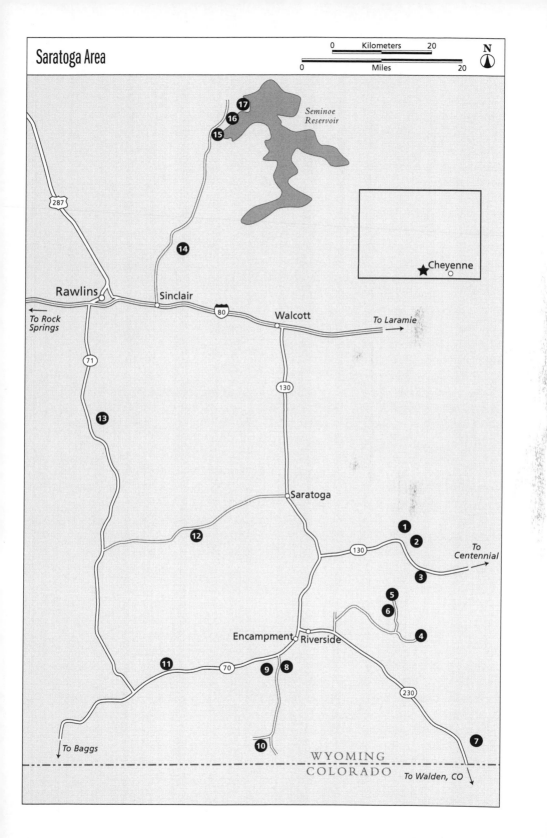

Saratoga Area

Seminoe
Reservoir

Cheyenne

287

To Rock
Springs

Rawlins

Sinclair

80

Walcott

To Laramie

71

130

13

Saratoga

12

130

1
2

To
Centennial

3

5
6

4

Encampment

Riverside

11

70

9
8

230

To Baggs

10

7

WYOMING

COLORADO

To Walden, CO

14

15
16
17

1 Lincoln Park

Location: 20 miles southeast of Saratoga
GPS: N41 22.46' / W106 30.87'
Facilities and amenities: Vault toilets, fire rings, trash receptacles, picnic tables, drinking water
Elevation: 8,090 feet
Road conditions: Gravel
Hookups: None
Sites: 12 basic sites
Maximum RV length: 32 feet long
Season: Mid-June through Sept, weather permitting
Fees: $ per night, $5 per additional vehicle, Golden Age and Access Passport holders half price
Maximum stay: 14 days
Management: Medicine Bow National Forest, Brush Creek/Hayden Ranger District, 2171 Highway 130, Saratoga, WY 82331; (307) 326-5258
Reservations: First-come, first-served
Pets: Pets must be leashed or under physical restrictive control.
Quiet hours: 10 p.m. to 6 a.m. (turn off generators)
ADA compliance: Yes
Activities: Hunting, fishing, OHV
Finding the campground: Take WY 130/230 south out of Saratoga for about 8 miles. Turn left onto WY 130 East and travel 20 miles. At the green camping sign, turn left. The FR 100 road sign will be on your right and is not visible from the main road. This paved road will change to gravel in short order. Travel 3 miles to the campground on the right side of the road.
About the campground: Pine and spruce trees live in the forest holding this campground. Willow brush outlines the creek banks flowing through, though the water flow is considerably lower than our first visit. In the right places fish can be seen, but getting the hook in front of them will be a challenge. There is a portion of the campground farther away from the road with less chance of traffic noise. Also, the lack of shade in the units farther away offers a better view of the night sky, which could be well worth enduring the sunshine. The wheelchair accessibility has been in much better shape. It is still doable, though holes created over the years have developed and could make things interesting.

2 South Brush Creek

Location: 21 miles southeast of Saratoga
GPS: N41 20.69' / W106 30.27'
Facilities and amenities: Vault toilets, fire rings, trash receptacles, picnic tables, drinking water
Elevation: 8,090 feet
Road conditions: Gravel
Hookups: None
Sites: 20 basic sites

Maximum RV length: 25 feet long

Season: Mid-May through mid-Sept, weather permitting

Fees: $ per night, $ per additional vehicle, Golden Age and Access Passport holders half price

Maximum stay: 14 days

Management: Medicine Bow National Forest, Brush Creek/Hayden Ranger District, 2171 Highway 130, Saratoga, WY 82331; (307) 326-5258

Reservations: First-come, first-served

Pets: Pets must be leashed or under physical restrictive control.

Quiet hours: 10 p.m. to 6 a.m. (turn off generators)

ADA compliance: No

Activities: Fishing, hiking, OHV, wildlife viewing

Finding the campground: Take WY 130/230 south out of Saratoga for about 8 miles. Turn left onto WY 130 East and travel 20 miles. At the green camping sign turn left. The FR 100 road sign will be on your right and is not visible from the main road. This paved road will change to gravel in short order. Travel about 0.2 mile to FR 200 and turn right. Travel down this rough gravel road for approximately 1.5 miles to the campground.

About the campground: There are taller trees in the distance with shorter ones present in the campground, hinting of shade, though at this elevation heat does not seem to be overbearing. There are plenty of boulders all over; the best benefit for those who choose to stay here is the crashing crunching of rock versus ice-cold water collisions for a nighttime audition. The grass and other assorted plants were quite tall as of our visit, even in the parking spurs indicating this campground hasn't had a lot of visitors yet. That could be a good thing if you are one of those that likes solitude. That is not a guarantee, however.

3 Ryan Park

Location: 23 miles east of Saratoga

GPS: N41 19.62' / W106 29.59'

Facilities and amenities: Vault toilets, fire rings, trash receptacles, picnic tables, drinking water

Elevation: 8,424 feet

Road conditions: Gravel

Hookups: None

Sites: 49 basic sites, 1 group site

Maximum RV length: 30 feet long

Season: June–Sept, weather permitting

Fees: $ per night, $ per additional vehicle, Golden Age and Access Passport holders half price

Maximum stay: 14 days

Management: Medicine Bow National Forest, Brush Creek / Hayden Ranger District, 2171 Highway 130, Saratoga, WY 82331; (307) 326-5258

Reservations: National Recreation Reservation Service toll-free at (877) 444-6777 or online at recreation.gov

Pets: Pets are allowed but must be kept on a leash no longer than 6 feet at all times.

Quiet hours: 10 p.m. to 6 a.m. Turn off generators. Keep voices and music down.

ADA compliance: No
Activities: Fishing, hiking
Finding the campground: Take WY 130/230 south out of Saratoga for about 8 miles. Turn left onto WY 130 East and travel 15 miles. The campground is east of the small community of Ryan Park on the right.
About the campground: This popular place seemed cramped, with a large number of tents mixed in with larger RVs. Trees are sporadic with open grassy areas, probably created by the past blow-downs. As of our visit, empty units were well marked designating the reservation dates. The campground was full or "accounted for." If this is an area of interest, making a reservation in advance could be considered a requirement. There tend to be a number of "younger" campers to share adventures with, so be on the alert when you have wheels turning.

4 French Creek

Location: 19 miles east of Riverside
GPS: N41 13.54' / W106 28.86'
Facilities and amenities: Vault toilet, fire rings, trash receptacles, picnic tables, drinking water
Elevation: 7,779 feet
Road conditions: Gravel to improved dirt
Hookups: None
Sites: 11 basic sites
Maximum RV length: 32 feet long
Season: June–Sept
Fees: $ per night, $ per additional vehicle, Golden Age and Access Passport holders half price
Maximum stay: 14 days
Management: Medicine Bow National Forest, Brush Creek / Hayden Ranger District, 2171 Highway 130, Saratoga, WY 82331; (307) 326-5258
Reservations: First-come, first-served
Pets: Pets must be leashed or under physical restrictive control.
Quiet hours: 10 p.m. to 6 a.m. (turn off generators)
ADA compliance: No
Activities: Hunting, fishing, hiking, OHV
Finding the campground: Take WY 130/230 south out of Saratoga for about 8 miles. Turn left onto WY 130 East and travel 15.4 miles (a little over 0.25 mile past the Ryan Park Campground entrance). Turn right onto the gravel South French Creek Road/FR 225 and travel 10 miles. At the three-way intersection, turn right onto the gravel road. This is FR 206, though we could find no sign. Travel down this gravel road for about 4 miles. The campground is on the right side.
About the campground: The aspen grove has gotten much taller since our first visit. Rosebushes share the space between trees with grass and an assortment of other plants. There is a lot of space between camping sites, but water and toilet facilities can be a pretty good hike from the far end. Nearby French Creek refreshes deer and plenty of other wildlife. If the trout prove too fussy, a quick wading spree could cool you off very quickly. The campground sign was missing upon our arrival, though it may be replaced by the time of yours.

5 Bennett Peak

Location: 23 miles east of Riverside
GPS: N41 16.22' / W106 35.35'
Facilities and amenities: Vault toilet, fire rings, picnic tables, trash receptacles, drinking water
Elevation: 7,144 feet
Road conditions: Gravel, with numerous washboard conditions
Hookups: None
Sites: 11 basic sites
Maximum RV length: 20 feet long
Season: June through mid-Nov, weather permitting
Fees: $ per night, Golden Age and Access Passport holders half price
Maximum stay: 14 days
Management: Bureau of Land Management, Rawlins Field Office, 1300 North 3rd St., Rawlins, WY 82301; (307) 328-4200; rawlins_wymail@blm.gov
Reservations: First-come, first-served
Pets: Pets must be on a leash and/or under control at all times.
Quiet hours: 10 p.m. to 6 a.m. (turn off generators)
ADA compliance: No. *Note:* There is fishing and restroom accessibility but not camping.
Activities: Fishing, hiking, mountain biking, wildlife viewing, picnicking, hunting
Finding the campground: Take WY 230 east out of Riverside for 4 miles. Turn left onto the gravel French Creek Road and travel a short distance. Turn right at the Bennett Peak sign onto CR 660 and travel 11 miles. Turn left onto the gravel BLM Road 3404 and travel 8 miles.
About the campground: Level, well-groomed parking spaces are well divided by an assortment of sagebrush, cedar, stunted pine, and sand. This very well-kept site has little shade but lots of river access. Surrounding cliffs and rock outcrops invite old and young alike to explore. After traveling the long and dusty badlands to get here, this oasis seems like the pot at the end of the rainbow. Pine trees and mature cedar add an enchanted sort of quality to this river canyon.

6 Corral Creek

Location: 22 miles east of Riverside
GPS: N41 15.80' / W106 34.36'
Facilities and amenities: Vault toilet, fire rings, picnic tables
Elevation: 7,205 feet
Road conditions: Gravel to improved dirt
Hookups: None
Sites: 6 basic sites
Maximum RV length: 20 feet long
Season: June through mid-Nov, weather permitting
Fees: $ per night, Golden Age and Access Passport holders half price
Maximum stay: 14 days

Management: Bureau of Land Management, Rawlins Field Office, 1300 North 3rd St., Rawlins, WY 82301; (307) 328-4200; rawlins_wymail@blm.gov
Reservations: First-come, first-served
Pets: Pets must be on a leash and/or under control at all times.
Quiet hours: 10 p.m. to 6 a.m. (turn off generators)
ADA compliance: No
Activities: Fishing, hiking, mountain biking, wildlife viewing, picnicking, hunting
Finding the campground: Take WY 230 east out of Riverside for 4 miles. Turn left onto the gravel French Creek Road and travel a short distance. Turn right at the Bennett Peak sign onto CR 660 and travel 11 miles. Turn left onto the gravel BLM Road 3404 and travel 7 miles.
About the campground: This campground appears to be older than nearby Bennett Peak. When we visited, a sign warned campers that water was not available for consumption and to use Bennet Peak pump water until further notice. Small cedar trees grow here and there among the unusual rock formations. The North Platte River meanders by within sight but not real close. The many rock formations appeal to young and old alike for photos or climbing.

7 Six Mile Gap

Location: 25 miles southeast of Riverside
GPS: N41 2.65' / W106 24.08'
Facilities and amenities: Vault toilet, fire rings, bear canisters for food storage, trash receptacles, picnic tables, drinking water
Elevation: 7,772 feet
Road conditions: Gravel
Hookups: None
Sites: 4 basic sites, 5 tents-only
Maximum RV length: 20 feet long
Season: Mid-June through mid-Sept, weather permitting
Fees: $ per night, $ per additional vehicle, Golden Age and Access Passport holders half price
Maximum stay: 14 days
Management: Medicine Bow National Forest, Brush Creek/Hayden Ranger District, 2171 Highway 130, Saratoga, WY 82331; (307) 326-5258
Reservations: First-come, first-served
Pets: Pets must be leashed or under physical restrictive control.
Quiet hours: 10 p.m. to 6 a.m. Turn off generators. Keep voices and music low.
ADA compliance: No
Activities: Fishing, hiking
Finding the campground: Take WY 230 east and south out of Riverside for 23 miles. Turn left onto the gravel Six Mile Road and travel 2 miles. Watch for the sign, as it tends to sneak up on you.
About the campground: Aspen trees hide the south-side units, with stairsteps leading up to the tables from the parking spot. Wide-open, semi-level spaces are on the opposite side. Sagebrush and grass inhabit the ridge on the open side. A grassy, gentle dip cuts directly through the center of the camping area. Just past the campground is a parking area for river access and the Six Mile Gap Trail. Tents could be very well placed in the aspen.

Fires ravaged the forest in this area some time ago, but recovery is underway. Fishing will require some physical effort and a need to stay alert to conditions. Falling trees can cause no small injury, especially if one is caught by surprise. Being in a hurry is not a condition one wants to develop in this area. This is a very good place to unplug from the "high-tech, high-speed" burnout similar to the fire-ravaged forest and join in the "new-growth, new beginning" so to speak.

8 Encampment River

Location: 2 miles southwest of Encampment
GPS: N41 11.12' / W106 47.84'
Facilities and amenities: Vault toilet, fire rings, picnic tables
Elevation: 7,727 feet
Road conditions: Do not attempt to drive this road when it's muddy because its steepness and depth of mud may make it temporarily impossible to get out again.
Hookups: None
Sites: 8 basic units
Maximum RV length: 30 feet long
Season: June through mid-Nov
Fees: $ per night, Golden Age and Access Passport holders half price
Maximum stay: 14 days
Management: Bureau of Land Management, Rawlins Field Office, 1300 North 3rd St., Rawlins, WY 82301; (307) 328-4200; rawlins_wymail@blm.gov
Reservations: First-come, first-served
Pets: Pets must be on a leash and/or under control at all times.
Quiet hours: 10 p.m. to 6 a.m. (turn off generators)
ADA compliance: No
Activities: Fishing, swimming, hiking, mountain biking, wildlife viewing, photography
Finding the campground: Travel on WY 70 south out of Encampment for 0.5 mile. Turn left at the Encampment River Trail sign onto the gravel road and travel 2 miles, bearing left.
About the campground: Huge mature cottonwood trees provide shade. Willow brush and young cottonwood trees conceal the river. All of the sites appear easy to level long RVs. The last part of the "road" leading into the campground is one lane with some encroaching tree branches and has a prominent blind spot—use caution. Upon arrival at the campground, all is forgiven. Firewood does not appear to be easily obtained. Steep badlands covered with sage and melted-looking rock produce little to roast marshmallows. Be sure to obtain enough before arriving, along with enough drinking water for your length of stay.

9 Bottle Creek

Location: 7 miles southwest of Encampment
GPS: N41 10.51' / W106 53.64'
Facilities and amenities: Vault toilets, fire rings, picnic tables, drinking water

Elevation: 8,720 feet
Road conditions: Narrow gravel road
Hookups: None
Sites: 12 basic sites
Maximum RV length: 32 feet long
Season: June–Sept, weather permitting
Fees: $ per night, $ per additional vehicle, Golden Age and Access Passport holders half price
Maximum stay: 14 days
Management: Medicine Bow National Forest, Brush Creek/Hayden Ranger District, 2171 Highway 130, Saratoga, WY 82331; (307) 326-5258
Reservations: First-come, first-served
Pets: Pets must be leashed or under physical restrictive control.
Quiet hours: 10 p.m. to 6 a.m. (turn off generators)
ADA compliance: No
Activities: Hiking
Finding the campground: Take WY 70 south out of Encampment for 7 miles. Turn left at the sign onto the gravel FR 550 and travel a short distance. The campground access is on the right side of the road. Turn right and travel about 0.5 mile.
About the campground: Men of the Civilian Conservation Corps camped here during the 1930s. From the Bottle Creek Camp, men would embark on a variety of projects for $30. Of that money, $25 would be sent to each family. Large aspen and pine trees cluster together on this otherwise sagebrush mountainside. Larger units could fit in the precious few sites that are likely to fill quickly. A large group of picnic tables allows people to meet in the center of the camp. The small bubbly stream was not wandering as of our visit, likely a victim of prolonged drought. There was also no identified host at the time. The drinking water emerges via a single hand pump close to the center of the campground. Leveling will prove to be a challenge for most of the sites.

10 Hog Park

Location: 23 miles southwest of Encampment
GPS: N41 1.44' / W106 51.98'
Facilities and amenities: Vault toilets, fire rings, picnic tables, boat ramp, drinking water. *Note:* There are no trash receptacles; this is a pack-it-in, pack-it-out area.
Elevation: 8,467 feet
Road conditions: The 18 miles of gravel road can have washboard conditions that will require slower speeds.
Hookups: None
Sites: 50 basic sites
Maximum RV length: 30 feet long
Season: Mid-June through Sept, weather permitting
Fees: $ per night, $ per additional vehicle, Golden Age and Access Passport holders half price
Maximum stay: 14 days

Management: Medicine Bow National Forest, Brush Creek/Hayden Ranger District, 2171 Highway 130, Saratoga, WY 82331; (307) 326-5258

Reservations: May be made up to 6 months in advance at recreation.gov or by calling the National Recreation Service at (877) 444-6777

Pets: Pets must be leashed or under physical restrictive control.

Quiet hours: 10 p.m. to 6 a.m. Turn off generators. Keep voices and music down.

ADA compliance: No

Activities: Fishing, boating, hiking, wildlife viewing, picnicking

Finding the campground: Take WY 70 west out of Encampment for 5 miles to FR 550. At the Hog Park Reservoir sign, turn left onto the gravel FR 550 and travel 17 miles. Bear left to get onto FR 496 and travel 1 mile. Turn right at the campground sign and travel across the dam to access the camping area.

About the campground: Several loops provide scenic views of Hog Park Reservoir, though they can get somewhat close to each other. The units are located on rolling small hills of sorts with some encroaching smaller trees and brush. Reservations are the best, if not the only way to have any assurance of a unit big enough for larger RVs. The first-come, first-served units are more suitable for shorter RVs. Fishing and boating are among the top choices with respect to activities. Deadfall from the lodgepole pine forest appeared to be fairly easy to pick up for firewood as of our visit. A host typically occupies one of the units, though as of our visit none was present.

11 Lost Creek

Location: 17 miles southwest of Encampment

GPS: N41 8.46' / W107 4.76'

Facilities and amenities: Vault toilet, fire rings, picnic tables, drinking water. *Note:* There are no trash receptacles; this is a pack-it-in, pack-it-out area.

Elevation: 8,748 feet

Road conditions: Gravel

Hookups: None

Sites: 13 basic sites

Maximum RV length: 22 feet long

Season: Mid-June through Oct, weather permitting

Fees: $ per night, Golden Age and Access Passport holders half price

Maximum stay: 14 days

Management: Medicine Bow National Forest, Brush Creek / Hayden Ranger District, 2171 Highway 130, Saratoga, WY 82331; (307) 326-5258

Reservations: First-come, first-served

Pets: Pets must be leashed or under physical restrictive control.

Quiet hours: 10 p.m. to 6 a.m. (turn off generators)

ADA compliance: No

Activities: Hiking, OHV, mountain biking

Finding the campground: Take WY 70 west out of Encampment for 17 miles. The campground is on the right side of the road.

About the campground: Spruce and some aspen still shade the unique parking arrangement of this aged camping area. Lost Creek bubbles pleasantly past on one side; though drought has diminished the bubbling, it still offers pleasant night music. Grass and other assorted plants stand tall where the sun sneaks through the thick needles. A host was not obviously present, though we may have arrived too early. Firewood may take some extra effort to locate but should not be a major issue.

12 Jack Creek

Location: 27 miles west of Saratoga
GPS: N41 17.16' / W107 7.29'
Facilities and amenities: Vault toilet, fire rings, trash receptacles, picnic tables, drinking water
Elevation: 8,397 feet
Road conditions: Gravel to improved dirt
Hookups: None
Sites: 16 basic sites
Maximum RV length: 45 feet long
Season: Mid-June through Oct, weather permitting
Fees: $ per night, $ per additional vehicle, Golden Age and Access Passport holders half price
Maximum stay: 14 days
Management: Medicine Bow National Forest, Brush Creek/Hayden Ranger District, 2171 Highway 130, Saratoga, WY 82331; (307) 326-5258
Reservations: First-come, first-served
Pets: Pets must be leashed or under physical restrictive control.
Quiet hours: 10 p.m. to 6 a.m. (turn off generators)
ADA compliance: No
Activities: Fishing, hiking, OHV, picnicking
Finding the campground: In Saratoga go west on the West Bridge Road, which turns into the gravel CR 500/Jack Creek Road for 19 miles. Bear left onto the gravel FR 452 and travel 8 miles.
About the campground: The crystal-clear waters of Jack Creek hide in the willow brush as they pass. Parking divides the pine forest adjacent to the creek with enough space to create a sense of privacy. The rolling forest surrounding the campground is splattered with grassy meadows. Aspen thickets join the lodgepole pine here and there, which adds another dimension to the meaning of beauty when they turn gold in the fall. This remote treasure fills quickly on weekends and holidays. This would be an ideal place for the days in between. It is also a popular base camp for ATV-OHV enthusiasts.

13 Teton Reservoir

Location: 15 miles south of Rawlins
GPS: N41 36.19' / W107 15.35'
Facilities and amenities: Vault toilet, fire rings, grills, picnic tables, boat ramp
Elevation: 7,056 feet
Road conditions: Access roads become impassable after heavy rain and snow melt due to muddy conditions.
Hookups: None
Sites: 5 basic sites
Maximum RV length: 40 feet long
Season: June through mid-Nov
Fees: None
Maximum stay: 14 days
Management: Bureau of Land Management, Rawlins Field Office, 1300 North 3rd St., Rawlins, WY 82301; (307) 328-4200; rawlins_wymail@blm.gov
Reservations: First-come, first-served
Pets: Pets must be on a leash and/or under control at all times.
Quiet hours: 10 p.m. to 6 a.m. (turn off generators)
ADA compliance: No
Activities: Fishing, hiking, water sports, wildlife viewing, photography
Finding the campground: At Rawlins take exit 214 from I-80 and travel north to Locust Road/WY 71 and turn left. Travel past the KOA for 15 miles. The campground is on the left.
About the campground: No shade or firewood are to be found here. Obviously, fishing brings campers out to this panoramic setting. Endless distant cliffs stretch out overlooking the sagebrush hills. Stars and coyotes can be expected in full force on just about any night in this country. This would be an excellent place to get a feel for what the pioneers experienced on their journeys to the West.

14 Dugway

Location: 7 miles north of Sinclair
GPS: N41 51.83' / W107 3.60'
Facilities and amenities: Vault toilet, fire rings, grills, picnic tables
Elevation: 6,410 feet
Road conditions: Improved dirt
Hookups: None
Sites: 5 basic sites
Maximum RV length: 60 feet long
Season: June–Oct, weather permitting
Fees: None

Maximum stay: 14 days
Management: Bureau of Land Management, Rawlins Field Office, 1300 North 3rd St., Rawlins, WY 82301; (307) 328-4200; rawlins_wymail@blm.gov
Reservations: First-come, first-served
Pets: Pets must be on a leash and/or under control at all times.
Quiet hours: 10 p.m. to 6 a.m. (turn off generators)
ADA compliance: No
Activities: Fishing, picnicking
Finding the campground: Take exit 219 off of I-80 at Sinclair. Follow directions toward Seminoe State Park and travel 7 miles. The campground is on the right side of the road.
About the campground: The North Platte River sleepily passes by in plain sight of this campground, but lack of shade could make this a very uncomfortable place on a late summer day. It could be a very pleasant place in the evening and an excellent place to stargaze. If you want a campfire, don't forget to bring the wood. Pronghorn look on, along with the available livestock nibbling on abundant sagebrush. Bugs can be very abundant in the late spring and early summer so be prepared.

Seminoe State Park

15 Sunshine Beach

Location: 35 miles north of Sinclair
GPS: N42 7.42' / W106 53.58'
Facilities and amenities: Vault toilets, fire rings, picnic tables, shelters
Elevation: 6,440 feet
Road conditions: Gravel
Hookups: None
Sites: 38 basic sites
Maximum RV length: 40 feet long
Season: Year-round
Fees: Resident camping fee $$ per day, nonresident camping fee $$$$. See the website for information on annual permits.
Maximum stay: 14 days
Management: Seminoe State Park, Seminoe Dam Route, Box 30, Sinclair, WY 82334; (307) 777-6323
Reservations: Book online 24/7 at wyo-park.com or by phone at (877) 996-7275.
Pets: Pets must be on a leash at all times.
Quiet hours: 10 p.m. to 6 a.m. (turn off generators)
ADA compliance: No
Activities: Fishing, boating, swimming, picnicking, OHV

Finding the campground: Take exit 219 off of I-80 at Sinclair and follow directions to access CR 351. Travel this paved road for 33 miles. Turn right and travel 2 miles.

About the campground: The name of this huge reservoir came from an early mountain man. This Frenchman camped here long before the dam existed, but the pronouncement of his name lives on. The desert badlands get hot under this huge expanse of open sky.

16 South Red Hills

Location: 34 miles north of Sinclair
GPS: N42 7.94' / W106 54.37'
Facilities and amenities: Vault toilets, fire rings, picnic tables, boat ramp, playground, shelters, drinking water
Elevation: 6,469 feet
Road conditions: Gravel
Hookups: None
Sites: 19 basic sites
Maximum RV length: 40 feet long
Season: Year-round
Fees: Resident camping fee $$ per day, nonresident camping fee $$$$. See the website for information on annual permits.
Maximum stay: 14 days
Management: Seminoe State Park, Seminoe Dam Route, Box 30, Sinclair, WY 82334; (307) 777-6323
Reservations: Book online 24/7 at wyo-park.com or by phone at (877) 996-7275.
Pets: Pets must be on a leash at all times.
Quiet hours: 10 p.m. to 6 a.m. (turn off generators)
ADA compliance: No
Activities: Fishing, boating, swimming, picnicking, OHV
Finding the campground: Take exit 219 off of I-80 at Sinclair and follow directions for 34 miles. The paved access road turns to gravel in 32 miles.
About the campground: Not all units have shelters. The ones closer to the shore of Seminoe Reservoir go quickly. The stark badlands and sage hills hint of intense sun and little rain. Forget about gathering firewood. There aren't even living trees here. Hiking might be a stretch for those who like wooded trails. In spite of the barren appearance, a lot of things remain to be discovered. When all else fails, the cold lake water takes the sting out of the hot sun.

17 Red Hills North

Location: 34 miles north of Sinclair
GPS: N42 8.15' / W106 53.65'
Facilities and amenities: Vault toilets, fire rings, picnic tables, picnic shelters, beach, boat dock, fishing pier, playgrounds, drinking water

Elevation: 6,434 feet

Road conditions: Paved to gravel

Hookups: 13 electricity (50 amp)

Sites: 30 basic sites

Maximum RV length: 40 feet long

Season: May–Sept

Fees: Resident camping fee $$ per day, nonresident camping fee $$$$. See the website for information on annual permits.

Maximum stay: 14 days

Management: Seminoe State Park, Seminoe Dam Route, Box 30, Sinclair, WY 82334; (307) 777-6323

Reservations: Book online 24/7 at wyo-park.com or by phone at (877) 996-7275.

Pets: Pets must be on a leash at all times.

Quiet hours: 10 p.m. to 6 a.m. (turn off generators)

ADA compliance: Yes

Activities: Fishing, boating, swimming, picnicking, OHV

Finding the campground: Take exit 219 off of I-80 at Sinclair and follow signs for 34 miles. The paved access road turns to gravel in 32 miles.

About the campground: The camping area here is a bit more compact than that of the adjacent South Red Hills. Parking is somewhat organized, with lots of room for multiple vehicles, trailers, or boats. Sagebrush carpets most of the rolling terrain. A few vacant units were present on our visit toward the end of a weekend. Most, if not all, campers found water recreation to be the activity of choice.

Sheridan Area

Stagecoaches of Old West fame opened the roadway leading to the majority of campgrounds in the northern Bighorns. All-terrain vehicles (ATVs) are quite popular here and work quite well on the designated trails. There are remote campgrounds in the area with access to the Cloud Peak Wilderness, though the access roads seem to be leftover unmaintained stagecoach roads. Classic western trout streams are abundant, with plenty of room for exploring.

Multiple dynamic canyons beckon to the adventuresome to discover the beauties resting in their shadows. A glimpse of their glory can be found near Shell, along the highway at the spectacular Shell Creek Falls. Campers can choose between camping along the roar of mountain snowmelt crashing over defiant boulders or having a placid ice-cold lake within walking distance. In more than a few places, the lakes are in view of camping areas and make for a beautiful sight opposite an evening campfire.

Water activities are the primary attraction at Sibley Lake.

#	Name	Group sites	Tents	RV sites	Total # of sites	Picnic area	Toilets	Hookups	Drinking water	Dump station	Phone	Handicap	Recreation	Fee	Season	Can reserve	Stay limit
1	Connor Battlefield Historic Site			20	20	X	V		X			X	FPiPg	$$–$$$	5/1–9/30	X	14
2	Sibley Lake		1	24	25	X	V	El	X			X	FBoSHiMPi	$$–$$$	6/1–9/30	X	14
3	Prune Creek			21	21		V		X			X	FHi	$$	6/1–9/30	X	14
4	North Tongue			12	12	X	V		X			X	FHiHuPiOhv	$$	6/1–9/30	X	14
5	Bald Mountain			15	15		V		X			X	FHiWHu	$$	6/1–9/30	X	14
6	Porcupine		2	14	16	X	V		X			X	HuHiPi	$$	6/1–9/30	X	14
7	Five Springs Falls		9	10	19	X	V		X			X	HuHiPiPh	$	6/1–9/30	X	14
8	Horseshoe Bend			68	68		Fl	El	X	X		X	FBoHiMPiW	$$$	Year-round	X	14
9	Barry's Landing & Trail Creek		16	14	30		V		X	X			FBoHiBiPiW	$$	Year-round		14
10	Owen Creek			8	8		V		X				HuFOhv	$$	6/1–9/30	X	14
11	Tie Flume		24	23	47	X	V		X			X	FHiMPiOhv	$$	6/1–9/30	X	14
12	Dead Swede		4	18	22	X	V		X			X	HuFHiPiOhv	$$	6/1–9/30	X	14
13	Shell Creek		2	13	15		V		X				HuFHiM	$$	6/1–9/30		14
14	Medicine Lodge Lake			14	14		V		X			X	FBoBrHi	$$	6/1–9/30		14
15	Lower Paint Rock Lake			5			V		X				FHi	$$	6/15–9/15		14

Bi = biking, Bo = boating, Br = boat ramp, El = electric hookups, F = fishing, Fl = flush toilet, Hi = hiking, Hu = hunting, M = mountain biking, Ohv = off highway vehicle,
Pg = playground, Ph = photography, Pi = picnicking, S = swimming, V = vault toilet, W = wildlife viewing

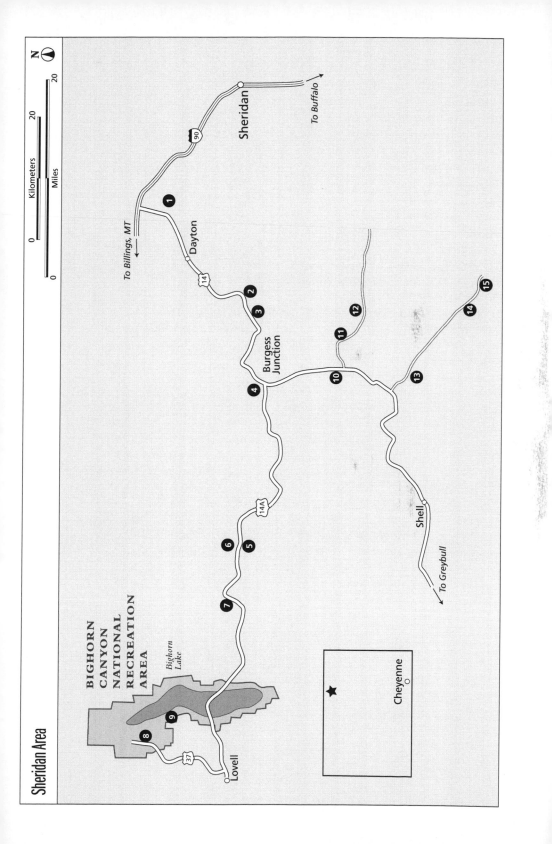

Sheridan Area

1 Connor Battlefield Historic Site

Location: In Ranchester, just off of I-90
GPS: N44 54.18' / W107 9.98'
Facilities and amenities: Restrooms, fire rings, grills, picnic tables, playground, drinking water
Elevation: 3,756 feet
Road conditions: Gravel
Hookups: None
Sites: 20 basic sites
Maximum RV length: 60 feet long
Season: May–Sept, weather permitting
Fees: Resident $$ per night, nonresident $$$ per night, not including the day pass fee
Maximum stay: 14 days
Management: Wyoming State Parks, Historic Sites & Trails, (307) 684-7629
Reservations: First-come, first-served
Pets: Pets must be on a leash and under physical control at all times.
Quiet hours: 10 p.m. to 6 a.m. Turn off generators. All generators and electronic devices or any actions that may disturb the peace are prohibited during these hours.
ADA compliance: Yes
Activities: Fishing, picnicking
Finding the campground: Take I-90 north out of Sheridan for 10 miles to the Ranchester exit/ exit 9. Turn left onto US 14 and travel for 1 mile to Ranchester. In Ranchester turn left onto Gillette Street and travel 1 mile. The campground will be on the left.
About the campground: Previous campers at this historic site were the Arapaho, led by Chief Black Bear. Camping duties changed on August 29, 1865, when Jim Bridger guided General Patrick E. Connor and his troops to the campsite. The Arapaho suffered but prevailed and forced Connor's troops to retreat. Ranchester sits peacefully across the Tongue River from this former battleground. Anglers test their skill along the mowed grassy banks, and children noisily play under the huge cottonwood trees. Under the noise of occasional traffic and a boom box, one can almost hear the echoes of Arapaho children running, jumping, and splashing in the water. Starving mosquitoes anxiously await your arrival, so take plenty of bug spray. If your hour is getting late and your "tin tepee" pulls hard on a mountain grade, this would be an excellent place to spend the night and reflect on the history of the area.

2 Sibley Lake

Location: 33 miles west of Sheridan
GPS: N44 45.62' / W107 26.58'
Facilities and amenities: Host on-site, vault toilets, fire rings, grills, trash receptacles, picnic tables, drinking water
Elevation: 7,993 feet
Road conditions: Gravel

Hookups: 15 sites with electric hookups (30- and 50-amp)

Sites: 24 basic sites, 1 tents-only

Maximum RV length: 50 feet long

Season: June–Sept, weather permitting

Fees: $$ per night, $$$ per night for electric service, Golden Age and Access Passport holders half price

Maximum stay: 14 days

Management: Bighorn National Forest, Tongue Ranger District, 2013 Eastside 2nd St., Sheridan, WY 82801; (307) 674-2600. Gallatin Canyon Campgrounds, (406) 587-9054; gccampgrounds 13@gmail.com (concessionaire).

Reservations: National Recreation Reservation Service toll-free at (877) 444-6777 or online at recreation.gov

Pets: Pets must be leashed and kept under physical control at all times.

Quiet hours: 10 p.m. to 6 a.m. (turn off generators)

ADA compliance: Yes

Activities: Fishing, boating, swimming, hiking, mountain biking, picnicking

Finding the campground: Take I-90 north out of Sheridan for 10 miles to the Ranchester exit/exit 9. Turn left onto US 14 and travel 23 miles. The campground access is on the left side of the highway.

About the campground: Laughter and pleasant echoes of recreation associated with cold water on a hot day replace war cries and gunfire. Chief White Antelope of the Cheyenne was killed near here during an attack on July 7, 1876. Lt. Frederick W. Sibley led a scouting party into this area, resulting in the subsequent attack. Members of the 2nd Cavalry were forced to abandon their horses and supplies. Hiking through the surrounding country reveals how difficult the soldiers found retreat out of the mountains with no supplies. Wind whispers through the needles of the slender, tall lodgepole pine forest that envelops both lake and campground with stories left to your imagination. Gathering firewood takes extra effort as the immediate area has been picked clean. A host is available, and there is access for the disabled for fishing and at other facilities. Reservations well in advance of your trip are a must if you want to spend time here.

3 Prune Creek

Location: 35 miles west of Sheridan

GPS: N44 46.20' / W107 28.15'

Facilities and amenities: Host on-site, vault toilets, fire rings, grills, trash receptacles, picnic tables, drinking water

Elevation: 7,687 feet

Road conditions: Gravel

Hookups: None

Sites: 21 basic sites

Maximum RV length: 50 feet long

Season: June–Sept, weather permitting

Fees: $$ per night, $ per night per additional vehicle, Golden Age and Access Passport holders half price

Maximum stay: 14 days
Management: Bighorn National Forest, Tongue Ranger District, 2013 Eastside 2nd St., Sheridan, WY 82801; (307) 674-2600. Gallatin Canyon Campgrounds, (406) 587-9054; gccamp grounds13@gmail.com (concessionaire).
Reservations: National Recreation Reservation Service toll-free at (877) 444-6777 or online at recreation.gov
Pets: Pets must be leashed and kept under physical control at all times.
Quiet hours: 10 p.m. to 6 a.m. (turn off generators)
ADA compliance: Yes
Activities: Fishing, hiking
Finding the campground: Take I-90 north out of Sheridan for 10 miles to the Ranchester exit/exit 9. Turn left onto US 14 and travel 25 miles. The campground is on the left side of the highway.
Note: As of our visit, the campground sign was not visible from the highway until we were too far past it to make the turn. Mark the mileage after passing the Sibley Lake Campground and be on the lookout for the gravel access road.
About the campground: Easy access and refreshing water recreation make this a popular place and one that fills quickly. Prune Creek rushes through the campground with willow brush and lodgepole pine sharing the bank. Pools captured by downfall and large boulders in the creek tempt angler and wader alike. Firewood will involve some footwork to gather. A host is available at this campground. The paved highway alongside the campground does not produce any dust, but traffic can be heavy during the day. As with other campgrounds along the roadways, the traffic generally dies off after dark. Any noise is soon forgotten with s'mores roasted over a crackling fire under a clear, star-filled night. The two loops have a turnaround at the end for easy trailer access and exit.

4 North Tongue

Location: 44 miles west of Sheridan
GPS: N44 46.87' / W107 32.05'
Facilities and amenities: Host on-site, vault toilets, fire rings, grills, trash receptacles, picnic tables, drinking water
Elevation: 7,883 feet
Road conditions: Gravel
Hookups: None
Sites: 12 basic sites
Maximum RV length: 100 feet long
Season: June–Sept, weather permitting
Fees: $$ per night, $ per night per additional vehicle, Golden Age and Access Passport holders half price
Maximum stay: 14 days
Management: Bighorn National Forest, Tongue Ranger District, 2013 Eastside 2nd St., Sheridan, WY 82801; (307) 674-2600. Gallatin Canyon Campgrounds, (406) 587-9054; gccamp grounds13@gmail.com (concessionaire).
Reservations: National Recreation Reservation Service toll-free at (877) 444-6777 or online at recreation.gov

Pets: Pets must be leashed and kept under physical control at all times.

Quiet hours: 10 p.m. to 6 a.m. (turn off generators)

ADA compliance: Yes

Activities: Fishing, hiking, hunting, picnicking, OHV

Finding the campground: Take I-90 north out of Sheridan for 10 miles to the Ranchester exit/exit 9. Turn left onto US 14 and travel 33 miles. Turn right onto US 14 Alternate and travel 0.5 mile. Turn right onto the gravel FR 15 and travel 1 mile. The campground is on the left.

About the campground: The main attraction of this area is the prime fishing in nearby streams. Douglas fir close in on the units here with lodgepole pine crowding up behind them on the ridges. A happy little creek is hard to see but easy to hear bouncing over rocks and logs; it pleasantly gurgles peacefully through the campground, quenching the thirst of tall grass and willow brush alike. A host is available at a nearby site. Firewood will take some footwork to gather. Trailers can enter and exit either of the two loops easily with a turnaround at the end. Traffic creates a whole lot of dust that can be very annoying on a busy weekend; however, as the sun drops, so does the dust, making for a pleasant evening. This area fills quickly so don't put off obtaining a unit.

5 Bald Mountain

Location: 70 miles west of Sheridan

GPS: N44 48.48' / W107 51.59'

Facilities and amenities: Host located at Porcupine campground, vault toilets, fire rings, trash receptacles, picnic tables, drinking water

Elevation: 9,098 feet

Road conditions: Gravel

Hookups: None

Sites: 15 basic sites

Maximum RV length: 50 feet long

Season: June–Sept, weather permitting

Fees: $$ per night, $ per night per additional vehicle, Golden Age and Access Passport holders half price

Maximum stay: 14 days

Management: Bighorn National Forest, Medicine Wheel Ranger District, 95 US 16/20, Greybull, WY 82426; (307) 765-4435. Gallatin Canyon Campgrounds, (406) 587-9054; gccampgrounds 13@gmail.com (concessionaire).

Reservations: National Recreation Reservation Service toll-free at (877) 444-6777 or online at recreation.gov

Pets: Pets must be leashed and kept under physical control at all times.

Quiet hours: 10 p.m. to 6 a.m. (turn off generators)

ADA compliance: Yes

Activities: Fishing, hiking, wildlife viewing, hunting

Finding the campground: Take I-90 north out of Sheridan for 10 miles to the Ranchester exit/exit 9. Turn left onto US 14 and travel 33 miles. Turn right onto US 14 Alternate and travel 27 miles. Turn left at the Bald Mountain Campground sign and travel 0.25 mile.

About the campground: Willow brush and a thick stand of fir trees share this camping area in the wide-open alpine meadow typical of the Bighorn Mountains. Gathering firewood will be difficult, though a short drive will take you to available deadfall. The wind cuts with a steely cold after sliding over any one of the remaining snow piles above. The vast meadows surrounding the area display plenty of wildflowers from late June to early July in an average year. Wildlife can be seen frequently, especially early in the evening. The highway is close enough to be convenient and far enough away for the campground to seem isolated.

6 Porcupine

Location: 70 miles west of Sheridan
GPS: N44 49.83' / W107 51.55'
Facilities and amenities: Host on-site, vault toilets, fire rings, trash receptacles, picnic tables, drinking water
Elevation: 8,785 feet
Road conditions: Gravel
Hookups: None
Sites: 14 basic sites, 2 tents-only
Maximum RV length: 40 feet long
Season: June–Sept, weather permitting
Fees: $$ per night, $ per night per additional vehicle, Golden Age and Access Passport holders half price
Maximum stay: 14 days
Management: Bighorn National Forest, Medicine Wheel Ranger District, 95 US 16/20, Greybull, WY 82426; (307) 765-4435. Gallatin Canyon Campgrounds, (406) 587-9054; gccamp grounds13@gmail.com (concessionaire).
Reservations: National Recreation Reservation Service toll-free at (877) 444-6777 or online at recreation.gov
Pets: Pets must be leashed and kept under physical control at all times.
Quiet hours: 10 p.m. to 6 a.m. (turn off generators)
ADA compliance: Yes
Activities: Hunting, hiking, picnicking
Finding the campground: Take I-90 north out of Sheridan for 10 miles to the Ranchester exit/exit 9. Turn left onto US 14 and travel 33 miles. Turn right onto US 14 Alternate and travel 27 miles. Turn right at the sign onto the gravel FR 13 and travel for 2 miles. The campground is on the left.
About the campground: The shade from the fir trees, which snag the incoming sun with no apologies, is almost unwelcome in this high altitude. Extra clothing and/or coats are a must in this mountain country where the fresh mountain air bites with a hard cold. Porcupine Creek is a short walk from the campground. Nearby trails lead the adventurous into some very rugged canyon country complete with torrential rapids and a waterfall. Depending upon the weather, this campground may not be open until the first part of July. Even on the Fourth of July, holiday piles of snow stubbornly hide in the shadows.

7 Five Springs Falls

Location: 79 miles west of Sheridan
GPS: N44 48.25' / W107 58.23'
Facilities and amenities: Vault toilets, fire rings, trash receptacles, picnic tables, drinking water
Elevation: 6,690 feet
Road conditions: Vehicles more than 25 feet long are not recommended. The old highway here is very steep with literal hairpin curves that require use of the whole road for longer rigs to go around.
Hookups: None
Sites: 10 basic sites, 9 tents-only
Maximum RV length: 25 feet long
Season: June–Sept, weather permitting
Fees: $ per night, Golden Age and Access Passport holders half price
Maximum stay: 14 days
Management: Bureau of Land Management, Cody Resource Area Office, (307) 587-2216
Reservations: First-come, first-served
Pets: Pets must be on a leash.
Quiet hours: 10 p.m. to 6 a.m. (turn off generators)
ADA compliance: Yes
Activities: Hunting, hiking, picnicking, photography
Finding the campground: Take I-90 west out of Sheridan for 10 miles to the Ranchester exit/exit 9. Turn left onto US 14 and travel 33 miles. Turn right onto US 14 Alternate and travel 34 miles. Turn right at the Five Springs Campground sign and travel 2 miles.
About the campground: Steep vertical cliffs hide forest and campground alike. Five Springs Creek rages through the combined camping-picnicking area, seemingly trying to be one of the big boys, but there just is not enough water. There is one parking spot that could be used for a pickup camper unit; you will have to share the rest of the parking area with those who access their tents. All in all, this seems to be a forgotten refuge. Five Springs Falls is a short hike up the narrowing canyon and well worth the time. Good photographs of the falls are hard to get. Most visitors don't know this waterfall exists.

8 Horseshoe Bend

Location: 14 miles north of Lovell
GPS: N44 57.55' / W108 17.29'
Facilities and amenities: Flush toilets, fire rings, trash receptacles, picnic tables, drinking water, RV dump station
Elevation: 3,718 feet
Road conditions: Gravel
Hookups: Electric hookups at 28 sites
Sites: 68 basic sites

Maximum RV length: 60 feet long

Season: Year-round. *Note:* Water availability is seasonal.

Fees: $$$ per night for improved sites, no discounts, $$ per night for unimproved sites

Maximum stay: 14 days

Management: Hidden Treasure Charters. Please contact them directly for more information, (307) 899-1401 or info@hiddentreasurecharters.com.

Reservations: First-come, first-served, with the exception of 10 sites that are reservable at horseshoebend-marina.com

Pets: Pets must be on a leash and may not be left unattended. Pet owners are responsible for cleanup and disposal of all pet feces.

Quiet hours: 10 p.m. to 6 a.m. Turn off generators. Idling of motor vehicles is not allowed during quiet hours.

ADA compliance: Yes

Activities: Fishing, boating, hiking, mountain biking, picnicking, wildlife viewing

Finding the campground: From the intersection of 14A E and 37, travel north on WY 37 for 9.7 miles. Look for the sign for Horseshoe Bend and turn right. Continue for 1.4 miles to campgrounds located to the left of the road prior to the marina.

About the campground: There are no trees here. The comfort stations offer running water and electricity. Parking spaces are well separated, with shade structures scattered about. Driftwood is collected over the year and placed in an access area; inquire at the ranger station across from the campground entrance. There is really no size limit, and that makes this an excellent place to park your trailer or RV and cruise the Bighorns. Bright stars in an unobstructed, warm badlands sky can be extremely refreshing after the freezing mountain air is left behind.

⑨ Barry's Landing & Trail Creek

Location: 27 miles north of Lovell

GPS: N45 5.75' / W108 12.61'

Facilities and amenities: Host on-site for summer, vault toilets, fire rings, trash receptacles, food-storage lockers, picnic tables

Elevation: 3,736 feet

Road conditions: Gravel

Hookups: None

Sites: 16 tents-only, 14 RV sites

Maximum RV length: 28 feet long

Season: Year-round

Fees: $$ per night, $ with NPS Senior Pass from mid-Apr through Sept, free from Oct through mid-Apr

Maximum stay: 14 days

Management: Hidden Treasure Charters. Please contact them directly for more information, (307) 899-1401 or info@hiddentreasurecharters.com.

Reservations: First-come, first-served

Pets: Pets must be on a leash and may not be left unattended. Pet owners are responsible for cleanup and disposal of all pet feces.

Quiet hours: 10 p.m. to 6 a.m. Turn off generators. Generators are permitted to run from 8 a.m. through 8 p.m. Idling of motor vehicles is not allowed during quiet hours.

ADA compliance: No

Activities: Fishing, boating, hiking, bicycling, picnicking, wildlife viewing

Finding the campground: From US 14A turn north on WY 37 and travel for approximately 22 miles. Turn right onto the Barry's Landing Road and travel about 2 miles. *Note:* If you miss the turn the paved WY 37 road will turn to gravel.

About the campground: The views are stunning with plenty of wildlife to tempt photographers. Be sure to bring plenty of drinking water as this country can get brutally hot with no mercy. The primary interests and activities of choice involve water sports. Be sure to bring bug spray, hats, and lots of sunscreen.

10 Owen Creek

Location: 50 miles west of Sheridan

GPS: N44 42.30' / W107 30.03'

Facilities and amenities: Host on-site, vault toilets, fire rings, grills, trash receptacles, picnic tables, drinking water

Elevation: 8,479 feet

Road conditions: Gravel

Hookups: None

Sites: 8 basic sites

Maximum RV length: 30 feet long

Season: June–Sept, weather permitting

Fees: $$ per night, $ per night per additional vehicle, Golden Age and Access Passport holders half price

Maximum stay: 14 days

Management: Bighorn National Forest, Tongue Ranger District, 2013 Eastside 2nd St., Sheridan, WY 82801; (307) 674-2600. Gallatin Canyon Campgrounds, (406) 587-9054; gccampgrounds 13@gmail.com (concessionaire).

Reservations: National Recreation Reservation Service toll-free at (877) 444-6777 or online at recreation.gov

Pets: Pets must be leashed and kept under physical control at all times.

Quiet hours: 10 p.m. to 6 a.m. (turn off generators)

ADA compliance: No

Activities: Hunting, fishing, OHV

Finding the campground: Take I-90 north out of Sheridan for 10 miles to the Ranchester exit/ exit 9. Turn left onto US 14 and travel 40 miles. Turn right at the Owen Creek Campground sign and travel 0.5 mile.

About the campground: A few Douglas fir trees share the area with lodgepole pines, shading the camping units. Owen Creek meanders through the grassy rolling meadow, with willow brush hugging the banks. A host is present in one of the seven available units. Gathering firewood requires some effort and may be done much more effectively by taking a drive. This campground is far enough off the highway to be quiet and close enough for easy access. If time is an issue, this may be the place to check in the early afternoon.

11 Tie Flume

Location: 52 miles west of Sheridan
GPS: N44 42.92' / W107 27.05'
Facilities and amenities: Host on-site, vault toilets, fire rings, grills, trash receptacles, picnic tables, drinking water
Elevation: 8,358 feet
Road conditions: Gravel
Hookups: None
Sites: 23 basic sites, 24 tents-only
Maximum RV length: 65 feet long
Season: June–Sept, weather permitting
Fees: $$ per night, $ per night per additional vehicle, Golden Age and Access Passport holders half price
Maximum stay: 14 days
Management: Bighorn National Forest, Tongue Ranger District, 2013 Eastside 2nd St., Sheridan, WY 82801; (307) 674-2600. Gallatin Canyon Campgrounds, (406) 587-9054; gccampgrounds 13@gmail.com (concessionaire).
Reservations: National Recreation Reservation Service toll-free at (877) 444-6777 or online at recreation.gov
Pets: Pets must be leashed and kept under physical control at all times.
Quiet hours: 10 p.m. to 6 a.m. (turn off generators)
ADA compliance: Yes
Activities: Fishing, hiking, mountain biking, picnicking, OHV
Finding the campground: Take I-90 north out of Sheridan for 10 miles to the Ranchester exit/exit 9. Turn left onto US 14 and travel 40 miles. Turn left onto the gravel FR 26 and travel 2 miles. Bear left onto FR 16 and travel 0.25 mile.
About the campground: This campground has been improved, especially with respect to ADA compliance. The road and walkways are all gravel but appeared to be well done. A lush grassy meadow runs along the bottom loop. The cool shade can be a precious commodity on a hot day, but when the sun goes down, don't have your coats very far away. There are a few first-come, first-served spots that fill very quickly in this popular campground. Reservations are required if one wants to ensure staying here. Keep in mind that internet access in the mountains is nonexistent. Crystal-clear water in nearby South Tongue River makes catching trout very challenging. It might be more fun to just join them in the water.

12 Dead Swede

Location: 56 miles west of Sheridan
GPS: N44 41.38' / W107 26.92'
Facilities and amenities: Host on-site, vault toilets, fire rings, grills, trash receptacles, picnic tables, drinking water
Elevation: 8,441 feet
Road conditions: Gravel
Hookups: None
Sites: 18 basic sites, 4 tents-only
Maximum RV length: 60 feet long
Season: June–Sept, weather permitting
Fees: $$ per night, $ per night per additional vehicle, Golden Age and Access Passport holders half price
Maximum stay: 14 days
Management: Bighorn National Forest, Tongue Ranger District, 2013 Eastside 2nd St., Sheridan, WY 82801; (307) 674-2600. Gallatin Canyon Campgrounds, (406) 587-9054; gccamp grounds13@gmail.com (concessionaire).
Reservations: National Recreation Reservation Service toll-free at (877) 444-6777 or online at recreation.gov
Pets: Pets must be leashed and kept under physical control at all times.
Quiet hours: 10 p.m. to 6 a.m. (turn off generators)
ADA compliance: Yes
Activities: Hunting, fishing, hiking, picnicking, OHV
Finding the campground: Take I-90 north out of Sheridan for 10 miles to the Ranchester exit/exit 9. Turn left onto US 14 and travel 40 miles. Turn left onto FR 26 and travel 6 miles. The campground is on the left side.
About the campground: The upper loop nestles into the lodgepole pine forest well away from the East Fork South Tongue River, though it is not out of reach. A number of improvements have been constructed here, making it a very desirable camping area. As such, there are a lot of return campers throughout the hotter days of summer escaping the heat at lower elevations. Reservations are required to make sure a spot is available.

13 Shell Creek

Location: 61 miles west of Sheridan
GPS: N44 33.11' / W107 31.11'
Facilities and amenities: Host on-site, vault toilets, fire rings, grills, trash receptacles, picnic tables, drinking water
Elevation: 7,558 feet
Road conditions: Gravel
Hookups: None
Sites: 13 basic sites, 2 tents-only

Maximum RV length: 40 feet long

Season: June–Sept, weather permitting

Fees: $$ per night, $ per night per additional vehicle, Golden Age and Access Passport holders half price

Maximum stay: 14 days

Management: Bighorn National Forest, Medicine Wheel Ranger District, 95 Highway 16/20, Greybull, WY 82426; (307) 765-4435. Gallatin Canyon Campgrounds, (406) 587-9054; gccamp grounds13@gmail.com (concessionaire).

Reservations: National Recreation Reservation Service toll-free at (877) 444-6777 or online at recreation.gov

Pets: Pets must be leashed and kept under physical control at all times.

Quiet hours: 10 p.m. to 6 a.m. (turn off generators)

ADA compliance: No

Activities: Hunting, fishing, hiking, mountain biking

Finding the campground: Take I-90 north out of Sheridan for 10 miles to the Ranchester exit/exit 9. Turn left onto US 14 and travel 50 miles. Turn left onto the gravel FR 17 and travel 1 mile. The campground is on the right.

About the campground: Forest meets grassy ridge along the crashing waters of Shell Creek. The tables and fire rings are tucked away just inside the fir and aspen groves. As the night sky lights up, you can steal away from the crackling fire and study the heavens just past the forest boundary. On the full moon, the stars are not easily seen, but other features of the surrounding nature are presented in a unique fashion. Shell Creek roars its complaint to all within earshot, seemingly not wanting to move out into the thirsty desert badlands below. If you like listening to powerful rapids with occasional interruptions due to passing wind, this is the place.

14 Medicine Lodge Lake

Location: 56 miles east of Greybull

GPS: N44 24.06' / W107 23.15'

Facilities and amenities: Vault toilets, fire rings, grills, trash receptacle, picnic tables, drinking water, boat ramp

Elevation: 9,283 feet

Road conditions: Gravel

Hookups: None

Sites: 14 basic sites

Maximum RV length: 40 feet long

Season: June–Sept, weather permitting

Fees: $$ per night, $ per night per additional vehicle, Golden Age and Access Passport holders half price

Maximum stay: 14 days

Management: Bighorn National Forest, Medicine Wheel District, (307) 765-4435. Gallatin Canyon Campgrounds, (406) 587-9054; gccampgrounds13@gmail.com (concessionaire).

Reservations: First-come, first-served

Pets: Pets must be leashed and kept under physical control at all times.

Quiet hours: 10 p.m. to 6 a.m. (turn off generators)

ADA compliance: Yes

Activities: Fishing, boating, hiking

Finding the campground: From Greybull travel east on US 14 for about 32 miles, then turn south onto FR 17 for 24 miles.

About the campground: Firewood was available as of our visit for $5 per bundle. An envelope was present for depositing the payment. Douglas fir mixed with aspen march right up the shoreline at Medicine Lodge Lake, which has 65 surface acres of trout-infested mountain water to invite anglers. Hikers can explore deep rugged canyons or high alpine meadows, depending on individual desires. The camping units settle in among the shade of the thick forest, providing a sort of seclusion from any passersby. The long gravel road leading to the end of the road does not see a lot of traffic, but those who do go by would not know of any campers here without actually driving through the camping area. This is a very good place to spend more than a few days; however, be sure to have all your needed supplies. It is a long way to any store, and it is especially difficult to find one still open after dark.

15 Lower Paint Rock Lake

Location: 86 miles west of Sheridan

GPS: N44 23.74' / W107 22.91'

Facilities and amenities: Host off-site at Medicine Lodge Lake Campground, vault toilet, fire rings, grills, trash receptacles, picnic tables, drinking water

Elevation: 9,200 feet

Road conditions: High-clearance 4-wheel-drive recommended on FR 17. Large RVs and trailers are not recommended.

Hookups: None

Sites: 5 basic sites

Maximum RV length: 45 feet long. *Note:* Getting to the campground can be an issue.

Season: Mid-June through mid-Sept, weather permitting

Fees: $$ per night, $ per night per additional vehicle, Golden Age and Access Passport holders half price

Maximum stay: 14 days

Management: Bighorn National Forest, Medicine Wheel District, (307) 765-4435. Gallatin Canyon Campgrounds, (406) 587-9054; gccampgrounds13@gmail.com (concessionaire).

Reservations: First-come, first-served

Pets: Pets must be leashed and kept under physical control at all times.

Quiet hours: 10 p.m. to 6 a.m. (turn off generators)

ADA compliance: No

Activities: Fishing, hiking

Finding the campground: Take I-90 north out of Sheridan for 10 miles to the Ranchester exit/exit 9. Turn left onto US 14 and travel 50 miles. Turn left onto the gravel FR 17 and travel 26 miles. The campground is at the end of the road.

About the campground: Longer RVs and trailers take extra effort to level because of the obvious slope of the parking area. That does not include the difficult 26-mile trek on FR 17 (more like a trail). The road leading into this area can be very trying, especially a private section of dirt that gets heavily rutted after any amount of moisture. This is a jumping-off place for entering the Cloud Peak Wilderness, complete with a loading/unloading area for horses. So be on the lookout for large livestock trailers on the move.

Douglas fir trees shade the tables in most spots, with a grassy slope down to the small but trout-inhabited Lower Paint Rock Lake. Firewood is available for purchase at the Medicine Lodge Lake campground. It is a quiet place that you want to spend some time at; if you need to be on the move the following morning, the long painstaking drive would not be worth it. This is one of those hideouts where you would want to forget about the calendar.

Yellowstone National Park

Major flooding in June of 2022 extended well beyond Yellowstone National Park boundaries and will likely continue to have future impacts for some time. The campgrounds that were open in Montana en route to the Northeast Park Entrance had maintenance issues, including trash removal (resulting in a "pack-it-in, pack-it-out" policy as of our visit) and some with drinking-water quality. These issues were not limited to the northeast.

There are around 3,500 miles of road that include mountain passes, sharp curves, and steep grades, with five entrances. The speed limit in the park is 45 mph unless otherwise posted. However, with the amount of construction and road damage from the flooding, the average speed could easily be more like 15 mph. Six of the twelve campgrounds were (and remain as of this writing) closed due to flood damage. Road construction, including bridges, impacted the travel time for both construction and those wishing to visit the park attractions. An unforeseen "side effect" of this park-wide construction is what seems to be a lack of wildlife available for photographs and observation while traveling through the park. Apparently, the wildlife residents don't like noise any more than we humans and have moved into more quiet areas. If seeing wildlife is important for your visit, it would be best to put off a trip until the roads and bridges are done. Especially if your trip is going to be a "once-in-a-lifetime" event.

Management: Yellowstone National Park, PO Box 168, Yellowstone National Park, WY 82190-0168; (307) 344-7381

Pets: Bringing a pet to Yellowstone may limit your activities in the park. Protect your pet and park wildlife by observing the following regulations:

- Pets may only accompany people in developed areas and must remain within 100 feet of roads, parking areas, and campgrounds.
- Pets must be physically controlled at all times. They must be in a car, in a crate, or on a leash no longer than 6 feet.
- Pets are not allowed on boardwalks, hiking trails, in the backcountry, or in thermal areas.
- Pets may not be left unattended or tied to an object.

- Pets may not be left in a situation where food, water, shade, ventilation, and other basic needs are inadequate. Pets may remain in vehicles for short periods of time, but we recommend that someone stay behind to personally ensure their well-being.
- Pet owners must bag and dispose of pet waste.

	Group sites	Tents	RV sites	Total # of sites	Hookups	Toilets	Showers	Drinking water	Dump station	Phone	Handicap	Recreation	Fee	Season	Can reserve	Stay limit
1 Fishing Bridge RV Park			310	310	A		X	X	X		X	WPh	$$$$$	5/15-9/30		14
2 Canyon			273	273		C	X	X	X		X	HiW	$$$	5/1-9/30	X	14
3 Madison	3	62	213	278		C		X	X	X	X	FHiW	$$$	5/1-10/31	X	14
4 Bridge Bay	4		400	404		C		X	X		X	FHiBoW	$$$	5/1-9/30	X	14
5 Grant Village			430	430		C		X	X		X	FHiBoW	$$$	6/1-10/31	X	14
6 Lewis Lake		17	68	85		V		X				FHiBoW	$$	6/15-10/31	X	14

A = all, Bo = boating, C = comfort stations, F = fishing, Hi = hiking, Ph = photography, V = vault toilet, W = wildlife viewing

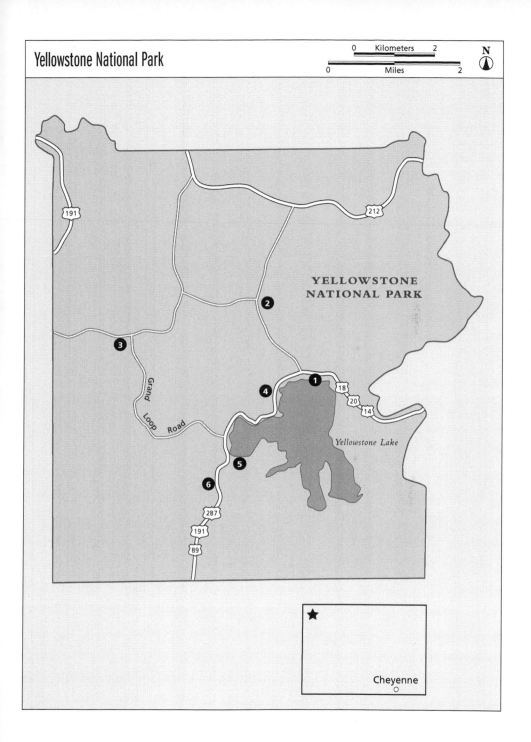

Yellowstone National Park

Kilometers

Miles

N

191

212

YELLOWSTONE
NATIONAL PARK

2

3

Grand
Loop Road

1

18

4

20

14

Yellowstone Lake

5

6

287

191

89

★

Cheyenne

1 Fishing Bridge RV Park

Location: 79 miles west of Cody
GPS: N44 33.78' / W110 22.21'
Facilities and amenities: Flush toilets, trash receptacles, laundry, dump station
Elevation: 7,769 feet
Road conditions: Paved
Hookups: Full hookups
Sites: 310 hard-sided RVs only
Maximum RV length: 40 feet long
Season: Mid-May through Sept, weather permitting
Fees: $$$$$$ per night
Maximum stay: None
Management: See introduction to this section.
Reservations: For campground and lodge reservations, go to yellowstonenationalparklodges.com.
Pets: See introduction to this section.
Quiet hours: Generators allowed only from 8 a.m. to 8 p.m. (60 db limit)
ADA compliance: Yes
Activities: Wildlife viewing, photography
Finding the campground: The East Entrance is 53 miles west of Cody. Take the East Entrance Road west from the fee booth for 26 miles.
About the campground: Campfires and picnic tables do not exist in this RV park. The parking is tight, but this really is the place for long RVs, as it is the one park campground truly designed for this kind of camping and has most amenities associated with RV camping (no cable TV—but who needs it with the park outside?). Campers who have discovered these conveniences make reservations up to 18 months in advance. Don't plan on pulling in here at the last minute.

2 Canyon

Location: 96 miles west of Cody
GPS: N44 44.07' / W110 29.25'
Facilities and amenities: Flush toilets, pay shower and laundry, fire rings, picnic tables, drinking water, dump station
Elevation: 8,006 feet
Road conditions: Gravel
Hookups: None
Sites: 273 basic sites. *Note:* Limited number of campsites set aside for bicyclists and hikers; check availability at campground.
Maximum RV length: Combined total length of 40 feet
Season: May–Sept, weather permitting
Fees: Rates do not include taxes or utility fees and are subject to change. Interagency Access and Senior Pass holders receive a 50% discount. $$$ per night, hiker/bicyclist $$ per person per night.

Maximum stay: 14 days
Management: See introduction to this section.
Reservations: For campground and lodge reservations, go to yellowstonenationalparklodges.com.
Pets: See introduction to this section.
Quiet hours: Generators only allowed from 8 a.m. to 8 p.m. (60 db limit)
ADA compliance: Yes
Activities: Hiking, wildlife viewing
Finding the campground: The East Entrance is 53 miles west of Cody. Take the East Entrance Road west from the fee booth for 27 miles. Turn right at the junction and travel 16 miles. Turn right at the sign and follow directions to the registration office on the left.
About the campground: Eleven separate loops wind through the pine forest here. Most of the units are back-in spots of various lengths. Tents seem to be the most common, though a few larger motor homes do manage. Canyon Village offers gift shops, a cafeteria, and other amenities nearby. A laundry and showers are available in the campground. Reservations are a must if you have definite plans to stay here.

3 Madison

Location: 14 miles east of West Yellowstone, MT
GPS: N44 38.77' / W110 51.66'
Facilities and amenities: Flush toilets, fire rings, food-storage lockers, trash receptacles, picnic tables, drinking water, dump station
Elevation: 6,835 feet
Road conditions: Paved
Hookups: None
Sites: 278 sites, 62 tents-only sites, 213 basic sites, and 3 group sites. *Note:* Both pull-through and back-in sites are available with limited width for slide-outs and various leveling challenges.
Maximum RV length: 30 feet total length
Season: May through mid-Oct, weather permitting
Fees: Rates do not include taxes or utility fees and are subject to change. Interagency Access and Senior Pass holders receive a 50% discount. $$$ per night, hiker/bicyclist $$ per person per night, group (1–19 individuals) $146, group (20–29 individuals) $219, group (30–39 individuals) $282, group (40–49 individuals) $356, group (50–60 individuals) $430.
Maximum stay: 14 days
Management: Contact information: (307) 344-7311, reserve-yp@xantera.com
Reservations: For campground and lodge reservations, go to yellowstonenationalparklodges.com.
Pets: See introduction to this section.
Quiet hours: Generators only allowed from 8 a.m. to 8 p.m. (60 db limit)
ADA compliance: 3 accessible sites
Activities: Fishing, hiking, wildlife viewing
Finding the campground: Take the West Entrance Road east of West Yellowstone for 14 miles. Turn right just before Madison Junction to access the campground.

Camping units here have a unique identity.

About the campground: Pine trees shade the asphalt access and parking area. Two of the ten loops are set aside for tents only, with the others turning into a sort of zoo. Larger RVs manage to find spaces, but it does crowd things. The Madison River rushes by just south of the campground, inviting anglers and wildlife watchers. This campground fills during the peak season as early as 7 a.m.

4 Bridge Bay

Location: 83 miles west of Cody
GPS: N44 32.09' / W110 26.06'
Facilities and amenities: Flush toilets, fire rings, trash receptacles, picnic tables, drinking water, dump station
Elevation: 7,780 feet
Road conditions: Paved
Hookups: None
Sites: 400 basic sites, 4 group sites. *Note:* Limited number of campsites set aside for bicyclists and hikers; check availability at campground.
Maximum RV length: Combined length of 40 feet
Season: May–Sept, weather permitting

Fees: Rates do not include taxes or utility fees and are subject to change. Interagency Access and Senior Pass holders receive a 50% discount. $$$ per night, hiker/bicyclist $$ per person per night, group (1–19 individuals) $146, group (20–29 individuals) $219, group (30–39 individuals) $282, group (40–49 individuals) $336, group (50–60 individuals) $430.

Maximum stay: 14 days

Management: See introduction to this section.

Reservations: For campground and lodge reservations, go to yellowstonenationalparklodges.com.

Pets: See introduction to this section.

Quiet hours: Generators only allowed from 8 a.m. to 8 p.m. (60 db limit)

ADA compliance: Yes

Activities: Fishing, hiking, boating, wildlife viewing

Finding the campground: The East Entrance is 53 miles west of Cody. Take the East Entrance Road west from the fee booth for 27 miles. Turn left at the junction (toward West Thumb) and travel 3 miles. The campground is on the right side of the road.

About the campground: Some sites have a distant view of Yellowstone Lake, but it is a pretty good hike. There is an assortment of wooded areas in the upper loops with fewer trees in the lower loops. Bear activity can alter camping unit availability earlier in the season so be prepared to alter your plans should that happen. The primary attractions here are fishing and boating, though some consider this a good position for a base camp to explore other features of the park.

5 Grant Village

Location: 80 miles north of Jackson

GPS: N44 23.51' / W110 33.56'

Facilities and amenities: Flush toilets, pay showers and laundry, dump station, group sites

Elevation: 7,792 feet

Road conditions: Paved and gravel

Hookups: None

Sites: 430 basic sites

Maximum RV length: 40 feet long

Season: June through mid-Sept

Fees: Rates do not include taxes or utility fees and are subject to change. Interagency Access and Senior Pass holders receive a 50% discount. $$$ per night, hiker/bicyclist $$ per person per night, group (1–19 individuals) $136, group (20–29 individuals) $199, group (30–39 individuals) $262, group (40–49 individuals) $336, group (50–60 individuals) $430.

Maximum stay: 14 days

Management: See introduction to this section.

Reservations: For campground and lodge reservations, go to yellowstonenationalparklodges.com.

Pets: See introduction to this section.

Quiet hours: Generators only allowed from 8 a.m. to 8 p.m. (60 db limit)

ADA compliance: Yes

Activities: Fishing, hiking, boating, wildlife viewing

Finding the campground: The South Entrance to Yellowstone National Park is 57 miles north of Jackson. Take the South Entrance Road north from the fee booth for 22 miles. Turn right at the Grant Village sign and travel 1 mile. Turn left at the well-marked campground entrance.

About the campground: This is one of the larger campgrounds with stores, gas station, restaurant, visitor center, and a boat ramp. A lodgepole pine forest occupies this camping area, providing the smells and other mountain features creating the fond memories associated with camping.

6 Lewis Lake

Location: 11 miles from the South Entrance
GPS: N44 16.99' / W110 37.60'
Facilities and amenities: Vault toilets, fire rings, food-storage lockers, trash receptacles, picnic tables, drinking water
Elevation: 7,300 feet
Road conditions: Gravel
Hookups: None
Sites: 85 basic sites including 17 walk-in sites
Maximum RV length: 25 feet total length
Season: Mid-June through Oct, weather permitting
Fees: $$ per night, hiker/bicyclist $ per night per person, Interagency Access and Senior Pass holders receive a 50% discount.
Maximum stay: 14 days
Management: Yellowstone National Park, PO Box 168, Yellowstone National Park, WY 82190-0168; (307) 344-7381
Reservations: For campground reservations, go to recreation.gov.
Pets: See introduction to this section.
Quiet hours: 10 p.m. to 6 a.m. *Note:* Use of generators not permitted in this campground.
ADA compliance: No
Activities: Fishing, boating, hiking, wildlife viewing
Finding the campground: The South Entrance to Yellowstone National Park is 57 miles north of Jackson. Take the South Entrance Road north from the fee booth for 11 miles. Turn left at the sign for Lewis Lake and travel a short distance. Turn left at the campground access.
About the campground: Pine and spruce trees shelter the RV sites in three confusing loops. Loop A bears left at the entrance with table designation open to interpretation, and twenty-four units haphazardly fit together like a jigsaw puzzle; the table could almost be divided in half the long way. The rolling knolls make it difficult for parking as well. Loop B takes up the center on a roller-coaster setting with similar conditions for sixteen sites. Loop C bears dead ahead with a tents-only section bearing to the right at the entrance. The lake nestles into place a pretty fair distance away. An active picnic area complete with boat ramp slides off to the right side just after leaving the highway.

Index